THE CAMBRIDGE
ANCIENT HISTORY

PLATES TO VOLUME IV

THE CAMBRIDGE ANCIENT HISTORY

PLATES TO VOLUME IV

Persia, Greece and the
Western Mediterranean
c. 525 to 479 B.C.

NEW EDITION

Edited by

JOHN BOARDMAN F.B.A.

*Lincoln Professor of Classical Archaeology and Art
in the University of Oxford*

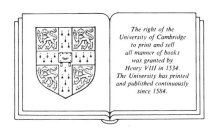

The right of the
University of Cambridge
to print and sell
all manner of books
was granted by
Henry VIII in 1534.
The University has printed
and published continuously
since 1584.

CAMBRIDGE UNIVERSITY PRESS

CAMBRIDGE

NEW YORK   NEW ROCHELLE

MELBOURNE   SYDNEY

Published by the Press Syndicate of the University of Cambridge
The Pitt Building, Trumpington Street, Cambridge CB2 1RP
32 East 57th Street, New York, NY 10022, USA
10 Stamford Road, Oakleigh, Melbourne 3166, Australia

First published 1988

Filmset and printed in Great Britain by
BAS Printers Limited, Over Wallop, Hampshire

Library of Congress catalogue card number: 77–378456

British Library cataloguing in publication data

The Cambridge ancient history. – New ed.
Vol. 4: Persia, Greece and the western Mediterranean,
c. 525 to 479 B.C. Plates
1. History, Ancient
I. Boardman, John
930   D57

ISBN 0 521 30580 2

CONTENTS

THE GREEK WORLD
by JOHN BOARDMAN

THE WEST

COINAGE
by M. JESSOP PRICE *Deputy Keeper,
Department of Coins and Medals, British Museum*

MAPS

ACKNOWLEDGEMENTS

Acknowledgement is due to the following for their permission to reproduce the photographs indicated.

Agrigento, Soprintendenza Archeologica: 257; Athens, American School of Classical Studies: 176a; Athens, French School: 125; Athens, German Archaeological Institute: 119, 120, 128–30, 135–6, 140, 173, 179, 237–8, 249; Athens, National Museum: 216; Basel, Antikenmuseum: 153, 180, 192; Berlin (East), Staatliche Museen: 138, 210; Berlin (West), Staatliche Museen: 182, 185, 194, 206, 213, 223, 260; J. Boardman: 78a, 79a, 114d, e, 160, 172; Bologna, Museo Civico: 275, 286–8, 293; Boston, Museum of Fine Arts: 168, 171, 174, 178, 196, 212; Bowdoin, College Museum of Art: 218; Brooklyn Museum: 58–9, 93; G. Buchner: 270; Cagliari, Soprintendenza Archeologica: 271; Chicago, Oriental Institute: 6, 7, 18, 24–39, 49, 52, 55, 73, 96–8, 100; Chieti, Soprintendenza Archeologica: 289, 299; A. Choremis: 126; Cleveland, Museum of Art: 156, 193; D. Content: 80b; T. Cuyler Young: 11–17; Florence, Soprintendenza Archeologica: 225, 284–5, 292; Fort Worth, Kimbell Art Museum: 147, 183; Hirmer Fotoarchiv, Munich: 117b, 118, 139, 141a, 191, 214, 220–1, 245, 248a, 250, 252–4, 265, 267; Istanbul, German Archaeological Institute: 127; Jerusalem, Israel Museum: 102; Jerusalem, Rockefeller Museum: 90; Karlsruhe, Badisches Landesmuseum: 170; Kassel, Staatliche Kunstsammlungen: 163; London, British Museum (courtesy of the Trustees): 41–2, 46b, 47, 51, 54, 61–3, 65–7, 69–72, 83–4, 86, 89, 95, 146, 155, 164, 187–9, 195, 197, 204–5, 208, 226–7, 235, 261–3, 269, 272, 279, 281, 298, 300a, b, 301; Malibu, J. Paul Getty Museum: 154; L. von Matt: 259, 266; Melbourne, National Gallery of Victoria: 277; M. Mellink: 81; D. Mertens: 251; Munich, Antikensammlungen: 122, 144, 162, 201, 231; New York, Metropolitan Museum of Art: 103, 186; P. Orlandini: 239; Oxford, Ashmolean Museum: 60, 68, 74, 88, 143, 236c, 300c; Paris, Louvre Museum: 19–21, 56–7, 75, 77, 85, 87, 99, 101, 190, 230, 236b, 242; Paris, Publ. d'Art et d'Archéologie: 50, 134; Philadelphia, University of Pennsylvania Museum: 94; Potenza, Soprintendenza Archeologica: 240, 255; Rome, British School: 283; Rome, Conservatori Museum: 121; Rome, Fondazione Lerici: 282; Rome, Soprintendenza Archeologica per l'Etruria Meridionale: 202, 268, 276, 278, 280, 290, 294–6, 297e–g; Rome, Università 'La Sapienza': 297b–d; N. Schimmel: 199; G. Scichilone: 274; Sofia, National Museum of History: 104, 105, 107a–b, 108d, e, 109, 110a, 111b, c, 112b, 113a; D. Stronach: 1–4, 7–10, 64, 92; Syracuse, Soprintendenza Archeologica: 241, 256; Taranto, Soprintendenza Archeologica: 264; Toronto, Royal Ontario Museum: 291; Viterbo, Museo Civico: 224; R. L. Wilkins: 48, 76b, c, 79b–d, 80a, c, 141b, 142, 145, 157–9, 161, 209, 229, 236a; R. J. A. Wilson: 243–4, 246–7, 258; Würzburg, Martin von Wagner Museum: 141b, 151, 169, 200, 211, 228; G. M. Young: 131; Zurich, Archaeological Institute: 46a.

PREFACE

The Cambridge Ancient History Volume IV, which is issued at the same time as this Plates Volume, describes the rise of the Persian Empire, its satrapies and its confrontations with the Greek homeland down to 479 B.C. The illustrations offered here include many from years later than 479, the intention being to make this volume the main visual demonstration of Achaemenid Persian archaeology and art in this series. The chapters on Greek history in *CAH* IV deal with the late Archaic period in Greece, down to 479. Some illustration of material relevant to this period has been included already in *Plates to Volume III*, while here there are also objects of relatively early date, but the emphasis is on Athens since this is a period in which the archaeology of the city is particularly rich, and its pottery particularly informative. In the sections on the Western Greeks and on Italy material from earlier periods has been included, for the westerners, to complement that on colonization in the previous volume, and for Italy to match the text chapters on the earlier history of the Italic peoples. Finally, coinage, though established long before the main period studied here, is reserved for a special section in this volume, with an account which is carried on into the fifth century and into Persian territory.

Timothy Taylor kindly provided illustrations and text for pls. 104–13, and John Morrison for pl. 181. The maps are by David Cox of Cox Cartographic Ltd and many of the line drawings have been specially prepared for this volume by Marion Cox. Authors and editors thank warmly the many institutions and scholars who have provided photographs and given permission for their use, not least the many who offered them for no charge.

Oxford, July 1987   J.B.

ABBREVIATIONS

AA	*Archäologischer Anzeiger*
ABFH	J. Boardman, *Athenian Black Figure Vases* (London, 1974)
ABV	J. D. Beazley, *Attic Black-Figure Vase-Painters* (Oxford, 1956)
AGGems	J. Boardman, *Archaic Greek Gems* (London, 1968)
AION	*Annali Istituto Orientale, Napoli: Sezione di Archeologia e Storia Antica*
AJA	*American Journal of Archaeology*
AK	*Antike Kunst*
Arch.Class.	*Archeologia Classica*
Arch.Delt.	*Archaiologikon Deltion*
Arch.Rep.	*Archaeological Reports*
ARFH	J. Boardman, *Athenian Red Figure Vases: The Archaic Period* (London, 1975)
ARV	J. D. Beazley, *Attic Red-Figure Vase-Painters* (Oxford, 1963)
AS Atene	*Annuario della Scuola Archeologica di Atene*
BCH	*Bulletin de Correspondance Hellénique*
BICS	*Bulletin of the Institute of Classical Studies, London*
BSA	*Annual of the British School at Athens*
BSR	*Papers of the British School at Rome*
Bull.Inst.	*Bullettino dell' Instituto di Corrispondenza Archeologica*
Cat.Arezzo 1985	*Santuari d' Etruria* (exhibition catalogue: Arezzo, 1985)
Cat. Bologna 1960	*Mostra dell' Etruria Padana e della città di Spina* (exhibition catalogue: Bologna, 1960)
Cat.Florence 1985	*Civiltà degli Etruschi* (exhibition catalogue: Florence, 1985)
CVA	*Corpus Vasorum Antiquorum*
Dalton, *Treasure*	O. M. Dalton, *The Treasure of the Oxus*[3] (London, 1964)
GGFR	J. Boardman, *Greek Gems and Finger Rings* (London, 1970)
GSAP	J. Boardman, *Greek Sculpture: The Archaic Period* (London, 1978)
GSCP	J. Boardman, *Greek Sculpture: The Classical Period* (London, 1986)
Hencken, *Tarquinia*	H. Hencken, *Tarquinia, Villanovans and Early Etruscans* (Cambridge, Mass., 1968)
Holloway, *GSSMG*	R. Ross Holloway, *Influences and Styles in the Late Archaic and Early Classical Greek Sculpture of Sicily and Magna Graecia* (Louvain, 1975)
IBR	D. and F. R. Ridgway (eds.), *Italy before the Romans* (London, New York, San Francisco, 1979)
JDAI	*Jahrbuch des Deutschen Archäologischen Instituts*
JHS	*Journal of Hellenic Studies*
JRS	*Journal of Roman Studies*
Kraay–Hirmer	C. M. Kraay and M. Hirmer, *Greek Coins* (London, 1966)
Langlotz–Hirmer	E. Langlotz and M. Hirmer, *The Art of Magna Graecia* (London, 1965)
LIMC	*Lexicon Iconographicum Mythologiae Classicae* (Zurich and Munich, 1981–)

MÉFRA	*Mélanges de l'École française de Rome, Antiquité*
Megale Hellas	G. Pugliese Carratelli et al., *Megale Hellas: storia e civiltà della Magna Graecia* (Milan, 1983)
Mon.Ant.	*Monumenti Antichi*
Not.Scav.	*Notizie degli Scavi di Antichità*
Para	J. D. Beazley, *Paralipomena* (Oxford, 1971)
Rasmussen, *Bucchero*	T. B. Rasmussen, *Bucchero Pottery from Southern Etruria* (Cambridge, 1979)
Robertson, *HGA*	M. Robertson, *A History of Greek Art* (Cambridge, 1975)
Röm.Mitt.	*Mitteilungen des Deutschen Archäologischen Instituts. Römische Abteilung*
Schmidt, *Persepolis*	E. F. Schmidt, *Persepolis* I: *Structures, Reliefs and Inscriptions* (Chicago, 1953); II: *Contents of the Treasury and other Discoveries* (Chicago, 1957); III: *The Royal Tombs and other Monuments* (Chicago, 1970)
Sikanie	G. Pugliese Carratelli et al., *Sikanie: storia e civiltà della Sicilia greca* (Milan, 1985)
Simon–Hirmer	E. Simon and M. & A. Hirmer, *Die griechischen Vasen* (Munich, 1976)
SSA 2	M. S. Balmuth (ed.), *Studies in Sardinian Archaeology* II: *Sardinia in the Mediterranean* (Ann Arbor, 1986)
Stud.Etr.	*Studi Etruschi*

THE PERSIAN EMPIRE

Introduction

The Achaemenid dynasty emerged from the Achaemenid clan of the Persian people to establish itself in the second half of the sixth century B.C. as the rulers of a vast and extremely diverse empire stretching from northern Greece in the west to the margins of Asiatic Russia in the east, from Caucasia in the north to the shores of the Indian Ocean in the south. It survived, for the most part intact, until the invasion of Alexander the Great in 331 B.C. It was a military autocracy, created and sustained by force of arms, structured and directed to exploit the resources of its diverse provinces, their towns and rural populations, for the benefit and security of the imperial authority. To this end its rulers sought order and stability largely within the existing politico-economic systems of the provinces. The early creative Achaemenid kings, notably Cyrus II and Darius I, gave their administrations a strong sense of purpose, a well-defined hierarchy and bureaucracy, and an imperial iconography, in which the Indo-Iranian traditions of the rulers were fused with the age-old political and cultural legacies of the ruled, to constitute a dominion wider and, to an extent, more enduring than any previously established in the region.

In many parts of this empire the period between the sixth and fourth centuries B.C. is archaeologically among the least well known. This is partly explained by the restricted character of the Persian impact on the material culture of the regions over which they ruled, partly by a concentration of modern archaeological research on major urban sites and, within those sites, on a few public buildings, where erosion or subsequent Hellenistic occupation has too often largely obliterated evidence for the Achaemenid period. In such urban centres, usually long established at key strategic points, the Persians appear generally to have done little more than reconstruct fortifications and administrative buildings to serve as centres for garrisons and administration, for tribute collection and storage. Local architectural styles often persisted unchanged. The well-known 'Persepolitan style' seems to have been used almost exclusively for the palaces and estates of the extended royal family; outside Babylon, Pasargadae, Persepolis and Susa they remain to be excavated.

It was the ruling Persian elites, wherever they were to be found across the empire, who set the fashions in costume and luxury goods that constitute the sharpest indicators of a Persian presence in the meagre surviving material record. It was parade weapons and finely engraved seals, tableware of precious metals and clear, cut glass, ornate personal ornaments and richly decorated textiles, furniture fittings and tent trappings, which took court fashions and taste deep into the Near East and often far beyond the borders of the empire to influence the art of inner Asia and continental Europe. Everywhere imitations of fine artefacts were produced in more common materials. But, as so often, luxury fashions passed with the rulers who patronized them and in the long run this Persian legacy was soon hellenized.

The archaeological record is at present negligible for the forts, small towns, villages and homesteads that formed the broader settlement patterns of the empire, within which moved even more archaeologically elusive nomadic populations. To understand in detail how the empire operated at this level and to assess the extent of actual Iranian settlement and penetration of local populations outside Iran, in short to establish how Persian the empire was, still remains a task primarily for the historian. In those regions where local material culture is relatively well known at this time the Persian impact varied considerably within the ruling group of any society, but in the lower social levels, those most commonly represented by the material culture present in excavations, local Iron Age traditions,

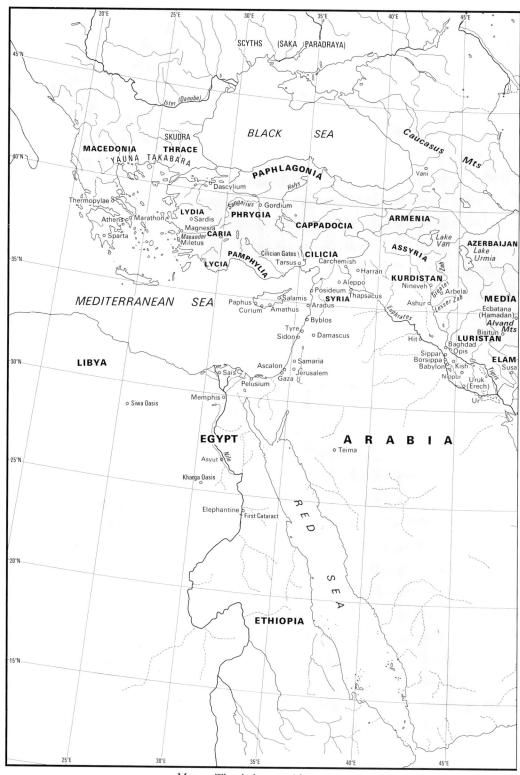

Map 1. The Achaemenid empire.

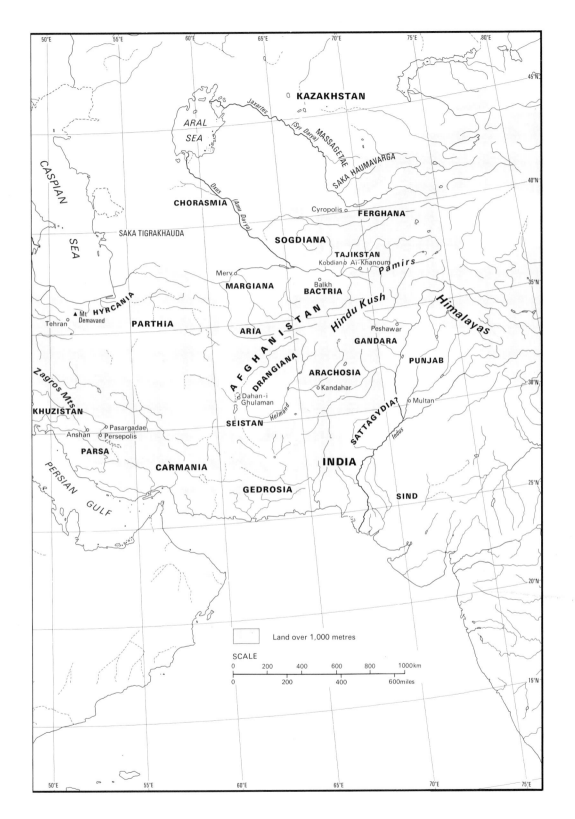

50°E   55°E   60°E   65°E   70°E   75°E   80°E

45°N

KAZAKHSTAN

ARAL
SEA

Jaxartes
(Syr Darya)

MASSAGETAE

SAKA HAUMAVARGA

40°N

CASPIAN

CHORASMIA

Oxus
(Amu Darya)

Cyropolis

FERGHANA

SEA

SAKA TIGRAKHAUDA

SOGDIANA

TAJIKSTAN

Kobdian Aï-Khanoum

Pamirs

35°N

Mervo

MARGIANA

Balkh

BACTRIA

Hindu Kush

Himalayas

▲ Mt
Demavand

HYRCANIA

Tehran

PARTHIA

ARIA

A F G H A N I S T A N

Peshawar

GANDARA

Zagros Mts

DRANGIANA

ARACHOSIA

PUNJAB

30°N

Dahan-i
Ghulaman

Kandahar

Multan

SATTAGYDIA?

Indus

KHUZISTAN

Pasargadae

Anshan   Persepolis

SEISTAN

Helmand

PARSA

CARMANIA

INDIA

PERSIAN

GEDROSIA

25°N

GULF

SIND

20°N

Land over 1,000 metres

SCALE

0   200   400   600   800   1000km

0   200   400   600miles

15°N

50°E   55°E   60°E   65°E   70°E   75°E

3

established in the previous two or three centuries, continued to mature with few signs of disruption or radical modification.

In such circumstances it seemed wisest to arrange a concise illustrated survey of material culture within the Persian empire thematically not topographically, as is possible for the subsequent Hellenistic period (cf. *CAH Pls. to Vol. VII.I* (1984)). The emphasis is laid here on tracing the emergence of a material culture distinctive of the Persian overlords and indicating impressionistically the ways and means by which it infiltrated the conquered territories, whose existing cultures were illustrated in *CAH Pls. to Vol. III* (1984). Sections on the great royal monuments of the empire are followed by a brief pictorial view of its enormously varied population, by illustrations of Persian cults, and by a survey of the crafts most often associated with the rule of the Achaemenids in western Asia. It is to be regretted that many of the best known of these have no archaeological context.

GENERAL BIBLIOGRAPHY

P. Briant, *Rois, tributs et paysans* (Paris, 1982); *États et pasteurs au Moyen-Orient ancien* (Cambridge, 1982); J. M. Cook, *The Persian Empire* (London, 1983); I. Gershevitch (ed.), *The Cambridge History of Iran* 2: *The Median and Achaemenian Periods* (Cambridge, 1985); R. N. Frye, *The Heritage of Persia* 2 (London, 1976); R. Ghirshman, *Persia: from the Origins to Alexander the Great* (London, 1964); A. T. Olmstead, *History of the Persian Empire* (Chicago, 1948); E. Porada, *Ancient Iran: The Art of Pre-Islamic Times* (London–New York, 1965); M. C. Root, *The King and Kingship in Achaemenid Art* (Leyden, 1979).

1. ARCHAEOLOGICAL SITES IN MEDIA

P. R. S. MOOREY

Until extensive and systematic excavations are conducted in occupational levels of the eighth and seventh centuries B.C. at the Median capital of Ecbatana (modern Hamadan) the material culture of the Medes, if it was indeed distinctive, will remain an enigma. At present there is no certain evidence for Median art or architecture. Within the area of western Iran known, from meagre documentary sources, to have been under Median control at this time, two archaeological sites in particular, the mud-brick citadels of Tepe Nush-i Jan and Godin Tepe, have been taken to exemplify the fortified Median towns represented on Assyrian palace sculptures. They are about equidistant from Hamadan, some 60 km to the south and south west respectively. Each has columned structures of a type evident earlier in the ninth century B.C. at Hasanlu to the north and fully developed later at Persepolis in the fifth century B.C. (see **23–25**). Attention has focused particularly on two buildings with comparable layout at Tepe Nush-i Jan, each equipped with an altar, though in one case only the plinth survived. What cult they served is unknown, as no other cult furniture was retrieved; but it is already clear that early attempts to associate them with the well-known fire altars of Zoroastrian worship take the evidence further than is at present justified.

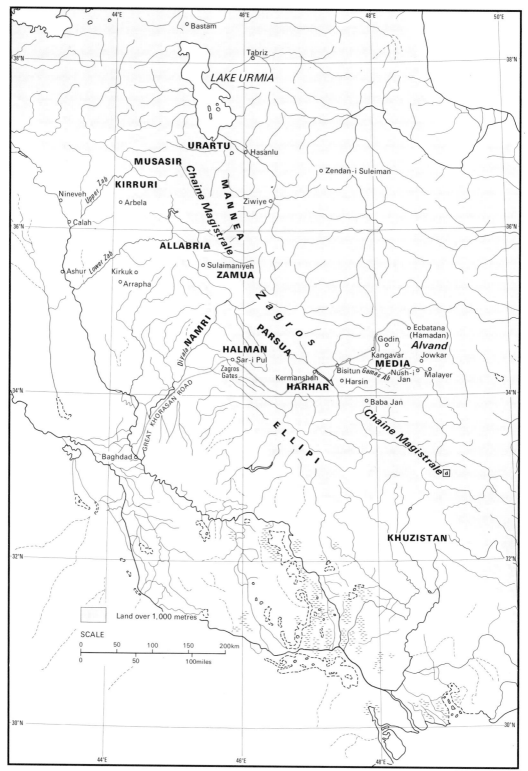

Map 2. Media.

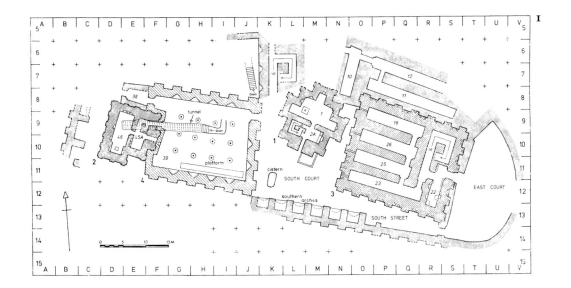

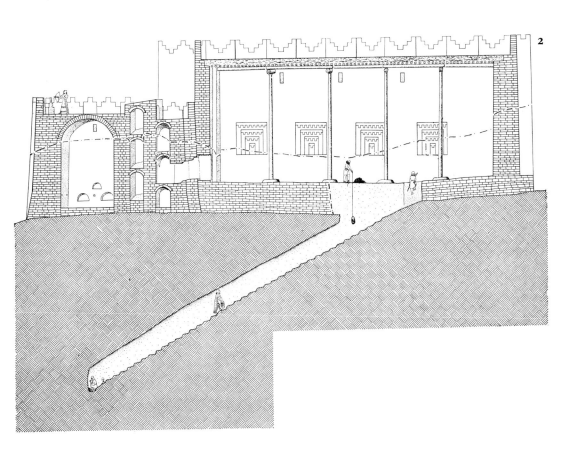

1. The eighth-century citadel of Tepe Nush-i Jan, set on a rocky outcrop, lies close to the centre of the fertile Malayer–Jowkar plain. In an area of about 100 × 40 m, as this plan shows, a mud-brick outer wall, decorated on the inner face with arches, enclosed at least four major structures: 1. Central Temple; 2. Old Western Building (Western Temple); 3. Fort; 4. Columned Hall.

D. Stronach, *Iran* 7 (1969) 1ff; M. Roaf and D. Stronach, *Iran* 11 (1973) 129ff; D. Stronach and M. Roaf, *Iran* 16 (1978) 1ff.

2. Reconstructed section and elevation (by M. Roaf) looking north on a line drawn through the Old Western Building, the Columned Hall and the unfinished tunnel at Tepe Nush-i Jan.

After *Iran* 16 (1978) fig. 3.

3. The eastern end of the Central Temple at Tepe Nush-i Jan seen from behind the altar. This view shows clearly the style of mud-brick architecture, unusually well preserved on this site, and the shale chips with which the shrine has been systematically packed after it passed out of use. The walls survived to a height of about 8.5 m.

Stronach and Roaf, *Iran* 16 (1978) pl. 8A.

4. The waist-high, plastered mud-brick altar in the Central Temple at Tepe Nush-i Jan, protected by a low mud-brick wall before being packed in shale. The top has a shallow cavity, with traces of burning; but it is not deep enough to hold the hot bed of ashes needed to sustain an ever-burning fire, so this shrine is better not described as a fire-temple. Burnt offerings were a common feature of many ancient Near Eastern cults, notably in Elam.

Stronach and Roaf, *Iran* 16 (1978) pl. 7A.

4

5. Plan of the structures in Level II at Godin Tepe, which is sited on the strategic route from Kermanshah to Hamadan on the bank of the Gamas Ab at the south-east corner of the Kangavar Valley. After a period of desertion a mud-brick citadel was erected on the top of the tell in the eighth century B.C. with a wall encircling a residence with columned halls, and extensive storerooms.

T. Cuyler Young, Jr and L. D. Levine, *Excavations of the Godin Project: Second Progress Report* (Royal Ontario Museum, Toronto, 1974) 29ff, fig. 37.

6. An oblique aerial view of Hamadan (taken in 1937) clearly showing to the left, in the middle distance, the barren slopes of the hill at Musalla, with the ground plan of a relatively modern fortress. This mound and the area immediately in front of it, now covered by housing, probably conceal the ruins of the Median capital.

The Median capital of Hamadan, ancient Hagmatana (Ecbatana) (The Place of Assembly), lies in central western Iran, on the main route from

5

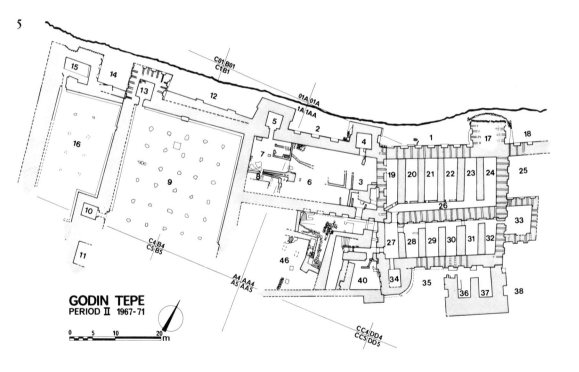

GODIN TEPE
PERIOD II 1967-71

0 5 10 20 m

the Iranian plateau down onto the Mesopotamian plain. It is one of the highest cities in Iran overshadowed by the impressive Mount Alvand (3,750 m high). It is pleasantly cool in summer, very cold in winter. According to Herodotus (1.96) this city was founded by the Median king Deioces. Greek authors describe the lavish construction of the city. It was the favourite summer residence of the Achaemenid kings. Ezra 6:2 recounts how a copy of Cyrus II's decree concerning the rebuilding of the Temple in Jerusalem was sought and found in archives at Ecbatana in the reign of Darius I.

No systematic excavations at Hamadan have reached Median levels. Unfortunately there is no certainty about the origin, even sometimes the authenticity, of a number of impressive objects of gold and silver, including royal inscriptions, said to have been found at Hamadan.

E. F. Schmidt, *Flights over Ancient Cities of Iran* (Chicago, 1940) pl. 92; *id.*, *Persepolis* I 36–9; R. G. Kent, *Old Persian* (New Haven, 1950) 107, 111, 113; O. Muscarella in D. Schmandt-Besserat, *Ancient Persia: The Art of an Empire* (Malibu, 1980) 31–5.

2. PASARGADAE, BISITUN, SUSA

P. R. S. MOOREY

(a) Pasargadae

The capital which Cyrus II founded in about 546 B.C., according to Strabo on the site of his crucial victory over the Medes, is situated at an altitude of 1,900 m in one of the most northerly and elevated plains of Fars; a cold spot for a capital in winter. It is about 30 km north east of Persepolis as the crow flies, twice that distance by the ancient road. Herodotus (1.125) lists the Pasargadae among the chief tribes of the Persians. It was the one to which the Achaemenid family itself belonged. However, one ancient Greek source gives as an etymology of the city's name 'camping ground of the Persians'. A series of excavations have added considerably to knowledge of the visible ruins, but have yielded no evidence of any overall plan or of an embracing city wall. The surviving monuments, widely scattered across the site (8), include four main complexes; a citadel (Tall-i Takht); a series of palaces and garden pavilions; The Sacred Precinct; and the tomb of Cyrus II. Confirmation of the identity of the site has been provided by its location, by descriptions in ancient authors, notably the historians of Alexander the Great, and indirectly by inscriptions from the site. It was to remain one of the empire's most important ceremonial centres, the town where the royal coronation took place, even after Darius founded Persepolis.

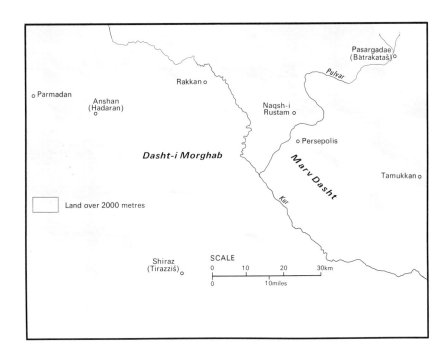

Map 3. Fars.

7. A view across the southern part of the site at Pasargadae, looking south west, with the tomb of Cyrus in the middle distance; taken in the 1930s.

E. F. Schmidt, *Flights Over Ancient Cities of Iran* (Chicago, 1940) pl. 14A.

8. Sketch plan of Pasargadae; after D. Stronach, *Iran* 3 (1965) fig. 1.

9. A view from the west across the ruins of the gateway (R) to the palace area at Pasargadae, showing the 'genius' carved on the east jamb of the north door. This is the most complete surviving fragment of relief attributed to the later part of the reign of Cyrus II (559–530 B.C.). It is much debated whether Cyrus himself or Darius was responsible for a trilingual inscription in Old Persian, Elamite and Akkadian, noted by early travellers and now lost, once inscribed above the figure: 'I, Cyrus, the King, an Achaemenian'. But it is now generally agreed that this text was meant to indicate the king as builder not to identify the figure, whose identity remains enigmatic. It looks inwards, not outwards as apotropaic

protective spirits at doorways in earlier buildings elsewhere normally did. It may represent the King, as a mythical being, or a syncretic deity. The figure's crown is a specifically Egyptian one, the robe is like that of Elamite kings, its wings are very reminiscent of 'genii' on Assyrian sculptures and its profile pose follows Neo-Babylonian rather than Neo-Assyrian practice. Its eclectic character epitomizes the initial stage of Achaemenid court art; but the choice of forms and their combination may already have conveyed to contemporaries a clear and distinct message peculiar to the new dynasty.

D. Stronach, *Pasargadae* (Oxford, 1978) 44ff, pl. 40; Root, *King and Kingship* 46–9, 300–3.

10. The building traditionally identified as the tomb of Cyrus at Pasargadae, seen from the west. It is a stone-built structure, resembling a house with a gabled roof, set on a platform of six receding tiers. There are the remains of a relief rosette at the point of the gable on the front. It stands apart from all other monuments on the site, dominating the plain. As earlier royal tombs are unknown in this region, the origin of the type

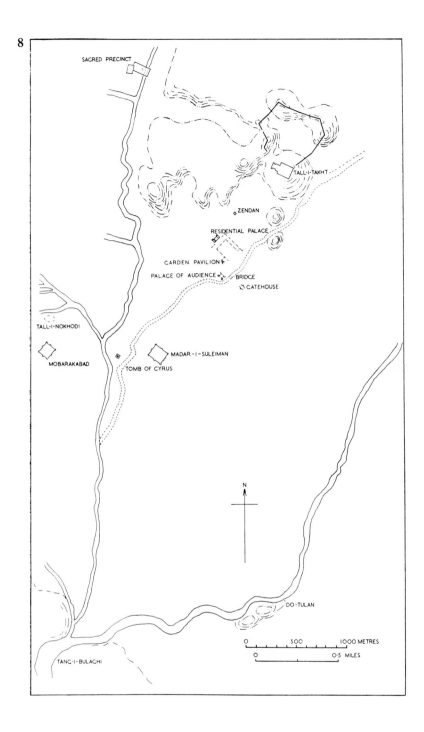

8

SACRED PRECINCT

TALL-I-TAKHT

ZENDAN

RESIDENTIAL PALACE

GARDEN PAVILION
PALACE OF AUDIENCE   BRIDGE
                    GATEHOUSE

TALL-I-NOKHODI

MOBARAKABAD
                    MADAR-I-SULEIMAN
            TOMB OF CYRUS

N

DO-TULAN

0   500   1000 METRES

0   0·5 MILES

TANG-I-BULAGHI

has been much disputed. Close analysis of its form, workmanship and dimensions suggests that Cyrus had been powerfully influenced by what he had seen in western Turkey, notably Lydia, and used craftsmen from that region for this work, as he did elsewhere at Pasargadae.

C. Nylander, *Ionians in Pasargadae* (Uppsala, 1970) 91ff; Stronach, *Pasargadae* 24ff.

(b) Bisitun

The relief and trilingual inscriptions cut between about 521/20 and 519/18 B.C. by order of Darius I high into the side of Mt Bisitun are the most famous single monument of the Achaemenid dynasty. They overlook the main route from the Iranian plateau down onto the Mesopotamian plain (from Ecbatana (Hamadan) to Babylon), just within the border of modern Iran. They are about 100 m above springs feeding a pool at the mountain's foot, occupying an area about 18 m long and 7.8 m high on the rock face. Why Darius chose this spot is not indicated in the inscriptions; perhaps because it overlooked the site of his decisive battle against the rebel Fravartish (Phraortes), who claimed to be Khashatreti (Khshathrita), a descendant of Cyaxares. Its inspiration is thought to have been the much older rock relief nearby at Sar-i Pul, north west of Bisitun, carved for King Anubanini fifteen hundred years earlier. No more certain are the methods employed by the workmen who undertook this intimidating and hazardous task, probably from some sort of precarious wooden scaffold.

Surviving royal inscriptions with any significant historical information are very rare in the Achaemenid empire. No Old Persian text compares in scope or historical importance with this one. But, as it is an obvious piece of royal propaganda, it has been, and remains, the source of considerable debate. Here Darius recorded the official version of the controversial events surrounding his accession to the throne (describing in some detail the role he had played in removing the Magian Gaumata, a Mede, from the throne), the events of the first three years of his rule and his claim to be the legitimate heir. A copy in stone of the relief and the inscription was set up at Babylon and a fragmentary Aramaic version of the inscription on papyrus has been found as far away as Elephantine in southern Egypt.

Through laborious and courageous efforts, between 1835 and 1847, Major-General (later Sir) Henry C. Rawlinson, a British officer, was the first to secure copies of the inscriptions. His decipherment of the Old Persian version was based on a combination of brilliant guesses, using the Achaemenid royal names and genealogy given in Herodotus, and a rare gift for understanding the meaning of a passage. By 1849, more significantly, he had unravelled much of the Babylonian (Akkadian) version, ensuring an enduring reputation as the 'Father of Assyriology'.

GENERAL BIBLIOGRAPHY

L. W. King and R. C. Thompson, *The Sculptures and Inscriptions of Darius the Great on the Rock of Behistun in Persia* (London, 1907); G. G. Cameron, *Journal of Cuneiform Studies* 5 (1951) 47–57; *id.*, 14 (1960) 59–68; H. Luschey, *Archäologische Mitteilungen aus Iran* 1 (1968) 63–94; M. A. Dandamaev, *Persien unter den ersten Achämeniden* (Wiesbaden, 1976) 1–90; E. N. von Voigtlander, *The Bisitun Inscription of Darius the Great: Babylonian Version* (London, 1978).

11. The Bisitun relief and inscriptions. The basic design was probably conceived as a relief panel (about 3 m high and 5.5 m long) flanked on the spectator's right by a text in Elamite. Then, to the left, on a projecting rock face was added a version in Babylonian (Akkadian). Subsequently, below the relief, an Old Persian text was carved in columns. The various captions appear to have been written in the same order. Of the Old Persian Darius said: 'I have made the writing of a different sort in Aryan, which did not exist before.' The rock on which the Babylonian text had been cut was undercut to provide a surface for a second Elamite version (an exact copy of the first) when the relief was extended, to insert the Scythian rebel king defeated in 519/18 B.C. after the original row of figures had been carved, thus mutilating the first Elamite version. The relief panel shows Darius at life size (about 1.75 m high) with the bearers of the royal bow and quiver and the royal spear behind him. The king stands holding a bow in his left hand whilst raising his right in a gesture of worship. His left foot is set on the abdomen of the rebel Gaumata, lying on the ground, behind whom, in a row, stand nine named rebels, roped at the necks, their hands tied behind their

backs. Above them hovers an anthropomorphic winged disk conventionally identified by western scholars as Ahura Mazda, though some now prefer to see in it either the spirit of the dead king (*fravahr*) or the god-given fortune (*farnah*) (khvarnah) of the living king.

12. Detail from 11 of the head of Darius wearing the battlemented royal crown. The hairstyle and full beard are strongly reminiscent of earlier portrayals of Assyrian kings, notably Ashurbanipal (*c.* 668–627 B.C.) (cf. for later rendering

of Achaemenid kings, **22, 29–31**). It is noticeable that Darius appears to look up towards the winged disk and holds his hand raised in a traditional gesture of prayer or obeisance; thus this is as much a depiction of an act of worship as of a triumph over defeated rebels.

13. Detail from **11** to show Darius trampling the rebel Gaumata, shown lying with his right leg up in the air; behind stands the first rebel: 'One, Acina by name, an Elamite . . .'

14. Detail from **11** of the winged disk showing how elements had to be let into the surface of the rock where it was faulty. They were secured with iron rivets leaded into place (cf. the iron pin on the top of the headdress). This relief, like that of the king, is more recognisably Assyrian in stylistic details than later sculptures of Darius I. Here the figure wears the horned crown of divinity, traditional in Mesopotamia, where the anthropomorphic winged disk represented the sun-god Shamash.

15. Detail from **11** of the royal bow-bearer, Aspathines, and the spear-bearer, Gobryas; they are also represented on the tomb of Darius I at

Naqsh-i Rustam. They wear the same type of bracelets as Ahura Mazda, but different from the single (damaged) circuit on the king's wrist.

16. Detail from **11** of three rebels under the winged disk with the inscription set unevenly round, and even across, them as happened on Assyrian reliefs. The figure to the left originally had the back of his head riveted into the rock surface. The height and contours of the relief carving are well illustrated here. Each of the rebels is dressed in the costume of the country he claimed to rule; here an Elamite (claiming Elam), a Babylonian claiming Babylonia, and a Persian (also claiming Elam).

17. Detail from **11** of Skunkha the Scythian added late to the relief, as is clear from the way the rock surface is cut back; the high pointed cap he wears is now known from excavations in Asiatic Russia.

(c) Susa

Susa in south-west Iran (Khuzistan) is one of the oldest cities in the Near East. It was under more or less continuous excavation by French expedi- tions between 1884 and the recent Iranian Revolution. This prosperous centre of the Elamite kingdom was sacked by the Assyrians under Ashurbanipal in 639 B.C.; these events were graphically depicted in palace sculptures at Nineveh in Iraq. A little over a century later Darius I began to turn the site into one of the capitals of the Achaemenid dynasty by creating a moated, walled city with a citadel and residen- tial palaces on and around the great mounds that represented millennia of previous occupation. Its location made Susa ideal for the purpose. It was a focal point for routes into and out of Iran, whether in the direction of Persepolis and Pasargadae, or of Hamadan, and it was easily linked to Babylon and, by the royal road, to Assyria and Turkey

GENERAL BIBLIOGRAPHY

M. K. Pillet, *Le Palais de Darius I à Suse* (Paris, 1914); Schmidt, *Persepolis* 1   29–36; R. de Mecquenem, *Mémoires . . . délégation en Perse* 30 (Paris, 1947) 1–119; R. Ghirshman, *Mémoires . . . délégation en Perse* 36 (1954) 1–78; A. Labrousse et R. Boucharlat, *Cahiers de la délégation française en Iran* 2 (1972) 61–167; J. Per- rot et al., *Cahiers de la délégation française en Iran* 4 (1974) 43–56.

16

17

18. Aerial view (taken in 1935) of the modern village and archaeological site at Susa. The main mound (Acropolis) in the centre is now crowned by a modern château, erected in the late nineteenth century by the French Archaeological Expedition. Immediately behind it is the Apadana Mound, site of the great royal palace created by Darius I, with an audience hall or throne room even larger than that at Persepolis (cf. **23, 24**). The plan of this palace is reminiscent of that at Babylon built for Nebuchadrezzar II (604–562 B.C.). In the main entrance gateway on the east side was found a headless monumental statue of Darius imported from Egypt (**22**). A trilingual building inscription describes the sources of the materials used in the construction of the palace and the diverse origins of the workmen employed there. In the reign of Darius, or later, there was another palace on the 'Donjon' (lower right in the photograph) and at least one more across the river to the north west of the 'Tomb of Daniel': the conical dome on the west side of the modern village. The lower palace-complex was set in gardens as a pleasant retreat near the river.

Schmidt, *Flights over Ancient Cities of Iran*, pl. 55.

19. *Restored* panel of glazed brick, said to have been excavated from the north east corner of the central courtyard of the Palace of Darius at Susa; winged human-headed lions, wearing the horned crown of divinity, with a winged disk above. These creatures, like the more familiar human-headed winged bulls (see **26**), were apotropaic figures; reign of Darius I(?).

Whereas at Persepolis, where a stone of good quality was readily available, the Achaemenid

palaces were decorated with relief sculpture, at Susa, in the plain, this was rare. Relief sculpture was replaced by friezes of polychrome moulded or painted glazed bricks, not, as previously, of baked clay but of sintered quartz (faience). This technique had a long history locally and in Babylonia, whence came, according to the foundation charter of the Palace of Darius 'the men who wrought the baked brick'. These friezes offer a rare glimpse of the colours and designs used in Achaemenid costume; the paint known to have been used on stone reliefs has usually worn off.

(Paris, Louvre. Height 1.22 m.)
  Encyclopédie photographique de l'art II (Louvre, Paris, 1936) pl. 58.

20. Part of a *restored* glazed brick frieze of guards in Persian costume reported to have been found in fragments 'beneath the substructure of a gate belonging to the palace of Artaxerxes II'. Each man carries a spear with a spherical 'silver' butt (according to Greek sources nine thousand of the ten thousand Immortals, constituting the King's guard, were so equipped), bows and quivers. Their garments are variously patterned with rosettes and small fortresses in square panels. Although Artaxerxes II (404–359 B.C.) is known to have restored the Apadana at Susa after destruction by fire, many of the elements of earlier work survived and these figures are now usually attributed to the earlier part of the reign of Darius I.

(Paris, Louvre. Height of guard 1.47 m.)
   M. Dieulafoy, *L'Acropole de Suse* (Paris, 1893) 280–5, pls. 6, 7 (colour); *Encyclopédie photographique de l'art* II, pls. 50–1; A. Farkas, *Achaemenid Sculpture* (Istanbul, 1974) 38ff; Stronach, *Pasargadae* 96–7; J. V. Canby, *Archäologische Mitteilungen aus Iran* 12 (1979) 315–20.

21. Bull-headed capital of grey marble from a tall column originally supporting the roof of the Apadana at Susa, built by Darius I and restored

21

by Artaxerxes II after a fire. This building covered about 1 ha; wooden roof beams were placed crossways, some resting on the saddle between the addorsed heads, some on their necks. Comparable capitals were used in the Apadana at Persepolis and the whole concept, like that of the columned hall itself, is Iranian, previously unknown in Mesopotamia.

(Paris, Louvre. Height 5.8 m.)
Encyclopédie photographique de l'art ii, pls. 48–9.

22. a, b. Photograph and drawings of the headless green schist statue of Darius I (522–486 B.C.) found in the Gateway of Darius which gave access to the palatial area at Susa, as did the Gateway of Xerxes at Persepolis. The statue stood on the outer (south) side of the west passage of the gate. It is set on a base (104 × 64 × 51 cm) carved with designs: on front and back, two Egyptian fertility figures binding the *sm₃* hieroglyph; on the sides, representations of the peoples ruled by the Persian king, each set in an oval fortress containing the name of his country in hieroglyphs (see **40**). The peoples are, from left to right in the drawing: 1. Persian; 2. Mede; 3. Elamite; 4. Arian; 5. Parthian; 6. Bactrian; 7. Sogdian; 8. Arachosian; 9. Drangian; 10. Sattagydian; 11. Chorasmian; 12. Sakan; 13. Babylonian; 14. Armenian; 15. Lydian; 16. Cappadocian; 17. Skudrian; 18. Assyrian; 19. Arabian; 20. Egyptian; 21. Libyan; 22. Nubian; 23. Makan; 24. Indian.

The style, the inscriptions and petrological study of the stone indicate that it was made in Egypt to be placed in a temple there, since, as the inscription says, 'the Persian man had conquered Egypt'. The figure of the king is rendered in Persian costume; but the back pillar and the style of base decoration is Egyptian, though not without Persian traits.

J. Perrot et al., *Journal Asiatique* 260 (1972) 235–66; id., *Cahiers de la délégation archéologique française en Iran* 4 (1974); H. Luschey, *Archäologische Mitteilungen aus Iran*, Ergänzungsband 10 (1983) 191ff.

3. PERSEPOLIS, NAQSH-I RUSTAM

P. R. S. MOOREY

(a) Persepolis

Persepolis lies about 55 km northeast of Shiraz in the wide, fertile plain of Marv Dasht in Fars. It was called Parsa by the Persians, Persai by the Greeks; both words also describe the land of the Persians. When Alexander the Great set fire to it in 330 B.C., perhaps at the whim of a courtesan during a feast or in revenge for the Persian sack of Athens in 480 B.C., he destroyed the heart of the Achaemenid empire, the most intimate and spectacular epitome of the Achaemenian dynasty's traditions and aspirations as a Persian ruling family. It was never one of the administrative centres of the empire, nor even a favoured summer residence, and Greek authors have virtually nothing to say about it. Created by Darius I about 515 B.C., it became the place where Achaemenid kings went at regular intervals to celebrate the achievements of their dynasty in religious ceremonies and diplomatic receptions, and where they were buried.

The principal buildings on the terrace, called a fortress in antiquity, were designed by Darius I (c. 522–486 B.C.); work on them continued through the reigns of Xerxes (486–465 B.C.) and Artaxerxes I (465/4–425 B.C.). Thereafter it seems to pass into eclipse, becoming a 'provincial Versailles' and after Darius II (423–405 B.C.) the kings were buried near the Persepolis platform not at Naqsh-i Rustam. Artaxerxes II (359/8–338 B.C.) undertook some alterations and rebuilding but otherwise the fifth-century buildings endured until Alexander's destruction. Thereafter the site was virtually untouched until excavated in modern times. It constitutes one of the most remarkable ruins in the Near East.

The palatial buildings occupied three sites: the platform (Takht-i Jamshid) onto which the main ceremonial buildings and the treasury were concentrated; parts of the plain to the south and west of the platform where the residential palaces probably stood; and the slope of the high hill to the east of it. Relief sculptures in stone, very stereotyped in style, are to be found in most of the dozen buildings on the platform. They were carved on façades, on staircases, and on door and window jambs. The site now has a skeletal look, as virtually all the mud-brick walls which formed the body of the structures have long since collapsed and been eroded away. Happily it was this debris overlying the sculptures that preserved so many of them. They are the only extensive sculptures to have survived in the Achaemenid Court Style; sites like Babylon and Susa have only yielded a few incoherent fragments. The full implications of the Old Persian words used for buildings here (and at Susa) are much debated: *tacara* (summer palace); *hadis* (royal residence or seat); *apadana* (courtyard).

Throughout the decoration of Persepolis the king dominates not so much as a personal, but as a dynastic image or as 'the Persian Man', who is master of a wide, cohesive and ordered realm. He is raised high, or honoured by his subject peoples with gifts; he in turn honours Ahura Mazda, from whom comes all his power and authority; and he or his representative destroys evil embodied in threatening monsters. Recent research had done nothing to modify Curzon's succinct verdict of 1892: 'Everything is devoted, with unashamed repetition, to a single purpose, viz. the delineation of majesty in its most imperial guise, the pomp and panoply of him who was well styled the Great King' (*Persia and the Persian Question* II, 195). It is unlikely that any of the reliefs illustrates an actual event or festival. Arguments that the Apadana reliefs should be associated with the New Year Festival, a ceremony reconstructed from later Sasanian sources, are not convincing.

GENERAL BIBLIOGRAPHY

Schmidt, *Persepolis* I–III; A. B. Tilia, *Studies and Restorations at Persepolis and Other Sites of Fars* I–II (ISMEO, Rome, 1972, 1978); A. Farkas, *Achaemenid Sculpture* (Leiden, 1974); Root, *King and Kingship*; M. D. Roaf, 'Sculptures and sculptors at Persepolis', *Iran* 21 (1983).

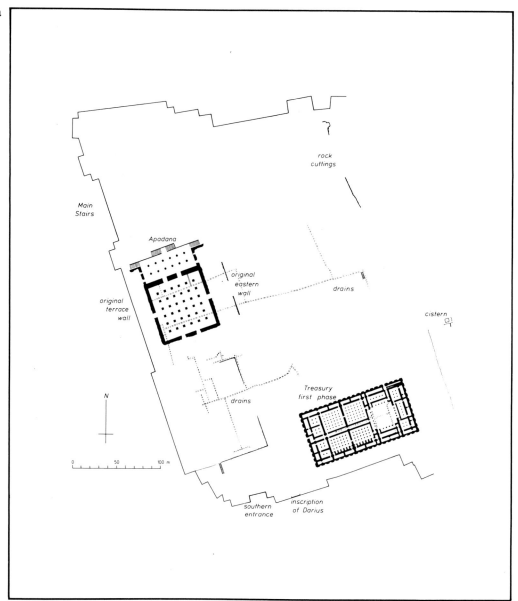

23. Plans of Persepolis (after Roaf, *Iran* 21) to show the architectural development of the platform.. (**a**) About 515–490 B.C. (**b**) About 490–480 B.C. (**c**) About 480–470 B.C. (**d**) About 470–450 B.C. (**e**) About 450–330 B.C.

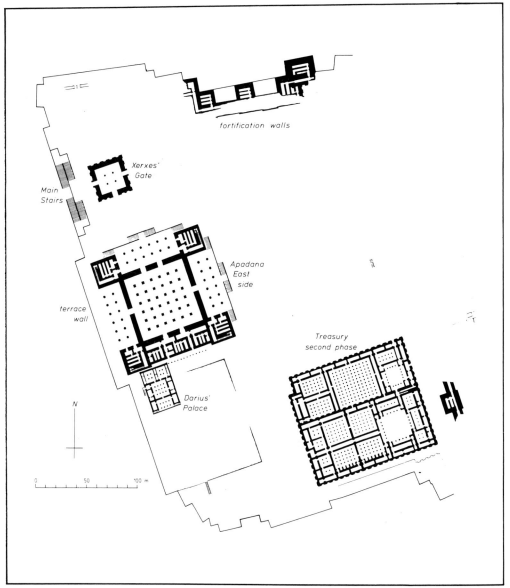

fortification walls

Xerxes' Gate

Main Stairs

Apadana East side

terrace wall

Treasury second phase

N

Darius' Palace

0   50   100 m

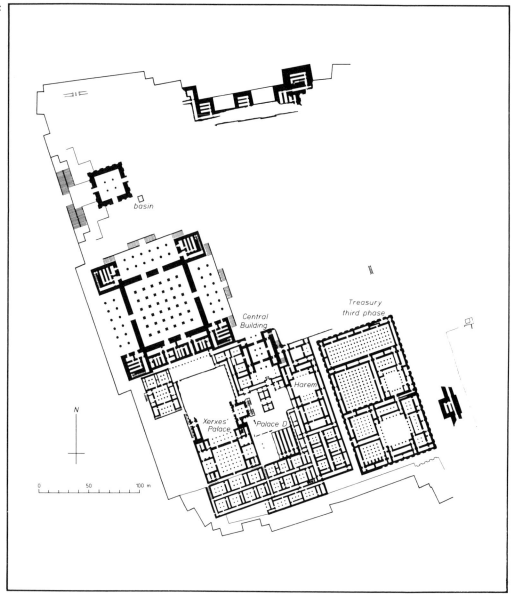

basin

Central
Building

Treasury
third phase

Harem

N

Xerxes'
Palace

Palace D

0   50   100 m

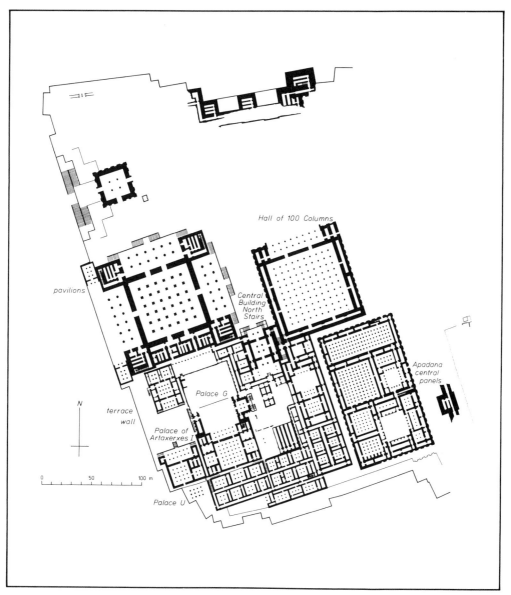

Hall of 100 Columns

pavilions

Central
Building
North
Stairs

Apadana
central
panels

N

terrace
wall

Palace G

Palace of
Artaxerxes I

0   50   100 m

Palace U

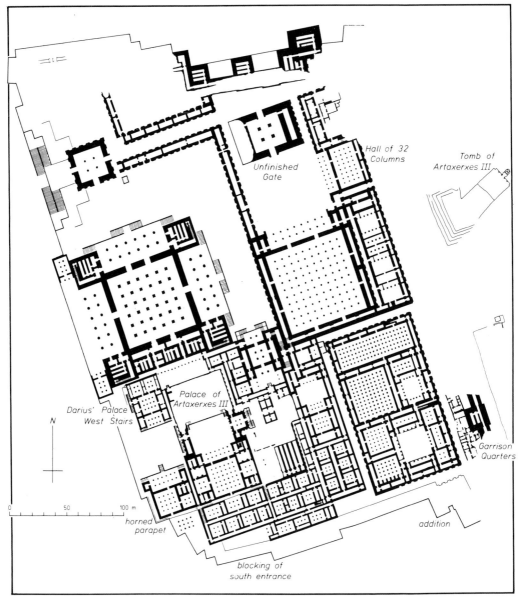

Hall of 32
Columns

Tomb of
Artaxerxes III

Unfinished
Gate

Darius' Palace
West Stairs

Palace of
Artaxerxes III

N

Garrison
Quarters

0   50   100 m

horned
parapet

addition

blocking of
south entrance

24. Oblique view of the platform at Persepolis during the American excavations in the 1930s. It rises over 10 m above the plain and occupies about 13 ha. The tall standing columns mark the Apadana; to the east of it are the lower column fragments and bases of the Hall of 100 Columns, or Throne Hall. The modern building in the foreground is office and museum accommodation.

Schmidt, *Persepolis* I, pl. 3.

25. General view of the western face of the platform with the columns of the Apadana above; access stairway to left; looking north east.

Schmidt, *Persepolis* I, pl. 18B.

26. Gate of All Lands, reign of Xerxes (485–465 B.C.) looking west-north-west. This was the main ceremonial entrance to the palace complex on the platform. The winged, human-headed bulls, wearing horned crowns of divinity, were traditional guardians of palace entrances in the Near East.

Schmidt, *Persepolis* I, pl. 12B.

27. Eastern stairway of the Apadana showing the central and northern parts with the Gate of All Lands in the right background; reigns of Darius and Xerxes. The central panel shown here, flanked by lion and bull motives, was a replacement for an original, showing the king and crown prince (see **29**), replaced in the second quarter of the fifth century B.C. Processions of tributaries (see **40**) are shown on the main façade.

Schmidt, *Persepolis* I, pl. 17A.

28. Lion and bull panel on the southern section of the central façade of the eastern stairway of the Apadana. This motif appears recurrently at Persepolis. It seems to have been a primary symbol of royal authority; in origin it goes back to the prehistoric period in Mesopotamia. It has been argued, by those who wish to associate these reliefs with the Persian New Year celebrations, that here it represents Leo and Taurus, constellations of the Zodiac, indicating the vernal equinox.

Schmidt, *Persepolis* I, pl. 20.

29. The southern relief found in the Treasury, where it was in a protected not an ignominious setting. A. B. Tilia demonstrated that this was originally the central panel, on the north side of the Apadana, towards which the procession of tributaries was conceived as moving. The king is shown enthroned, with the crown prince standing behind him, attended by his weapon and towel bearers. In front, beyond a pair of incense burners, a court dignitary, perhaps the grand marshal of the procession, is shown in the respectful attitude adopted when addressing the king. The royal figures, as is typical, are represented larger than the others. It is not known when this panel was displaced; to judge by the style of the replacement panel it was probably under Artaxerxes I. Whether the relief shows Darius and the Crown Prince Xerxes, or Xerxes and his eldest son Darius is not clear.

Schmidt, *Persepolis* I, pl. 149.

30. The king, originally carrying a staff and a lotus blossom, attended by the bearers of his sunshade, and of his towel and fly-whisk, under an anthropomorphic winged disk, facing the same way as the king. This relief is on the west jamb of the southern doorway of the main hall of the Central Building (Schmidt's 'Council Hall'); the figures are shown leaving the building. The identity of this king is debated; the relief was prob-ably carved towards the end of the reign of Xerxes. As has been noted (see 11) opinions on the identity of the anthropomorphic winged disk are divergent. Here, by contrast with Bisitun, the figure does not wear a divine horned headdress, rather a royal one.

Schmidt, *Persepolis* I, pl. 75.

32

pare the royal tomb façades (**36**, **38**). Again Darius or Xerxes might be intended here.

Schmidt, *Persepolis* I, pl. 78A.

32. Hero grasping the horn of a winged leonine monster in his left hand and stabbing it with his right; on the south jamb of the eastern doorway of the 'Harem' of Xerxes. As the human figure does not wear the headdress, or the type of shoes, worn elsewhere by kings at Persepolis, his identity is a matter of discussion. In Assyria kings had only been shown fighting real animals; gods, genii and mythical heroes fought monsters. Either this is an unidentified mythical figure or possibly a king conceived as the 'Persian Man', a phrase used by Darius in his tomb inscription to describe his exploits.

Schmidt, *Persepolis* I, pl. 196B.

33. Persian and Median dignitaries on the east wing of the northern stairway of the Apadana. One of the most striking features of the Persepolis reliefs is these files of court attendants depicted in variations of stock gestures: holding hands; touching one's neighbour; stroking one's beard or fingering one's cloak strap; holding a flower; turning to speak. It is not certain that the riding habit necessarily denotes a Mede, or the robe a Persian, as has been long assumed; if this is not the implied distinction, it may be that between military and non-military court personnel or between military dress and court dress.

Schmidt, *Persepolis* I, pl. 65C.

34. Beardless attendant, perhaps a youth or a eunuch, with an unguent jar (?alabaster) and a towel, on the south jamb of the western door of Room 12 in the Palace of Darius; matching figures elsewhere carry pails and incense burners.

Schmidt, *Persepolis* I, pl. 149.

31. The king enthroned, facing inwards, with his crown prince, under a canopy bearing a plain winged disk; Ahura Mazda above; on the south jamb of the eastern doorway of the main hall of the Central Building. A dais supports the royalty; it is slightly raised off the ground (cf. **38**) by 28 bearers in 3 tiers (9:10:9), who represent peoples of different regions in the empire. Com-

35. Two important archives of inscribed tablets were found at Persepolis. The Fortification Texts, dating between 509 and 494 B.C., are mainly concerned with ration issues and food transferred, yielding considerable information on administration in the area around Persepolis. The Treasury Texts, dating from 492–458 B.C.,

deal with issues of silver and have a more limited geographical scope. A number of famous individuals appear in these documents; sealings associated with three of the most renowned are illustrated here.

(**a**, **b**) impressions of two seals of Parnaka (Pharnaces), both inscribed in Aramaic on tablets from the Fortification archive; one reads Parnaka, the other Parnaka, son of Arsames; it is the latter inscription that suggests he was a brother of Darius' father Hystaspes, both sons of Arsames. Parnaka was a sort of controller-general of the administration of Persis (Fars) until about 497 B.C. The highest places in the empire's administration were allocated to members of the king's extended family.

(**c**) sealing on a tablet concerning Gobryas (Gubaru) from the Fortification archive; this is presumably the father-in-law of Darius who was satrap of Babylon and Abarnahara (*ebir nari*) (Syria). He had helped Darius to seize the throne after the death of Cambyses and became the spear-bearer of the new king (cf. Bisitun (**15**) and the tomb of Darius I at Naqsh-i Rustam).

(Persepolis T-974, seal 16; PF-1796, seal 9; PF-688.)

R. T. Hallock, *Persepolis Fortification Texts* (Chicago, 1969); G. G. Cameron, *Persepolis Treasury Tablets* (Chicago, 1948).

(b) Naqsh-i Rustam

A cliff face, about 6 km north-north-west of the platform at Persepolis, known as Naqsh-i Rustam, contains the tombs of four Achaemenid kings cut to virtually identical designs. Only that of Darius I is inscribed; consequently, attributions of the others, and the three royal tombs (one unfinished) near the Persepolis platform, are conjectural. Although it is only assumed that Cambyses had a tomb (its location is unknown) like that of Cyrus II (10), it seems that Darius I introduced a new type of rock-hewn royal burial. It was also probably Darius I who ordered the erection of the free-standing Ka'bah-i Zardusht, which is a replica of the Zendan at Pasargadae. Cyrus (10) had been inspired by west Anatolian architecture; what inspired the change effected by Darius I remains uncertain – possibly Urartian rock-cut tombs. Much controversy has

raged round these tombs, and that of Cyrus, as the royal bodies were apparently embalmed or covered with wax (Hdt. 1.140; Strabo XV.20; Curtius XII.12.13), not exposed, as in later orthodox Zoroastrianism; but what this indicates about royal religious practice is uncertain, since reference to exposure of the dead is not found in the old part of the Avesta.

36. Panoramic view of the cliff face at Naqsh-i Rustam showing the rock-cut tombs (from the right) of Darius I (identified by inscription) and those attributed to Artaxerxes I and Darius II; that of Xerxes, further to the right, is not shown here. The Ka'bah-i Zardusht is the free-standing rectangular stone structure on the extreme left. The carved reliefs set low on the rock face were put there by Sasanian kings. Tombs attributed to Artaxerxes II and III and to Darius III (unfinished) lie behind the platform at Persepolis.

Schmidt, *Persepolis* III, pl. 1; P. Calmeyer, *Archäologische Mitteilungen aus Iran* 8 (1975) 99ff.

35a

35b

35c

37. The Ka'bah-i Zardusht after excavation by the American Expedition (looking south east). It was probably built in the reign of Darius I to serve the same purpose as the Zendan at Pasargadae, built in the second half of the reign of Cyrus II. These virtually identical buildings have no known parallels; both have a single room at the top, in an otherwise solid mass of masonry, accessible through a single door, approached up a tall, monumental stairway. An inscription of Kartir, founder of the Sasanian state church, on the lower part of the Ka'bah, refers to a 'foundation house'. This is the only real clue to the function of these remarkable structures. It is taken to indicate that they are more likely to have been repositories for valuable objects or manuscripts of dynastic or religious importance rather than fire-temples or royal tombs; but the problem remains unsolved.

Schmidt, *Persepolis* III, pl. 13.

38. Detail of the façade of the tomb ascribed to Xerxes, about 100 m east-north-east of that of Darius I. In design all four royal tomb façades at Naqsh-i Rustam are basically the same: A Greek cross, about 18 m wide and 21 m high, cut into the rock face; the upper vertical space (as here) is carved with a couch-like dais held

36

37

38

just off the ground by 30 bearers (identified by labels on the tomb of Darius I), each representing one of the peoples of the empire. Two stepped *podia* are set on this, facing one another at a short distance; on the left the king stands, on the right a flaming altar; above the gap hovers Ahura Mazda with, behind him, a disk with a crescent inscribed within it. Various figures are cut to left and right.

Schmidt, *Persepolis* III, pl. 42A.

39. View of the horizontal bar on the tomb attributed to Xerxes carved to resemble a portico, with central doorway leading to the tomb chamber. Attached columns with bull capitals support the horizontal beams of the roof. The rock-cut chamber within, as in all cases, is now completely empty; rock-cut niches, some with stone covers, are cut on each side. The lower vertical bar is always plain.

Schmidt, *Persepolis* III, pl. 42B.

4. THE PEOPLES OF THE EMPIRE

P. R. S. MOOREY

40. One of the most characteristic features of Achaemenid monuments is the listing and illustration of subject peoples. As these lists almost certainly do not correspond to any political or financial divisions of the Persian empire (despite many suggestions to the contrary), they need not list every subject group. Yet they may still be taken to give a very direct impression of how rulers from Darius I to Artaxerxes I wished their vast realm to be seen by posterity. From Egypt, where the very idea may have originated, come the labelled figures of peoples represented on the base of the statue of Darius I found at Susa (**22**) and those on a series of stelae set up by the same king to commemorate the building of a canal from the Nile to the Red Sea. At Naqsh-i Rustam and at Persepolis they appear as bearers on the royal tomb façades. On the platform at Persepolis, where in all cases they are not identified by inscriptions, they appear, as dais supporters, on the Central Building (**31**) and on the Hall of 100 Columns and, as tribute bearers, on the Apadana reliefs (north and east sides), on the west stairs of the Palace of Darius and on the Palace of Artaxerxes I.

As the identity of the individual delegations on the Apadana is not given, they have to be compared to the labelled tomb representations of supporters (cf.**38**); but, as the correspondences are not exact, some margin of doubt persists. In the following section the reliefs of tribute bearers on the Apadana are used to provide a panorama of the Achaemenid empire. The Apadana (**25–29**) was started by Darius I and completed by Xerxes. The reliefs on the north side are a mirror image of those on the east side, now better preserved. Twenty-three groups, excluding the Persians, are shown in a processional frieze dressed in their national costumes bringing a selection of items – national dress, animals from their homeland, precious materials and fine manufactured objects – as gifts or tribute for the king.

GENERAL BIBLIOGRAPHY

R. G. Kent, *Journal of Near Eastern Studies* 2 (1943) 302ff; G. Walser, *Die Völkerschaften auf den Reliefs von Persepolis* (Berlin, 1966); G. G. Cameron, *Journal of Near Eastern Studies* 32 (1973) 47ff; Schmidt, *Persepolis* III, 108ff; M. Roaf, 'The Subject Peoples on the base of the statue of Darius', *Cahiers de la délégation archéologique française en Iran* 4 (1974) 73ff (who discusses the degrees of uncertainty in identification).

IV   II

V   III

VI

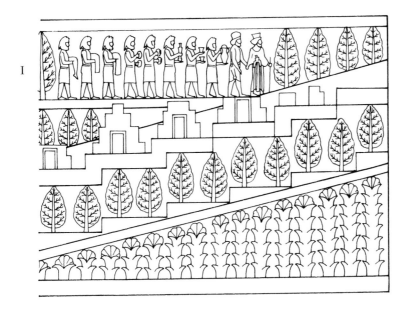

I

XVI

XVII

XVIII

XIII

XIV

XV

X

XI

XII

VII

VIII

IX

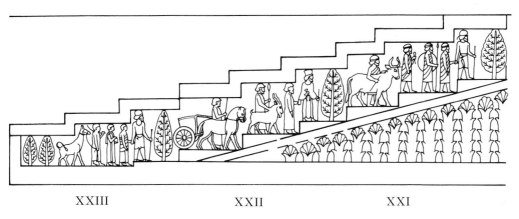

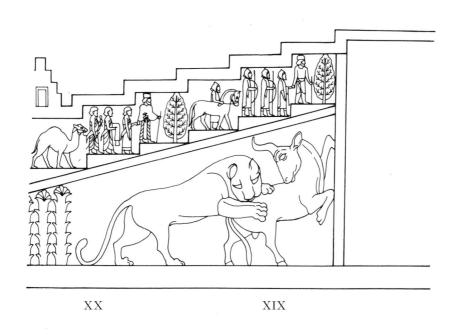

XXIII XXII XXI

XX XIX

I: *The Medes*; an accepted identification.

II: *The Elamites*; an accepted identification.

III: *The Armenians*; an accepted identification.

IV: *The Arians or Arachosians*; a probable identification.

V: *The Babylonians*; an accepted identification.

VI: *The Lydians*; a debated identification; the hair braid is distinctive.

VII: *The Drangians*; a possible identification; they wear garments similar to their Arian and Arachosian neighbours (cf. IV).

VIII: *The Assyrians*; a debated identification; they wear a distinctive fillet on the head.

IX: *The Cappadocians*; a disputed identification turning on the ethnic relationship of the fibula they wear.

X: *The Egyptians*; an accepted identification (heads are destroyed on the Apadana).

XI: *Saka tigrakhauda* (the pointed-hat Scythians); an accepted identification.

XII: *Ionians*; an accepted identification.

XIII: *Bactrians*; this is only a possible identification as the Bactrians and the Parthians are difficult to distinguish (cf. XV).

XIV: *Gandarans*; only a possible identification; might be *Maka*.

XV: *Parthians*; only a possible identification (cf. XIII).

XVI: *Sagartians*; a doubtful identification.

XVII: *Sogdians and Chorasmians*; a probable identification.

XVIII: *Indians*; this delegation may combine Gandarans and Sattagydians.

XIX: *Skudrians/Thracians*; a probable identification.

XX: *Arabians*; an accepted identification.

XXI: *Carians*; a doubtful identification.

XXII: *Libyans*; an accepted identification; the cap with its serrated border is distinctive.

XXIII: *Nubians/Ethiopians*; an accepted identification.

5. RELIGION AND THE RULERS

P. R. S. MOOREY

On account of the release of the Jews from captivity in Babylon, authorized by Cyrus, honoured by Darius I (Ezra 1:1; 6), the rulers of the Persian empire have an enduring reputation for religious tolerance. Wherever evidence survives elsewhere, this view is largely sustained. Traditional cults flourished unchallenged throughout the empire. There is no evidence for an orthodox imperial religion imposed through an elaborate establishment of priests. Whether among the Elamites of Fars in Iran, as revealed by tablets from Persepolis, or among a Jewish mercenary community on the southern frontier of Egypt, as in the papyri from Elephantine, the beliefs and practices of numerous traditional local cults were respected and protected. The rarely recorded exceptions serve only to emphasize the more usual official tolerance.

Intense scholarly controversy surrounds the religious beliefs of the king and his court. Did they simply observe the traditional beliefs and practices of the Indo-Iranian peoples or were they adherents of the reformed religion taught, at an unknown time before Cyrus, by Zoroaster? If they were Zoroastrians, was this the case from as early as Cyrus or from later time; if so, when? It is, to a considerable extent, a debate about definitions, since there is so little firm evidence for the nature of early Zoroastrian cult practice. Current reconstructions rest upon knowledge of more recent Zoroastrian rites and doctrines whose precise antiquity is unknown. Relevant Greco-Roman textual references to Iranian religion, in the absence of local sources from which to check them, confuse as often as they illuminate the problem.

As Achaemenid royal inscriptions are so few and cryptic they offer little guidance. Art reveals something of religious ceremonies; when it does, the cult practices are Indo-Iranian rather than specifically Zoroastrian. From Darius I to Artaxerxes II inscriptions extol Ahura Mazda, with occasional, but explicit, references to 'other gods who are'; it is not until Artaxerxes II that the god Mithra and the goddess Anahita are also actually named. Before him the rulers may have ignored rather than rejected them, since among the common people, at least in Fars, there is some evidence they were worshipped earlier.

The Persepolis tablets of the earlier fifth century reveal multi-faceted worship and a marked degree of syncretism. Cult scenes on sculptures and seals reveal a variety of practices, many traditional, involving altars, priests and shrines. The single most common icon, worship at a fire-altar, had long been popular among the Elamites and was not unknown in other parts of the ancient Near East. Apart from the so-called 'sacred precinct' at Pasargadae, archaeology has so far revealed little or nothing of the setting for such cult practices.

The message of Zoroaster was grafted onto age-old Iranian beliefs and practices with varying speed and intensity during the Achaemenid period; its precise impact among Iranians, let alone other members of the empire, may not be accurately gauged from present evidence.

GENERAL BIBLIOGRAPHY

E. Beveniste, *The Persian Religion according to the Chief Greek Texts* (Paris, 1929); M. Boyce, *A History of Zoroastrianism* I–II (Leyden, 1975, 1982); J. Duchesne-Guillemin, *La religion de l'Iran ancien* (Paris, 1962), and *Historia* Einzelschrift 18 (1972) 59–82.

42

41. Gold statuette of a man in 'Median' costume, with *kandys* (coat) over his shoulders, holding a bunch of twigs(?); he wears a hood-like cap, with flaps brought round to cover his mouth; probably a *magus*, one of the clan or tribe who were the officiating priests, rather than the theologians, of the old Persian religion; fourth century B.C.(?).

(London, British Museum WA 123902. Height 5.6 cm.)
 Dalton, *Treasure*, no. 2, pl. 13.

42. Gold plaque showing a man in 'Median' costume carrying a bundle of twigs or rods, probably the barsom (baresman): originally a handful of grasses strewn during Indo-Iranian sacrificial rites that became a common priestly attribute. Whether a figure such as this, armed with an *akinakes* (short sword), should be described as a *magus* or priest is open to debate; fourth century B.C.

(London, British Museum WA 123949, Height 15 cm.)
 Boyce, *History of Zoroastrianism* I, 167; II, 5ff; Dalton, *Treasure*, no. 48, pl. 14.

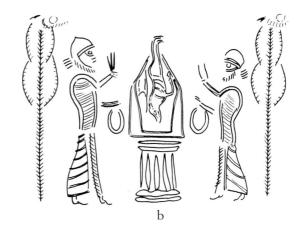

a

b

c

d

43. A limestone altar from Bünyän, near Kayseri, in Turkey, showing a bearded man in 'Median' costume with *kandys*; he wears a hat with side flaps turned back and carries a barsom in his right hand whilst raising his left in salutation. Repeated round the other sides of the altar. As the top is damaged, identification as a fire-altar is conjectural; fourth century B.C.

(Ankara Museum. Height 55 cm.)
E. Akurgal, *Die Kunst Anatoliens von Homer bis Alexander* (Berlin, 1961) 173–4, pl. 120.

44. Four drawings of designs on Achaemenid seals to show the variety of cults associated with the fire-altar.

((**a**) British Museum WA 128849 (attributed to Babylon); (**b**) Ashmolean Museum 1892.1416 (bought in Egypt); (**c**) Private Collection: A. Parrot, *Nineveh and Babylon* (London, 1961) fig. 160; (**d**) Orien-

tal Institute, Chicago: *American Journal of Scientific Languages* 44 (1927–8) 249, no. 59.)
(Cf. P. R. S. Moorey, *Archäologische Mitteilungen aus Iran*, Ergänzungsband 6 (Berlin, 1979) pp. 218–26.)

45. Fragmentary stone relief from Dascylium in Turkey showing two *magi*, dressed in tunic and trousers, with *kandys* and hat, its flap tied so as to cover nose and mouth. Both hold a long, thick, scroll-like object (barsom) and both raise their open hand in gesture. Heads of ox and ram on a wattle-like structure outside a tomb door; perhaps showing the consecration to the yazata Haoma of the heads of sacrificed animals; an observance for the souls of the dead; fifth century B.C.

(Istanbul Museum. Height 67 cm.)
Th. Macridy, *BCH* 37 (1913) 348ff, pl. 8; A. U. Pope, *Survey of Persian Art* IV (Oxford, 1939) pl. 103B; A. Büsing-Kolbe, *JDAI* 92 (1977) 120.

46. (a) Ritual meal on a rock crystal cylinder-seal of the fifth century B.C. from Iraq; the scene has exact precursors in Mesopotamia, but here a single winged disk replaces the multiple deity symbols used earlier and the costume is distinctively Iranian.

(Archäologisches Institut der Universität Zürich no.1961. Height 22.5 mm.)

A. Boisser, *Notice sur quelques monuments assyriens à l'Université de Zurich* (Geneva, 1912) 35, no.5; P. R. S. Moorey, *op cit.* **44**, 218–19, pl. 1.

(b) For comparison, an earlier Babylonian seal.

(London, British Museum WA 89590. Height 4.5 cm.)

D. J. Wiseman, *Cylinder Seals of Western Asia* (London, 1958) pl. 81.

47. Two modern impressions from cylinder-seals with scenes of worship in which an anthropomorphic winged disk appears alone and in combination with an 'encircled bust'; the identity of these symbols is debated.

(London, British Museum WA 89422, 89852. Heights 2.0 cm, 2.0 cm.)

Wiseman, *op cit.*, pls. 101, 102, 106.

 46a

46b

48

49

47

ing the Mesopotamian goddess Ishtar, she is probably Anahita.

(Leningrad, Hermitage Museum. Height 29 mm.)
E. Minns, *Scythians and Greeks* (Cambridge, 1913) 410–11, fig.298; *GGFR*, pl. 878.

49. Green chert pestle and mortar from Arachosia found with many such objects in the 'Treasury' at Persepolis; inscriptions in ink in Aramaic on the base of the mortar and on the head of the pestle. First read as a record of haoma ritual, the text formula was subsequently recognized as a routine administrative notation. There is no firm evidence that these utensils were intended for ritual purposes; kitchen or pharmacy service may be as likely. They had never been used.

(Tehran, Iran Bastan Museum.)
Schmidt, *Persepolis* II, pl. 23:1–2; R. A. Bowman, *Aramaic Ritual Texts from Persepolis* (Chicago, 1970); B. A. Levine, *Journal of the American Oriental Society* 92 (1972) 70ff; J. Naveh and S. Shaked, *Orientalia* 42 (1973) 445ff; W. Hinz, *Acta Iranica* 4 (1975) 371ff.

48. Fourth-century B.C. blue chalcedony cylinder-seal found in a grave at Anapa in south Russia, but probably made for a Persian in Turkey. An Achaemenid king worshipping a female deity, in a nimbus, set on the back of a lion. As this is the traditional way for represent-

50. A copy of the Daiva inscription of Xerxes in Old Persian on a grey limestone foundation tablet re-used as a drain cover in the citadel at Pasargadae; the same inscription is found at Persepolis in Akkadian and Elamite, as well as in Old Persian. Here Xerxes abominates the false gods (*daivas*) worshipped at one specific place; whether they were Indo-Iranian gods rejected by Zoroastrians or foreign gods is unknown. This act has been taken to identify Xerxes as a Zoroastrian.

(Tehran, Iran Bastan Museum.)

D. Stronach, *Pasargadae* (Oxford, 1978) 152, pls. 122b, 161b; R. G. Kent, *Old Persian* (New Haven, 1950) 151–2; G. G. Cameron, *Die Welt des Orients* 2 (1954–9) 470ff.

51. Two modern impressions of cylinder-seals showing the Achaemenid king or royal hero in scenes derived directly from traditional Near Eastern iconography.

(London, British Museum WA 89337, 89352. Heights 4 cm, 3 cm.)

Wiseman, *op cit.* **46b**, pls. 105. 106.

51a

51b

6. ASPECTS OF LIFE AND CRAFTS

P. R. S. MOOREY

(**76–82** *by John Boardman*; **104–113** *by T. F. Taylor*)

The life-style distinctive of the Persians as controllers of an empire was that of a military elite; its most conspicuous features were widely copied and emulated by their subjects. In the Iranian tradition, from an early age, male children were trained hard in the required physical skills and in learning the accepted code of behaviour: speaking the truth and observing precepts provided by legends and the example of their elders. Each man aspired to what Darius I proclaimed in his tomb inscription; 'Trained am I both with hands and with feet; as a horseman I am a good horseman; as a bowman I am a good bowman, both afoot and on horseback; as a spearman I am a good spearman, both afoot and on horseback' (Kent's translation). Such also are the virtues commended in the young Cyrus by Xenophon about a century later (*Anab.* I. 9.3–4): '... remarkable for his fondness for horses and being able to manage them extremely well. In the military arts also of archery and spear-throwing they judged him to be the most eager to learn and the most willing to practise them. When he got to the age for hunting, he was most enthusiastic about it, and only too ready to take risks ...'

Intellectual pursuits and literary achievements were not part of this life-style; reading and writing were left to scribes: 'it was inscribed and was read off before me' (Darius I in the Bisitun inscription). There is no indication of any Persian inclination to scientific pursuits or to philosophical speculations. As all surviving religious literature from Iran is known only from much later versions, the earlier elements within it are notoriously difficult to date and attribute.

The following, inevitably very selective, set of illustrations from art and material culture, attempts to offer a sketch of the most distinctive aspects of the Persian way of life. As was explained in the introduction, the nature of the sources and restricted space preclude any realistic representation of life at other levels in the numerous provinces of the empire. In some, notably Egypt, the material record shows scarcely any trace of a Persian impact (cf. J. D. Cooney, *Bulletin of the American Research Center in Cairo* 4 (1965) 39ff); in others, as in Turkey (C. G. Starr, *Iranica Antiqua* 11 (1975) 39ff; 12 (1977) 49ff) there was a subtle and fascinatingly various interaction of the new and the old in many aspects of daily life. There is no standard pattern and the scattered archaeological records of each region require detailed attention. Very few have yet received it (cf. E. Stern, *The Material Culture of the Land of the Bible in the Persian Period, 538–332 B.C.* (Warminster 1982)). Very broadly speaking, in archaeological terms, the material culture of the sixth, fifth and much of the fourth centuries B.C. follows on from the preceding phase of the mature Iron Age.

Here, first costume and personal ornaments, much worn by the male aristocracy as marks of wealth, rank and royal favour, are surveyed; then the role of horses and chariots in hunting and combat and the personal arms particularly appropriate to horsemen, most closely associated with the Medes and Persians; and finally in this section the view of court life in Persian Anatolia given by the so-called Greco-Persian arts. It is the sumptuary crafts which complete the section that have long epitomized the aristocratic way of life in the Achaemenid empire. Such products, including lavish and impressive table-ware in a variety of metals, perishable materials like carpets and wall-hangings, fine clothes and richly decorated tents, were widely distributed across the empire by serving soldiers and administrators, by rich gifts to secure alliances, often far beyond the empire's borders, and by deposit in temple and palace treasuries. Social bonding within the ruling group was secured through gift-giving. At the top of the social hierarchy, status with the king, to whom loyalty was absolute, meant everything. It was secured and conspicuously demonstrated through rich material rewards (and fearsome punishments) and, in general, by a legendary element of luxurious living.

Two hoards are important sources for objects illustrated here and deserve explanation:

The Treasure of the Oxus (54, 61–3, 66, 69, 71, 83, 235)

The heterogeneous collection of gold and silver objects now in the British Museum popularly known as 'The Treasure of Oxus' was found by chance in 1877, but the precise site of its discovery is disputed. The Treasure was brought out of the Oxus valley to Kabul in Afghanistan, and thence to Peshawar in modern Pakistan where it was sold. Following recent Russian excavations it is now assumed that the original find was most probably made near Kobdian (Mikojanabad), north of the river Oxus in modern Tajikstan, ancient Bactria. The integrity of the hoard as first published by Dalton in 1905 has never been established. Indeed it is very doubtful. The whole group is best treated as an assembly of individual objects whose original association is not proved. The coins which reached Europe in company with the hoard extend in date from the early fifth to about the end of the third century B.C. Although a majority of the objects probably date to the fifth and fourth centuries B.C., there are one or two that may well be post-Achaemenid. Suggestions that a few items, notably the gold cover for an *akinakes* scabbard, are sixth-century and possibly Median have not met with general support.

Russian scholars, particularly, now argue that many of the vessels and much of the jewellery in the Treasure were the work of craftsmen active in Bactria, not imports from production centres farther west in the Achaemenid empire. Although Bactria did not actually produce gold for the Persian kings, it was the entrepôt for Siberian gold. Delegations XIII and XV on the Apadana at Persepolis (see 40), who have been particularly associated with Bactria and Parthia, both bring vessels assumed to be made of precious metals, presumably gold if judged fit for the Great King. It is also likely that some of the more spectacular metal vessels acquired by the nomads of inner Asia, and recovered from graves in modern times in the region, came originally from workshops in Bactria.

O. M. Dalton, *The Treasure of the Oxus*[3] (British Museum, London, 1964); B. A. Litvinsky and I. R. Pichikiyan, 'The Temple of the Oxus', *Journal of the Royal Asiatic Society* 1981, 133ff.

The Pasargadae Hoard (64, 92)

Finds of gold and silver jewellery of the Achaemenid period are extremely rare in controlled excavations, particularly in Iran. In the course of the British excavations at Pasargadae from 1961 to 1963, directed by David Stronach, a hoard of personal ornaments was recovered from the base of a large pottery water-jar, the upper part of which was lost. This jar had originally been set near the exterior of one of the garden pavilions adjacent to palaces S and P. It was presumably used as a convenient place of concealment at a time of crisis. Apart from hundreds of beads in gold, silver, lapis lazuli, amethyst, coral and pearl, the hoard included: a pair of gold bracelets with detachable, ibex-headed terminals, a number of pairs of penannular gold ear-rings with pendants and two silver spoons. The hoard was probably concealed during the fourth century B.C., though some of the contents may have been made in the second half of the previous century.

D. Stronach, *Pasargadae* (Oxford, 1978) 168ff, pls. 146–60.

(a) Costume

52. Two armed men, to the left in Median, to the right in Persian costume, shown on the east face of the east wing of the north stairway of the Central Building (Council Hall) at Persepolis; such alternating figures seem only to occur on buildings associated with Artaxerxes I (464–424 B.C.). Traditional usage in Achaemenid studies labels as 'Median' any person wearing the tailored knee-length riding tunic and trousers, to which the long-sleeved *kandys* (coat) is sometimes added; as 'Persian' anyone wearing the draped robe with patterned folds more typical of earlier Near Eastern dress and perhaps related to the Elamite costume. Whether this was made of one or two pieces of cloth is debated. Herodotus (1.135) maintains that the Persians had borrowed Median costume, probably indicating that tunic and trousers, traditional Iranian riding habit, was the more common attire for men, at least in military contexts. It is almost

certain that the men wearing 'Median' costume at Persepolis were not necessarily meant to represent Medes; indeed Medes may have been rare in court circles and the ruling class predominantly Persian.

Schmidt, *Persepolis* I pl. 65c; G. Widengren, *Studia Ethnographica Upsaliensis* 11 (1956) 228ff; P. Beck, *Iranica Antiqua* 9 (1972) 116–22; M. C. Root, *Acta Iranica* 9 (1979) 279–82.

53. Drawing of the king's Weapon-Bearer as represented at Persepolis on the original main panels of the Apadana friezes (cf. **40**), primarily from the northern panel, but details restored from the eastern version. The short-sword (*akinakes*), battle-axe and *gorytus*, a case to carry both a composite bow and its arrows, are typical Median military equipment, as is the costume; early fifth century B.C.

Schmidt, *Persepolis* I, pls. 119–23.

54. Silver, partially gilded, statuette of a man from the Oxus Treasure; a flat band of gold round his head is engraved with crenellations suggesting royal status. The full-sleeved and

pleated costume, in the Persian mode, and the headdress are uncanonical, perhaps indicating provincial rather than Persepolitan fashion. In his left hand he grasps what may be a stylized lotus, as does the king at Persepolis (cf. **29**) rather than the barsom (cf. **42**); sixth to fifth century B.C.

(London, British Museum WA 123901. Height 14.8 cm.)
   Dalton, *Treasure*, pl. 2.1.

55. Hollow terracotta head of a man, perhaps from a vessel, found among the Fortification Tablets at Persepolis; the fur-trimmed hat is distinctive; it may be a more commonplace version of the headdress shown in **54**; fifth century B.C.

Schmidt, *Persepolis* II, 68, pl. 32.

54

56

55

57ª

56. Limestone head of a Persian; bought in Paris, but usually attributed to Egypt. The style of the headdress and the cut of the beard are exactly like those of the 'royal heroes' on the reliefs of the Palace of Darius at Persepolis; fifth to fourth century B.C.

(Paris, Louvre.)
Ghirshman, *Persia: from the Origins to Alexander the Great* 244, fig. 293; R. L. Scheurleer, *Revue d'Égyptologie* 26 (1974) 90.

57. Fragmentary statuette in hippopotamus ivory and wood of a standing man in pleated costume with a short-sword of Persian type in his belt; reported to be from Egypt; fifth to fourth century B.C.

(Paris, Louvre.)
R. A. Stucky, *AK* 28 (1985) no. 5, pl. 3.

58. Fragmentary dark grey-brown schist statue of Ptahhotpe, Treasurer of Egypt under Darius I (521–486 B.C.); the sleeved jacket, the neck torc (see detail) and the bracelets are fashions reflecting the impact of Persia on Egypt. A long, mainly autobiographical, hieroglyphic inscription on the back pillar of the statue reports the work he did in the temples of Memphis. Detail (**b**): recumbent mouflon at the ends of the torc (probably a royal gift indicating his rank) and an Egyptian pectoral showing a king, presumably Darius, before the two Memphite deities, Ptah (in a shrine) and Sekhmet.

(New York, Brooklyn Museum 37.353. Height 85 cm.)
B. V. Bothmer, *Egyptian Sculpture of the Late Period 700 B.C. to A.D. 100* (Brooklyn, 1960) no. 64, pls. 60–1.

58a

b

59

monly found in Egypt. Representations of women in Achaemenid art are extremely rare (cf. **60**, **78b**, **c**); it is not certain whether this is a secular figure or a representation of the goddess Anahita; fourth century B.C.

(New York, Brooklyn Museum 63.37. Height 15 cm.)

J. D. Cooney, *Journal of the American Research Center in Egypt* 46 (1965–7) p. 26; A. Spycket, 'Women in Persian art' in D. Schmandt-Besserat (ed.), *Ancient Persia: The Art of an Empire* (Malibu, 1980) 43–5; H. Sancisi-Weerdenburg in A. Cameron and A. Kuhrt (eds.), *Images of Women in Antiquity* (London 1983) 22–3.

60. Bronze kohl tube in the form of a standing woman, bought at Aleppo in Syria; she wears a simplified version of the garment shown in **59**; fifth to fourth centuries B.C.

(Oxford, Ashmolean Museum 1889.794. Height 8.2 cm.)

D. B. Harden, *The Phoenicians* (London, 1962) pls. 84–5; W. Culican, *Iranica Antiqua* 11 (1975) 104, fig. 3; P. R. S. Moorey, *Levant* 16 (1984) 87, no. 41.

59. Limestone plaque with a high relief figure of a woman in the female version of the Persian costume; this type of 'trial piece' is most com-

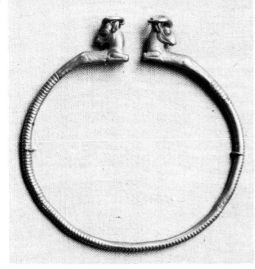

(b) Personal ornaments

61. One of a pair of heavy gold bracelets from the Oxus Treasure, originally inlaid with coloured stones, glass or faience; terminals cast as leaping lion-griffins. This, one of the finest surviving pieces of Achaemenid jewellery, reveals something of its exuberant design and polychrome splendour; sixth to fifth centuries B.C.

(London, British Museum WA 124017. Width 11.5 cm.)
 Dalton, *Treasure*, no. 116, pl. 1.

62. Gold bracelet from the Oxus Treasure with terminals cast as winged goats leaping forward; sixth to fifth centuries B.C.

(London, British Museum WA 124040. Width 8.3 cm.)
 Dalton, *Treasure*, no. 137, pl. 21.

63. A gold torc, twisted out of shape, or a spiral bracelet, terminating in lions' heads with cavities for polychrome inlays, from the Oxus Treasure; sixth to fifth centuries B.C.

(London, British Museum WA 124018. Width 10.35 cm.)
  Dalton, *Treasure*, no. 117, fig. 65.

64. Jewellery from the Pasargadae Hoard, fourth century B.C. In the bottom of a tall, buff-ware water-jar, near the south-west portico of the garden pavilion at Pasargadae, the British excavators found 1,162 objects in all, comprising bracelets, ear-rings, two silver spoons (cf. **92**), numerous beads and pendants:
  (**a**) Pair of gold bracelets with detachable ibex-head terminals; 6.5 cm and 7 cm diameter.

63

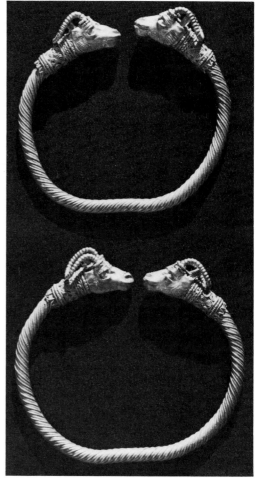

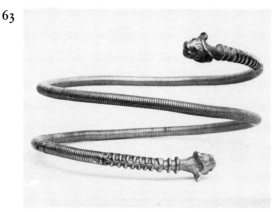

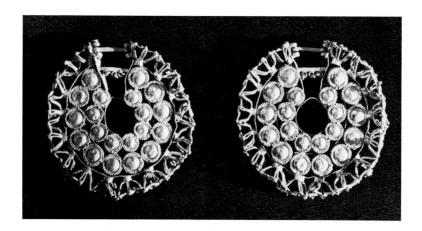

(b) Pair of gold ear-rings each with a hollow mesh on the outside, three rows of gold pendants in the centre and a large gold and lapis lazuli pendant at the base; 5.1 cm diameter. (c) Pair of gold ear-rings each with sixteen free-standing openwork rosettes round the outside and two concentric circles of small disks round an open centre; 4.9 cm diameter.

(Tehran, Iran Bastan Museum.)

Stronach, *Pasargadae*, pls. 146–9, figs. 85.4 (**a**), 85.1 (**b**), 85.2 (**c**).

(c) Aristocratic life

(i) *Hunting*

65. Modern impression from an agate cylinder-seal, reported to be from Egypt, inscribed for 'Darius the Great King' in Old Persian, Elamite and Babylonian cuneiform; this is assumed to be Darius I. The royal lion-hunt was a traditional Near Eastern and Egyptian symbol of royal power.

(London, British Museum WA 89132. Height 3.3 cm.)

J. Yoyotte, *Revue d'Assyriologie* 46 (1952) 165–7; D. J. Wiseman, *Cylinder Seals of Western Asia* (London, 1958) pl. 100.

66. Gold chariot model from the Oxus Treasure; driver and seated man in heavy chariot with large wheels, drawn by pony-sized horses as on **65**; Bes-like head on the front, sixth to fifth centuries B.C.

(London, British Museum WA 123908. Length 18.8 cm.)

Dalton, *Treasure*, no. 7, pl. 4, fig. 20; M. A. Littauer and J. H. Crouwel, *Wheeled Vehicles and Ridden Animals in the Ancient Near East* (Leyden, 1979) 145ff, fig. 82.

67. Bronze horseman, originally the handle of a metal object(?), wearing Median costume and a short-sword (*akinakes*); note the decorated saddle cloth and the absence of saddle and stirrups, both later inventions; fifth to fourth centuries B.C.

(London, British Museum WA 117760. Height 8.5 cm.)

Ghirshman, *Persia: from the Origins to Alexander the Great* 261, fig. 315.

68. Bronze horse-bit of typical Achaemenid type from what may have been a military cemetery at Deve Hüyük near Carchemish (Jerablus) in Turkey; cheekpieces tipped at one end with a phallus, a hoof at the other; fifth century B.C.

(Oxford, Ashmolean Museum 1913.717. Width 10.8 cm.)

C. L. Woolley, *Liverpool Annals* 7 (1914–16) pl. 24.3; P. R. S. Moorey, *Cemeteries of the First Millenium B.C. at Deve Hüyük* (Oxford, 1980) no. 227.

69. Silver, partially gilded, disk from the Oxus Treasure, of uncertain purposes (possibly a shield-boss) decorated with a scene of hunting, where both spear and composite bow are used; sixth to fifth centuries B.C.

(London, British Museum WA 123925. Diam. 8.65 cm.)

Dalton, *Treasure*, no. 24, pl. 9.

70

70. Modern impression from a chalcedony cylinder-seal showing a man in Median costume hunting wild boar; inscribed in Aramaic with a name: *wyzk*; perhaps made in Turkey; fifth to fourth centuries B.C.

(London, British Museum WA 89144. Height 2.8 cm.)
Wiseman, *op. cit.* **65**, pl. 111.

(ii) *Fighting*

71. Chalcedony cylinder-seal (and a modern impression from it) showing a king in Persian costume twice triumphant over his foes, set below a variety of religious symbols; from the Oxus Treasure; sixth to fifth centuries B.C.

(London, British Museum WA 124015. Height 3.7 cm.)
Dalton, *Treasure*, no. 114, pl. 16.

72. Modern impression from a chalcedony cylinder-seal showing a Persian (left) and a Greek (right) in combat; probably made in Turkey; fifth to fourth centuries B.C.

(London, British Museum WA 89333. Height 3.1 cm.)
Wiseman, *op. cit.* **65**, pl. 117.

73. Detail of the *akinakes* or short-sword of the king's weapon-bearer on the original central panel of the Apadana friezes at Persepolis; the decoration is probably on sheet gold over the wood or leather of the scabbard; early fifth century B.C.

Schmidt, *Persepolis* I, pl. 120.

74. Two iron short-swords from graves in a cemetery at Deve Hüyük, near Carchemish (Jerablus) in Turkey, with associated chapes, one of bronze, the other of ivory (repaired in antiquity); both are decorated with a curled animal motif of Scythian ancestry.

(Oxford, Ashmolean Museum 1913.705A, 1913.582, 1913.584, 1913.639. Lengths 34.6, 28.8 cm. Heights of chapes 4.2, 6.8 cm.)
    C. L. Woolley, *Liverpool Annals* 7 (1914–16) pls. 25H, 22.2, 23.1; Moorey, *op. cit.* **68**, nos. 149–50; 156–7.

75. Addorsed calf-heads; ivory; probably the T-shaped pommel from an *akinakes*. This decorative device was typical of Iranian art: a miniature version of the great bull-head capitals (cf. **21**); source unknown; fifth to fourth centuries B.C.

(Paris, Louvre MN 1343 = N 8331 = Longpérier 403. Length 4.7 cm.)
    R. A. Stucky, *AK* 28 (1985) no. 15, pl. 8.

(iii) *Greco-Persian Anatolia* (by J. Boardman)

In Anatolia the Persians had their closest contact both with the Greek cities of the west coast and with native kingdoms which had to varying degrees been infiltrated by Greek arts since the seventh century, or which had shared a lively archaic culture with their Greek neighbours in which it is not always easy to distinguish Greek from Anatolian. This was especially true in Lydia (see *Pls. to Vol. III*, ch. 10 and pls. 282–7, 300a, 314). The result is a series of monuments in various media and mixed in style and content. Stamp-seals of Mesopotamian form are made in the Lydian capital of Sardis, some with Greek motifs, most with Persian, but some carrying inscriptions or symbols indicating their use by Lydians in Persian service (**76**). These begin in the sixth century, and in the fifth are followed by the so-called 'Greco-Persian' gems which are still generally in the favourite eastern material, blue chalcedony, but in the new, large scaraboid shape also favoured for Classical Greek works. Their subject matter is the hunt and fighting (**79, 80**), as it was for many cylinder-seals of the Persian homeland, but we find also domestic scenes, with figures in Persian dress (**78**), and these must owe something to Greek inspiration, just as the style does. They are finely cut stones, with figures more boldly patterned than their pure Greek contemporaries and in this respect closer to Persian Court Style, but they could never be mistaken for native Persian products. Most seem to come from the prosperous kingdoms of south Anatolia which were allowed considerable independence by the Persians and could even strike their own coinage, sometimes with motifs resembling those of the gems.

Wall-painting had enjoyed a long history in Anatolia, starting probably in the Bronze Age with the Hittites, and attested in the sixth century by the finds at Gordium and Sardis. In Lycia there have been important finds of painting which include the banqueter (**81**), but in the same tomb are subjects of pure Greek derivation. Votive and grave reliefs have a long Anatolian history; for the new empire they carry Persian and local subjects in a mixed style (**82**, and cf. **43, 45**).

GENERAL BIBLIOGRAPHY

Seals and gems: J. Boardman, *Greek Gems and Finger Rings* (London, 1970) ch. 6; *id., Iran* 8 (1970) 19–45; *id., Rev. Arch.* 1976, 45–54. Reliefs: E. Akurgal, *Die Kunst Anatoliens* (Berlin, 1900) 167–74. General: C. G. Starr, *Iranica Antiqua* 11 (1975) 39–99, 12 (1976) 49–115.

77. Cylinder-seal of blue chalcedony, fifth century B.C.(?). A man ploughing with a pair of zebu bulls, the style is eastern.

(Paris, Louvre AO 2282. Height 3.0 cm.)
  L. Delaporte, *Catalogue des cylindres* II (Paris, 1923) pl. 91.

77

78. (a) Scaraboid of grey-white chalcedony. A Persian dancing in a whirling eastern posture, not unknown in Greece. (b) Scaraboid of blue chalcedony. A Persian woman, pigtailed and of characteristically robust physique, holding flowers; from Eretria. (c) Pear-shaped pendant of pink chalcedony, from Cyprus. On one side a Persian with his wife; on the other a Persian mother with her little daughter, holding for her a flower and a pet bird. All fifth/fourth century B.C.

((a) Malibu, Getty Museum. Height 2.5 cm. (b) London, British Museum 434. Height 1.8 cm; (c) London, British Museum 436. Height 2.6 cm.)
  J. Boardman, *Intaglios and Rings* (London, 1975) no. 88 (a); *GGFR* pls. 879, 891 (b, c).

79. (a) Tabloid seal of blue chalcedony. A Persian horseman hunts a lion. Other facets of the seal carry figures of an antelope, a fox, a calf and a bear. (b) Scaraboid of white jasper, from the Peloponnese. A Persian returning from the hunt with his bow and his bag (one small bird!). (c) Scaraboid of chalcedony from Ithome (Greece), Persian hunters with a dead fox. Notice the trident spear with which the fox had been hunted from horseback. (d) Scaraboid of blue chalcedony. A Persian spears a wild boar. All fifth/fourth century B.C.

76. (a) Lydian stamp-seal of blue chalcedony, late sixth century B.C. An East Greek version of the god Hermes, with winged hat and shoes, holding caduceus and flower, with a bird. The dress is Greek, its treatment, as that of the bird, eastern. (b) Lydian stamp-seal of blue chalcedony, late sixth century B.C. Lion and lioness, and two symbols, probably indicating ownership, as does the inscription in Lydian letters, *sivamlin atelis*, 'of Sivams son of Ates' (Lydian names).

((a) New York, Metropolitan Museum 86.1.3. Height 1.7 cm. (b) Naples, Mus. Naz. 1475. Height 1.6 cm.)
  J. Boardman, *Iran* 8 (1970) pls. 1–2, nos. 11, 3; *GGFR* pl. 845 (a).

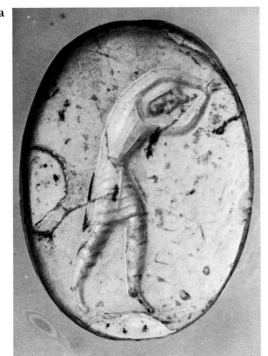

79a

79b

79c

79d

80a

((a) Malibu, Getty Museum. 1.4 × 1.9 cm. (b) Oxford, Ashmolean Museum 1892. 1482. Length 2.6 cm. (c) Berlin, Staatliche Museen F 183. Length 2.5 cm. (d) Athens, National Museum. Length 2.3 cm.)

Boardman, op. cit. **78**, no. 89 (**a**); *GGFR* pls. 853, 890, 925 (**b–d**).

80. (**a**) Scaraboid of onyx from Caria, late sixth century B.C. A Persian ruler spears a collapsing Greek hoplite (naked but for shield and helmet). (**b**) Barrel-shaped gem of blue chalcedony, late fifth century B.C. A Persian horseman attacks a Greek hoplite, the group depicted as in a Classical Greek combat scene. (**c**) Scaraboid of cor-

nelian, carved on the back, from Mesopotamia, fourth century B.C. A Persian horseman pursues two Persians in a chariot.

((**a**) Once Arndt Collection A 1410. Height 1.6 cm. (**b**) Houlton (Maine), Derek Content Coll. (**c**) London, British Museum 435. Length 2.4 cm.)
  GGFR pls. 849, 864 (**a**, **c**).

81. Wall painting from a tomb (tumulus II) at Karaburun near Elmali in Lycia, early fifth century B.C. The tomb-owner, though not a Persian, is shown as an easterner, wearing zoomorphic bracelets and ear-rings and holding a fluted bowl. No such scenes are yet known in the Achaemenid Court Style but the practice of reclining at banquet had been adopted by the Greeks from the east by 600 B.C. (cf. *CAH* III².3, 452–3; *Pls. to Vol. III*, pl. 50) and had been used for images of the heroized dead in Anatolia. See *CAH* IV², 222–3.

  M. Mellink in *Mélanges Mansel* (Ankara, 1974) 1 537–47, pl. 168.

82. Limestone stela from a grave at Dascylium in north-west Anatolia, fifth century B.C. In the top register a funeral cart; below, a husband and wife feasting. A provincial style echoing Persian fashions.

(Istanbul. Arch. Mus.)
  H. Möbius, *AA* 1971, 442–5.

(d) International craft traditions

(i) In the East and Egypt

83. Gold jug with cast lion-headed handle from the Oxus Treasure; decorative horizontal ribbing was especially popular in Achaemenid workshops; sixth to fifth centuries B.C.

(London, British Museum WA 123918. Height 13 cm.)
  Dalton, *Treasure*, no. 17, pl. 7.

84. A rhyton, the bull protome of sheet gold, the horn of sheet silver; said to have been found at Marash in Turkey; sixth to fifth centuries B.C.

(London, British Museum WA 116411. Height 22.2 cm.)
  C. L. Woolley, *Liverpool Annals* 10 (1923) 69ff, pl. 6°.

ob

oc

84

85

85. Silver rhyton with gazelle (?) protome; said to be from Turkey; fifth to fourth centuries B.C.

(Paris, Louvre. Height 30 cm.)
 G. Contenau, *Musée du Louvre: Les Antiquités orientales* (Paris, 1930) pl. 52; P. Amiet, *L'Art antique du Proche-Orient* (Paris, 1977) pl. 724.

86. Silver, partially gilded, rhyton with a winged griffin protome, said to have been found in Turkey; fifth to fourth centuries B.C.

(London, British Museum WA 124081. Height 25 cm.)
 Dalton, *Treasure*, no. 178, pl. 22.

87. Bronze rhyton with goat-shaped protome; source unknown.

(Paris, Louvre. Height 24 cm.)
 Contenau, *op. cit.* **85**, pl. 51; Amiet, *op. cit.* **85**, pl. 722.

88. Burnished light brown terracotta rhyton terminating in a horned (restored) head, from Deve Hüyük, near Carchemish, in Turkey. This illustrates how this very popular metal shape was imitated in cheap materials.

(Oxford, Ashmolean Museum 1913.636. Length 34.6 cm.)
 C. L. Woolley, *Liverpool Annals* 7 (1914–16) pl. 27.15; Moorey, *op. cit.* **68**, no. 66, fig. 5.

89. Cast hemispherical silver bowl with friezes of a Persian king or hero between borders, formed of sheet gold appliqués; source unknown.

(London, British Museum WA 134740. Height 6.9 cm.)
 J. Curtis, *British Museum Quarterly* 37 (1973) 126.

90. Silver phiale and ladle from tomb 650 at Tell el-Farah (south) in Israel. The phiale is the type of metal bowl (also imitated in glass and baked clay) most widely used for drinking in the Persian empire (cf. **81**). The ladle has a nude, swimming girl in Egyptian style and, just under the circular loop, addorsed calf or bullock heads (cf. **75**).

(Jerusalem, Rockefeller Museum. Diam. of phiale 17.5 cm. Length of ladle 21.5 cm.)
 W. M. F. Petrie, *Beth-Pelet* I (London, 1930) 14, pls. 44, 45; J. H. Iliffe, *Quarterly of the Department of Antiquities of Palestine* 4 (1935) 182ff, pls. 90, 91.

87

88

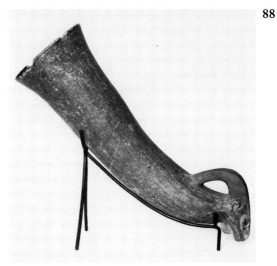

90

89

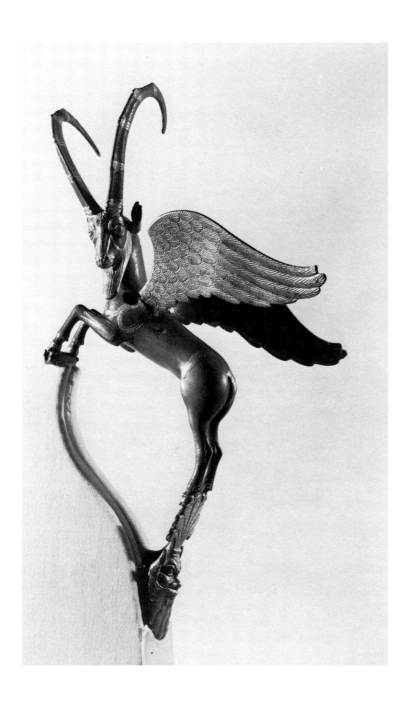

91. Silver, partially gilded, handle in the shape of a rampant winged goat from a vessel, perhaps an amphora-rhyton. This is one of the most famous examples of the Greco-Persian style in fine metalwork. The mask at the base of the handle (a Greek trait) combines features of the Phoenicio-Egyptian Bes and the Greek Silenus; fourth century B.C.

(Paris, Louvre.)
P. Amandry, *AK*2 (1959) 50, pls. 26.2, 27.2–3.

92. Silver spoon with a duck or swan's head, from the Pasargadae Hoard.

(Tehran, Iran Bastan Museum. Length 15 cm.)
Stronach, *Pasargadae* 168–9, pls. 150b, 151.

92

93c

93a

93c

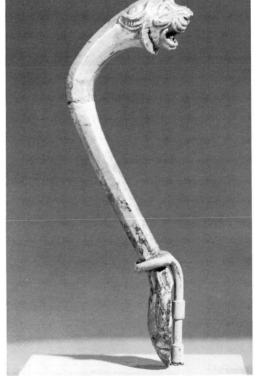

93b

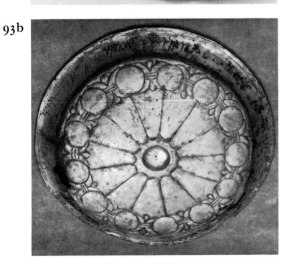

73

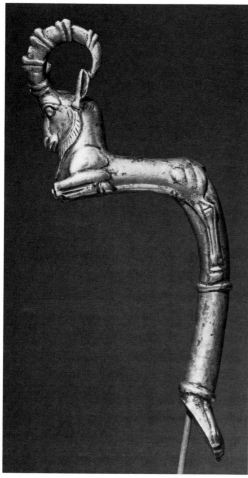

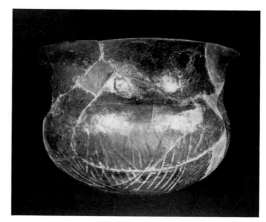

(b) Shallow silver bowl inscribed in Aramaic: 'That which Qaynu, son of Gašmu, king of Qedar, brought in offering to Han-ʿIlat.' The Gašmu mentioned here is probably identical with the man of that name who figures prominently in the Old Testament as an opponent of Nehemiah (2:19–20; cf. 6:1–9).
(c) Silver jug with cast lion-head handle (illustrated separately here); the vessel has a traditional Egyptian form; but Achaemenid Persian influence is evident in the handle.
(d) Cast silver vessel handle in the shape of a springing wild goat; a traditional Iranian motif.

((a) New York, Brooklyn Museum 54-50-32. (b) New York, Brooklyn Museum 54-50-34. (c) New York, Brooklyn Museum 54-50-39; 54-50-42. (d) New York, Brooklyn Museum 54-50-41.)

(a) I. Rabinowitz, *Journal of Near Eastern Studies* 15 (1956) 2, pls. 4, 5; W. J. Dumbrell, *Bulletin of the American School of Oriental Research* 203 (1971) 35, fig. 2. (b) Rabinowitz, *op. cit.*, 2, pls. 6, 7; Dumbrell, *op. cit.*, 37, fig. 3. (c) Cooney, pls. 73–4 (right). (d) Cooney, pl. 74 (left).

93. Items of silver plate, part of a group of some nine or more vessels, some of which bear Aramaic inscriptions, said to have been found in 1947 at Tell el-Maskhuta, near Ismaïlia in Lower Egypt (E. S. G. Robinson, *Numismatic Chronicle* 7 (1947) 115–21; J. Cooney, *Five Years of Collecting Egyptian Art 1951–1956* (Brooklyn Museum, 1956)). The dedicatory inscriptions are to the goddess Han-ʿIlat, so these are votive gifts to a shrine, not part of a table service. These vessels exhibit a blend of traditional Egyptian forms and decorations with traits of the international Achaemenid Court Style. Collectively this has become known as the Pithom Hoard; but its integrity is uncertain.
(a) Deep silver bowl with lotus decoration on the lower sides; inscribed in Aramaic: 'That which Sehaʿ, son of Abd-Amru brought in offering to Han-ʿIlat.'

94. Colourless cut-glass bowl restored from sherds found at Nippur in Iraq: rosette on the base, lotus leaves on the side. In Aristophanes' *Acharnians* (line 74) Greek ambassadors to the court of the Persian king boast of drinking from 'goblets of glass and of gold' as if they were regarded as luxury materials of comparable value; fifth to fourth centuries B.C.

(Philadelphia, University Museum. Nippur B.2349. Diam. max. 11.3 cm.)

D. Barag, *Journal of Glass Studies* 10 (1968) 17ff; A. Oliver, *Journal of Glass Studies* 12 (1970) 9ff; S. M. Goldstein in D. Schmandt-Besserat (ed.), *Ancient Persia: The Art of an Empire* (Malibu, 1980) 47ff.

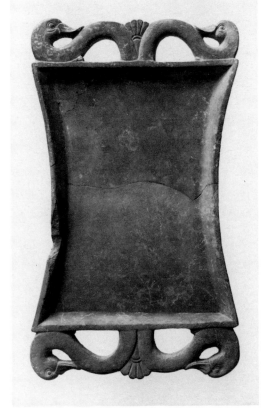

97. Tray of grey calcareous stone, decorated with swan's heads, found in the hall of the Treasury at Persepolis; fifth to fourth centuries B.C.

(Tehran, Iran Bastan Museum. Length 38 cm.)
Schmidt, *Persepolis* II, pl. 53.2.

95. Wooden door from a small Egyptian shrine with a design in polychrome glass inlays: Darius I, identified by the cartouche near his head, worshipping the enthroned Anubis, behind whom stands Isis grasping a long staff.

(London, British Museum WA 37496. Height about 30 cm.)
J. D. Cooney in W. K. Simpson and W. M. Davis (ed.), *Studies in Ancient Egypt, the Aegean and the Sudan* (Boston, 1981) 32–3, fig. 2.

98. Partially restored translucent alabaster unguent bottle found in the Treasury at Persepolis; such vessels are represented in the hands of royal servants at Persepolis; fifth to fourth centuries B.C.

(Diam. of mouth 8 cm.)
Schmidt, *Persepolis* II, pl. 65.12.

96. Restored speckled black-and-white pedestal dish found in the hall of the Treasury at Persepolis; fifth to fourth centuries B.C.

(Tehran, Iran Bastan Museum. Height 12.6 cm.)
Schmidt, *Persepolis* II, pl. 57.1.

99. Fragment of a carved ivory comb from Susa; traces of the teeth above and below: on one face a winged bull either attacked by a griffin

(head only survives) or with a griffin head on its wing tip; on the other a human-headed winged lion, wearing a horned crown with similar griffin head.

(Paris, Louvre 2811. Height 6 cm.)

P. Amiet, *Syria* 49 (1972) 184–5, pl. 3 a–b; R. de Mecquenem, *Mémoires* 30 (1947) 88, fig. 56(1–2); Ghirshman, *Persia: from the Origins to Alexander the Great*, figs. 561–2.

100. Limestone plaque, reported to have been acquired in Egypt, showing friezes of winged lion-griffins, lions attacking gazelles and winged bulls in the Achaemenid Court Style. Frankfort called it a 'goldsmith's trial-piece'; it might simply be a sculptor's exercise or model, since the statue of Darius I, made in Egypt (cf. **22**), has comparable decoration on the upper part of the sword scabbard.

(Chicago, Oriental Institute A27978. 17.7 × 20.4 cm.)

H. Frankfort, *Journal of Near Eastern Studies* 9 (1950) 111ff, pl. 3.

101. Lion-shaped bronze weight, found at Susa, weighing four talents (121 kg); this magnificent object follows a tradition established in Neo-Assyrian times for casting standard sets of weights in the shape of recumbent lions. There is a comparable weight, of one talent, inscribed in Aramaic, from Abydus on the Dardanelles, now in the British Museum (E.32625: T. C. Mitchell, *Iran* 11 (1973) 173ff); sixth or fifth century B.C.

(Paris, Louvre. Height 29.5 cm.)

G. Lampre, *Mémoires . . . délégation en Perse* 8 (1905) 171–6, pl. 9; *Encyclopédie photographique de l'art* 11 (Louvre, 1936) pl. 59.

102. Cast bronze fittings from the leg of a throne said to come from Samaria; such fittings are clearly shown on the royal thrones depicted at Persepolis. As Samaria was the home of a Persian governor, such objects are appropriate there. At Tell el-Farah (south), in Israel, comparable fittings from a throne indicate that such furniture was placed in tombs of officials of the Persian administration (cf. Petrie, *op. cit.* **90**, pl. 46: probably not a couch); fifth to fourth centuries B.C.

(Israel Museum no. 70.92. Height of paw 13.7 cm. Height of cylinder 22 cm.)

M. Tadmor, *Israel Exploration Journal* 24 (1974) 37ff.

103. Cast bronze head of an ibex, hollow, with holes round the base of the neck for attachment, possibly to a piece of furniture. The horns and ears were cast separately and joined to the head by fusion welding. This fine piece epitomizes the tradition of animal decoration so distinctive of Iranian art; sixth to fifth centuries B.C.

(New York, Metropolitan Museum of Art 56.45. Height 34 cm.)

C. K. Wilkinson, *Bulletin of the Metropolitan Museum of Art* 15 (3) (1956) 72–8.

(ii) In Europe (by Timothy Taylor)

The degree to which various areas of Europe were affected by Achaemenid Persian style, in art as well as life, is a matter of controversy. The style of objects such as the Trichtingen ring or the Klein Aspergle drinking horns, from Celtic central Europe, is more likely to be due to contact with Thracian south-east Europe than to any direct Persian influence. South-east Europe is the most likely place of origin for the Gundestrup cauldron, and the oriental motifs which it carries are best seen as a product of the direct connexion between Persia and Thrace, when silversmithing first arose there three centuries earlier. An understanding of the nature of this connexion is therefore a necessary preliminary to any proper assessment of apparently oriental features on artefacts from elsewhere in Europe during the same period.

Ancient Thrace was the country stretching from the Danube delta in the north to the Aegean coast in the south, and from the Iron Gates in the west to the Bosporus in the east. At times, Thracian-speaking tribes occupied areas beyond these boundaries – Transylvania in the far north west, and Mysia and Bithynia in Asia Minor, to the south east. A large part of Thrace lies within the modern boundaries of Romania and Bulgaria. Recent archaeological research in these countries has filled out the picture of Thracian daily life, only roughly sketched by the Greek authors. Thucydides tells us (II.97) that the amount of tribute demanded in one year

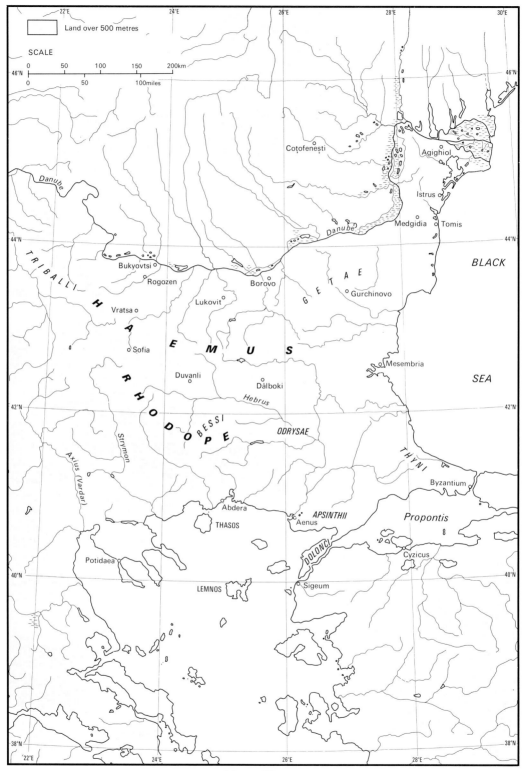

Map 4. Thrace.

by Seuthes, king of the Odrysian Thracians, from the Hellenic cities and the provinces, was 400 talents in gold and silver; that a person had to give gifts in Thrace if he wanted anything done; and that such gifts would be made of gold or silver. Whilst excavations of Thracian burial mounds (*Mogili*) have produced some support for this, it has been the chance discovery of large hoards of gold and silver drinking vessels that has really demonstrated the plausibility of the historical account. The recently discovered hoard from Rogozen, in north-west Bulgaria, contained 165 silver drinking vessels, many of them decorated with gold, weighing a total of 20 kilograms.

Thrace has preserved more prehistoric gold and silver artefacts than anywhere else in the ancient world, but it is even more remarkable that the majority date to a relatively short period. Before the Persian occupation of Thrace, between about 513 and 480 B.C., silver appears to have been completely unknown.

The explanation for this lack lies as much with history as with archaeology. The patterns of distribution of the material cannot be easily understood outside the historical framework of conquests, expeditions and alliances provided by surviving textual accounts. In this, Darius' expedition against the Scythians is of fundamental importance. As Powell pointed out, 'thirty years of Achaemenid presence, and the great wealth of booty passing through barbarian hands on the withdrawal of Xerxes, cannot but have had new formative influences'. One such influence may be detected in the adoption of the phiale form of drinking cup, and another in the emergence of an explicit iconography of the 'Royal Hunt'. From the fifth century B.C. onwards a school of native Thracian silver-smithing emerged, often taking objects wrought in the Persian style for its models. Thus, from amongst the known material, we can distinguish both a small number of exotic oriental objects, and a larger corpus of objects made locally in response.

GENERAL BIBLIOGRAPHY

P. Amandry, 'Toreutique achéménide', *AK* 2 (1959) 38–56, pls. 20–30; D. Berciu, *Arta Traco-Getică* (Bucharest, 1969); A. K. Bergquist and T.F. Taylor, 'The origin of the Gundestrup cauldron', *Antiquity* 61 (1987) 10–24; K. Bittel, *Der Trichtinger Ring und seine Probleme* (Heidenheim, 1978); A. Fol and I. Marazov, *Thrace and the Thracians* (New York, 1977); R. F. Hoddinott, *The Thracians* (London, 1981); J. V. S. Megaw, *Art of the European Iron Age* (Bath, 1970); T. G. E. Powell, 'From Urartu to Gundestrup: the agency of Thracian metal-work', in J. Boardman et al. (eds.), *The European Community in Later Prehistory* (London, 1971) 183–210; I. Venedikov and T. Gerassimov, *Thracian Art Treasures* (Sofia and London, 1975).

104. Sheet goldworking began very early in Bulgaria, and is represented in the 4th-millennium B.C. Chalcolithic cemetery at Varna on the Black Sea coast (*Plates to Vol. III*, ch. 1). Sheet gold work was deposited at various times throughout the Bronze Age in south-east Europe, but in the later Bronze Age and earlier Iron Age (the first half of the 1st millennium B.C.) there is little evidence for it. Two finds which attest to a renewal of interest in gold-smithing around the mid-1st millennium B.C. come from near to the route which Darius' army followed through Thrace. They are both of oriental inspiration, if not manufacture, and could well be directly related to the production of prestige objects during the period of the invasion. (**a**) Bronze object, probably a 'matrix' or former, over which soft sheet metal can be beaten. Found without context at Gurchinovo (Bulgaria). There has been some debate over whether the matrix served to shape a single object, or whether particular elements were used as needed, in the manner of a pattern book. The close grouping of the figures over the surface precludes the latter, on technical grounds alone. If the matrix shaped a single sheet of metal, what function would be served? Experiment supports the view that a single sheet made on the matrix would be of the right size and shape to be bent round on itself to form the cone of a decorated rhyton. The piece is unique in Thrace. Its bestiary is oriental, but stylistically it has no precise parallels in Scythia or Persia. A date around 500 B.C. seems acceptable. It is the earliest hunt-related scene known from Thrace. It couples natural observation with a number of metamorphic conventions: the stag's antlers become rams' heads, its shoulder a hawk's head with curved beak.

(**b**) Detail of (**a**). The lower register of the matrix shows a wild boar, and behind it a strange beast; is it a horned bull, a horse with a top-knot, or is it the earliest known representation of a unicorn?

(c) Bronze 'sword emblem' from near Medgidia (Romanian Dobrudja); probably also a matrix, used for forming a precious metal sheath cover, such as were common in the East. Actual examples are known from Scythia, and they are shown on many of the Apadana reliefs at Persepolis (see **53, 73**). Whether the matrix can be termed 'Persian' is less important than its status as a unique piece within Thrace, without stylistic progenitors or progeny.

(a, b) Sofia, Bulgarian National Museum of History. Length *c.* 30 cm. (c) Bucharest, Romanian National Museum of History. Length 46.7 cm.)
(a, b) N. Fettich, *Der scythische Fund von Gartschinovo* (Budapest, 1935). (c) D. Berciu, *Studii şi Cercetări de Istoria Veche* 10 (1959) 7–18.

105. A problem in considering 'Persian' style is that so little portable material survives from the heartlands of the empire. Only on the periphery, in the tribal confederacies and emergent states of Thrace for example, have precious metal objects in a Persian style been found in securely dated contexts. But where were they made? The tribute which the empire expected stimulated the growth of what may be termed 'prestige goods economies' among the tributary peoples, and required that the tribute should take a specific form.

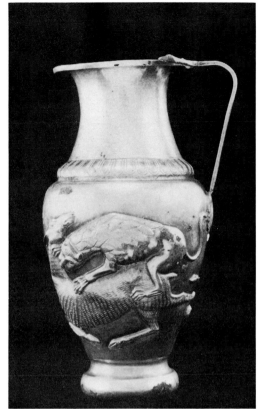

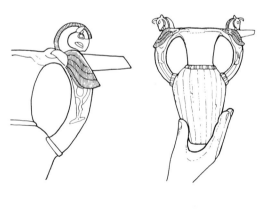

(a) Partially gilded silver spouted amphora from the Kukuva Mogila in the barrow cemetery of Duvanli. This is certainly not of local manufacture. Assuming the grave context is secure, a date of deposition around 450 B.C. is probable, making this one of the earliest examples of the silversmith's art in Thrace. The construction of the body is masterly: beaten up from a single sheet of silver, a sharp angle has been formed between the shoulder and the neck with only a small decorated band between to give 'spring' to it. The surface has been beaten up in a light repoussé to form two bands of lotus and palmette decoration, and beaten down into vertical cannelures beneath them. Hammer-marks are all but invisible, except in places on the inside.

(b) Detail of (a). The handles are made in the form of winged lions with ibex horns (missing from one). The animals are partially gilded and finished with traced and punched decoration. One of the handles served as a pouring spout, no doubt for red wine – a prerequisite for banqueting in the Persian style, a custom clearly adopted by the local elite who emerged after the occupation. The vessel was probably made in the third quarter of the fifth century B.C., perhaps a little later than the ones shown on the Apadana reliefs in the hands of (probably) an Armenian and a Lydian (shown here in drawings: **40** III, VI). Filov, the excavator of Duvanli, favoured the Bosporan city of Cyzicus as the place of manufacture, and this is not impossible. However, the very high standard of the workmanship – surpassing other known vessels of the type (*amphore à bec*; e.g., Amandry, pls. 22.1, 23.1), and worked into a sharper and more closed form than is apparent on the Apadana representations of provincial work – could perhaps support a more central origin.

(c) Silver jug from Rogozen (Bulgaria), decorated with gold leaf, mid-fourth century B.C. Particular iconographic groups in the Persepolis reliefs (see **28**: lion and bull) attest preoccupation with certain themes, so often repeated that they take on a hieratic appearance, which must have had distinct symbolic connotations. A similar group appears on the side of this jug, although with a deer rather than a bull under attack. This is a native Thracian synthesis of the amphora and oenochoe (Beazley form 8) vessel types. The mouth is round and regular, but there is no sharp division of neck and shoulder nor a second, pouring handle. Both these features are remark-

ably difficult to achieve, and may have been beyond the competence of local, possibly itinerant, silversmiths. Although the vessel owes a technical debt to metropolitan workshops, and its social role was similar to what it would have been in Persia, its formal aspects, including its iconography, are a local adaptation.

((a, b) Sofia, National Museum of History 189 (6137). Height 27 cm. (c) Sofia National Museum of History 22456. Height 13 cm.)
(a, b) B. Filov, *Die Grabhügelnekropole bei Duvanlij in Südbulgarien* (Sofia, 1934) 199ff, pl. 3; for attribution see O. W. Muscarella in D. Schmandt-Besserat (ed.), *Ancient Persia: the Art of an Empire* (Malibu, 1980) 25. (c) A. Fol, B. Nikolov, R. F. Hoddinott, *The New Thracian Treasure from Rogozen, Bulgaria* (London, 1986) no. 156.

106. That very little of the tribute brought to Persepolis survives may in great part be due to the success of Alexander's conquest of Asia, in which great hoards of Achaemenid gold and silver work were collected. Some material has certainly survived from Hamadan, along with other genuine Achaemenian pieces which have been ascribed to it and to other sites. If treated critically, these offer useful stylistic and technical information for identifying imports in Thrace and assessing the degree of eastern influence there.

(a) Gold rhyton, possibly from Hamadan. Protome in the form of a winged lion, but without any pouring spout between the front legs; the protome is separated from the cup by an internal diaphragm; probably used in the manner of a drinking horn. Analysis of the 44 rows of fine double-stranded gold wire, used to decorate the rim, strongly suggests that the piece is authentic. (b) Partially gilded silver rhyton from an unknown location in Anatolia. Mountain goat protome, extending backwards to the hind legs over the cone of the rhyton. The rim has a palmette and lotus border similar to **105a**, though not in raised repoussé, and can be dated similarly. The protome has been cast in two pieces, joined along the central axis, with the hollow beaten horn fitted to it. Both rhyta have horizontal rills rather than vertical cannelures.

((a) New York, Metropolitan Museum of Art 54.3.3. Height 17.1 cm. (b) New York, Schimmel Collection. Height about 20 cm.)
(a) C. K. Wilkinson, *Bulletin of the Metropolitan Museum of Art, New York* 8 (1954/5) 222. (b) O. W.

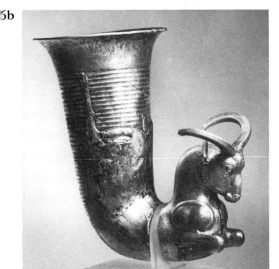

Muscarella, ed., *Ancient Art, the Norbert Schimmel Collection* (Mainz, 1974) no. 155; for animal-headed rhyta in general see K. Tuchelt, *Gefäße in Tier und Protomengestalt* (Berlin, 1962).

107. Almost as little precious metalwork has survived from the Greek world as from the Persian, making it unclear how much they influenced each other. Further, as with core and periphery within the Persian empire, no adequate criteria can be drawn up for distinguishing between the production of the Greek Black Sea colonies and that of the homeland states.

(a) Three partially gilded silver rhyta: part of a hoard from Borovo (north-east Bulgaria). All are constructed with beaten horn sections and two-piece *cire perdue* cast protomes; the sphinx's wings are not integral. Two of the rhyta have

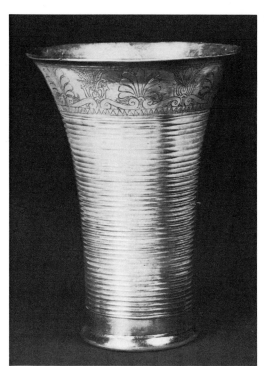

vertical cannelures and decorated borders. When found they were in pieces, with the protomes and the horns separated, and were initially reconstructed wrongly. That this was possible (i.e., that practically the horns are interchangeable) suggests that they both came from the same workshop.

(b) Bull protome rhyton from hoard (a), with plain rim and horizontal rilling. Its style is Persian, whereas the style of the others is Greek. The contoured decoration at the midpoint of the

bull's cheeks shows considerable wear, consistent with extensive use of the vessel for drinking. The soldered join down the bull's chest is disguised by a double band of decorated gold leaf. Cf. the Susa bull protome, **21**, details of which not only place the rhyton firmly in Persian stylistic milieu, but also suggest that the carving itself follows a metal prototype: the decorated vertical bands on its chest are the same as on (**b**) and on bronze column capitals, but otherwise serve no function.

(**c**) Silver beaker from Bukyovtsi (Bulgaria). Possible mercury-gilded (parcel gilt). This may well have originated in a Greek Black Sea atelier: not all horizontally rilled vessels from Thrace need be considered fully Persian in style. As Shefton has pointed out, the extent to which eastern conventions had been adopted by Greek silversmiths can only be gauged through indirect evidence from within the Greek world, for instance in an Attic black-glaze mug (**d**) which follows a metal prototype. The Bukyovtsi beaker, however, preserved in a Thracian hoard, provides us with a Greek original.

((**a, b**) Sofia, Bulgarian National Museum of History II–357 to II–359. Height (Greek rhyta) 21 cm, (Persian rhyton) 17 cm. (**c**) Sofia, Archaeological Museum 6694. Height 12.2 cm. (**d**) Karlsruhe, Badisches Landesmuseum B881. Height 9 cm.)

(**a, b**) D. Ivanov, *Izkustvo* 1975 (3–4), 14–21, pls. 3–4; I. Marazov, *Ritonite v Drevna Trakiya* (Sofia, 1978). (**c**) I. Velkov and H. Danov, *Izvestiya na Bulgarskiya Arkheologicheski Institut* 12 (1939) 435. (**d**) *CVA* Karlsruhe 1 pl. 34.11; B. B. Shefton, *Annales Archéologiques Arabes Syriennes* 21 (1971) 109–11, pl. 20.7.

108. The small phiale, or handleless drinking cup, made up part of the standard drinking set in the Persian world. Its precursors go back at least as far as eighth-century B.C. Assyria (*Plates to Vol. III*, ch. 2). In the Greek world the standard forms of drinking cup were handled vessels, whilst large phialai were used only for libation. In Thrace it was the Persian form that was adopted. Although Luschey thought that the phialai found in Thrace were actually of Persian manufacture, it seems clear that most were locally made.

(**a**) Gold bowl, possibly from Hamadan. This is not a typical phiale form, but is interesting because it carries a cuneiform inscription naming Darius in Old Persian, Babylonian and Elamite. It is similar to others with Xerxes inscriptions. Its authenticity is supported by the fact that its weight, 1,100 gm, is equal to 130 darics at 8.46 gm (i.e., freshly minted coin).

(**b**) Small bronze double phiale from a grave at Deve Hüyük. Fifth century B.C. This shows

how incised palmettes and lotuses could be interspersed between more pointed bosses. The decorated bowl is attached to, and covers, an integral plain bodied vessel.

(**c**) Silver phiale from the grave of Agighiol (Romanian Dobrudja, just south of the Danube delta), about 350 B.C. The grave contained some spectacular silver objects including four phialai. Most were of local Thracian manufacture, but the one illustrated was of a higher technical standard, decorated in repoussé and very carefully finished. It could well have been made in the Greek colony of Histria, where Greek silversmiths might have worked in the Persian style for the Thracian market.

(**d**) Thracian-made phiale from the Mushovitsa Mogila at Duvanli, earlier fifth century B.C. This illustrates well the difference in

108a

108b

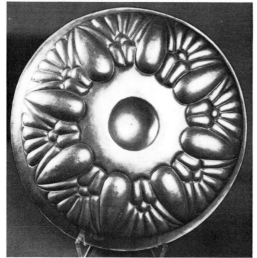

108c

108d

108e

technical accomplishment between local and colonial silversmithing.

(e) Partially gilded phiale from the Lukovit hoard, with rows of faces in place of bosses. An example of the specifically local vessel types that had emerged in the mid-fourth century B.C. This decoration was popular, sometimes combined with animal heads in the distinctive 'Thracian Animal Style'.

((a) New York, Metropolitan Museum of Art 54.3.1. Height 11.4 cm. (b) Oxford, Ashmolean Museum 1913.595. Height 5.6 cm. (c) Bucharest, Romanian National Museum of History. Height 4.3 cm. (d, e) Sofia, Bulgarian National Museum of History 1539, 8226. Heights 4.6 cm, 7 cm.)

H. Luschey, *Die Phiale* (Bleicherode am Harz, 1939). (a) Wilkinson, *op. cit.* **106**, 224; for ascription see Muscarella, *op. cit.* **105**; for metrology see M. Vickers, *American Journal of Ancient History* (forthcoming). (b) C. L. Woolley, *Liverpool Annals* 7 (1914–16) 119, grave 15. (c) D. Berciu, *Bericht der Römisch-Germanischen Kommission* 50 (1969) 209–65. (d) Filov, *op. cit.* **105**, 82ff, pl. 110; cf. C. Ewigleben in J. Hodgson et al. (eds.), *The First Millennium BC in Europe* (Oxford, 1988). (e) D. P. Dimitrov, *Izkustvoto i kulturata na trakite. Arkheologicheski Otkritiya* (Sofia, 1956); for Thracian Animal Style see Taylor in I. Hodder (ed.), *The Archaeology of Contextual Meanings* (Cambridge, 1987) 117–32.

109. Phiale from the Vratsa grave, about 360 B.C. Thracian culture was eclectic. Whilst the standard drinking vessel was a borrowing from Persia, the alphabet with which it was inscribed was Greek. Many undecorated phialai from Thrace are inscribed with what appear to be Greek words linking Thracian names. The name ΚΟΤΥΟΣ occurs quite often, as here, (e.g., on the Greek rhyta of **107a**) and perhaps refers to Kotys I, king of the Odrysae (c. 384–359 B.C.). However, no satisfactory theory of the inscriptions' meaning has yet been proposed.

(Sofia, National Museum of History B-468. Height 4.5 cm.)

I. Venedikov, *Arkheologiya* (Sofia) 8(1) (1966), 7–15; Venedikov–Gerassimov, *Thracian Art Treasures*, no. 152; for the Rogozen inscriptions see S. Mashov *Izkustvo* 1986 (6) and Fol in Fol, Nikolov and Hoddinott, *op. cit.* **105**, 11ff.

110. Imports and influence are complementary. It is not just objects which are imported, but also the iconography, systems of decoration and principles of symmetry which they carry. And

objects themselves are not the sole agency of stylistic transmission; artisans, too, may have travelled. As in Renaissance Italy, a first-class goldsmith of the Achaemenid period might have dined at the tables of kings, and chosen his patron. Or again, as in Egypt, he might have been tied to his patron in such a way that he could be given to someone from another country. In either case, travelling as a freeman or as a chattel, he would have required apprentices and met other goldsmiths, whom he would have influenced as they, in turn, influenced him.

(a) Silver vessel from the Rogozen hoard, decorated with gold leaf. This is a technical masterpiece. It is designed with eight horned and winged lions whose tails curve up and spray out, each to form one side of a palmette. They are rendered in such a way as to appear almost identical, yet they are not matrix-worked. They appear the same on the outside as well as on the inside of the vessel, yet it is not the heavier for this, as the thin sheet has been bent back upon itself (through its section, so to speak) where necessary, and projects equally from either side. Who made it, and where, are matters of conjecture, but it could well have originated in one of the metropolitan centres of Persia proper. That such objects found their way into north-western

Bulgaria attests the economic strength of the Thracians in the fifth and fourth centuries B.C. That it was not melted down attests their connoisseurship of fine metalwork. It must have left a great impression on native Thracian silversmiths.

(b) Sheet gold bridle frontlet, possibly from Hamadan. Horned and winged lions are symmetrically paired in a rather different fashion from (a). Similar frontlets may have been seen by Thracians on the horses of Darius. (c) Sheet silver bridle frontlet, from the Lukovit hoard (northern Bulgaria). The silversmith who made this had either seen a frontlet of type (b) or copies of it at various removes. Although the lions have become beaked griffins and their posture has changed, the symmetry of the original is recognizable. The frontlet contrasts strongly with more common examples of Thraco-Scythian asymmetric pairs.

((a) Sofia, Bulgarian National Museum of History 22397. Diameter 18.8 cm. (b) New York, Metropolitan Museum of Art 54.3.2. (c) Sofia, Archaeological Museum 317. Length 11 cm.)
(a) Fol, Nikolov and Hoddinott, *op. cit.* **105**, no. 97. (b) Wilkinson, *op. cit.* **106**, 223. (c) Dimitrov, *op. cit.* **108**, 69.

90

a

III. Persian influences on Thrace were not narrowly stylistic. The adoption of oriental style in the form of drinking vessels indicates a willingness to adopt eastern customs too; perhaps, even, eastern mythologies. Both Persians and Thracians were mobile pastoralists at heart, concerned with maintaining flocks and breeding horses. Neither society was fully mobile, unlike the nomad Scythians of the steppes, nor were they enclosed like the Greeks of the mainland city states or Aegean islands. A degree of cultural empathy might therefore be expected between their peoples.

(**a**) Sheet gold helmet, from Coţofeneşti (Romanian Moldavia). One of five 'eyed' helmets known from northern Thrace (one of the others is from Agighiol). On its neckguard three predatory beasts are represented, with four man-predators above them. The latter recall the sphinxes at Susa (**19**) which suggests some connexion. The cheekpieces show what may be the sacrifice of a ram.

(**b, c**) Partially gilded silver jug from the Rogozen hoard. A further Thracian example of the theme, this time combined with another representation, widespread in the orient: the outward facing figure holding two animals. In central and western Europe this group is almost unknown. It appears in silver on the Gundestrup cauldron – a piece probably made in Thrace – whilst a similar scene occurs on a rare Celtic wood carving from Fellbach-Schmidten in Germany.

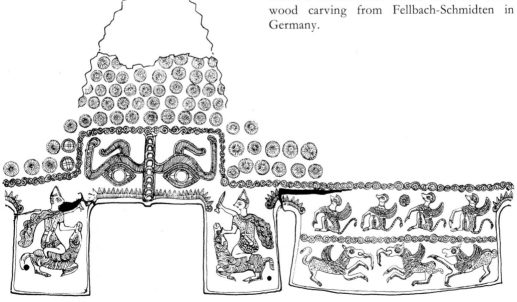

((a) Bucharest, Romanian National Museum of History. Height 25 cm. (**b**, **c**) Sofia, Bulgarian National Museum of History 22458. Height 11.5 cm.)

(**a**) Berciu, *Arta Traco-Getică* 77ff, pls. 55–61; for iconographic interpretations, see I. Marazov, *Semaines Philippopolitaines de l'Histoire et de la Culture Thrace (Pulpudeva)* 3 (1978) 81–101 and Taylor, *op. cit.* **108**, 127ff. (**b**, **c**) Fol, Nikolov and Hoddinott, *op. cit.* **105**, no. 158; for Gundestrup see Bergquist–Taylor, 'Gundestrup cauldron', fig. 1; for Fellbach-Schmidten see D. Planck, *Germania* 60 (1982) 105ff, figs. 22–6.

111b

112. Although fourth-century B.C. Thracian culture was eclectic, it was also individual. Artistic motifs from Persia, Scythia and Greece were not just borrowed piecemeal, but chosen for their appropriateness and then synthesized. What emerged may be termed the 'Thracian Animal Style'.

(**a**) Silver greave from the Vratsa tumulus, decorated with sheet gold overlays. Influence from all three alien cultures is evident, yet the final manifestation is strikingly original.

(**b**) Silver beaker from Rogozen, decorated with thin sheet gold overlays. Made about 360 B.C.; deposited about 330 B.C. One of four known: two others from Agighiol, and a third, said to be from the Danube in the Iron Gates gorge but quite possibly also from Agighiol; none of these has gold decoration. The iconography, with eight-legged stag and horned predatory bird grasping a hare in its claws and fish in its mouth, does not appear derivative, even though many of the motifs have been borrowed from elsewhere.

((a) Vratsa, Archaeological Museum B-231. Height 46 cm. (**b**) Sofia, National Museum of History B-593. Height *c.* 20 cm.)

(**a**) Venedikov, *op. cit.* **109**, pl. 3; I. Marazov, *Nakolennikut ot Vratsa* (Sofia, 1980). (**b**) Fol, Nikolov and Hoddinott, *op. cit.* **105**, no. 165; T. F. Taylor in B. F. Cook (ed.), *Proc. of the British Museum Rogozen Conference* (forthcoming); for Agighiol see Berciu, *Arta Traco-Getică*, figs. 26–38; for 'Iron Gates' see B. Goldman, *Jahrbuch für Praehistorische und Ethnographische Kunst* 22 (1966/69) 67–75; for comparative reassessment and chronology see Taylor, *op. cit.* **108**, 119ff., figs. 12.2 (b), 12.3–12.7.

111c

113. It was perhaps Persian culture which exercised the most profound influence over Thrace during the mid-first millennium B.C. In this period Thrace is perhaps better seen as an extension of Asia, rather than the furthest edge of Europe. The Persian occupation in Thrace was the immediate precursor of the formation of the Odrysian state, and this, in turn, adopted Persian style in its court and preserved it in its burial ritual. Gold- and silver-smiths emerged to work with previously unknown techniques.

(**a**) Pectoral from the Bashova Mogila at Duvanli. Late fifth century B.C. The earliest surviving example of sheet gold matrix work in Thrace; a pattern punch has been used around the edge. Probably originally mounted on leather. A rough but visually commanding version of the more sophisticated pectorals known from the east (e.g. 'Ziwiye').

(**b**) Sheet gold pectoral from the grave of Dălboki, buried around 430 B.C. This is worked over its entire surface with small pattern-punches, some in the form of lion heads. The presence of this beast alone demonstrates the

eastern connexions of the piece (see **28**; later, in fourth-century B.C. Thrace, the lion was superseded by the griffin). Pattern-punches became a favourite tool of the Thracian silversmiths during the fourth century B.C. A gold pectoral occurred also in the cemetery of Trebenishte, but they are unknown in the rest of Europe. Their local manufacture is a further example of the uniqueness of Thrace in this period, when every local ruler wanted to be a Xerxes.

((**a**) Sofia, Bulgarian National Museum of History 1514. Width 13.8 cm. (**b**) Oxford, Ashmolean Museum 1948.96. Width 36 cm.)

(**a**) Filov, *op. cit.* **105**, 59ff, pl. 2.1; for Ziwiye see O. W. Muscarella, *Journal of Field Archaeology* 4(2) (1977) 197–219. (**b**) B. Filov, *Izvestiya na Bulgarskiya Arkheologicheski Institut* 6 (1930–31) 45–46; T. F. Taylor, *Oxford Journal of Archaeology* 4 (1985) 293–304 for dating; B. Filov, *Die Archäische Nekropol von Trebenischte am Ochrida-See* (Berlin–Leipzig, 1927) no. 4.

7. ART

JOHN BOARDMAN

(a) Architecture

By the late Archaic period the basic elements of the Doric and Ionic orders had been established and variants were minor and local. It had become commoner for marble to be employed for temples, both for structure and for decorative sculpture (treated separately here, below). Monumental architecture was still confined largely to sanctuaries for temples, treasuries, altars and stoai, although in Athens at least the new Agora area was beginning to attract imposing buildings devoted to state business. For the larger sanctuary projects the problems of the provision of labour probably outdid those of engineering, and in tyrant-controlled states major buildings were surely regarded as a good way of distributing wealth and keeping the populace employed, as well as a means of displaying wealth and authority, even piety. At the national sanctuaries this could be done by building treasuries. The layout of the major national sanctuaries was described in *Pls. to Vol. III*, pls. 304, 309, with pl. 313 for the beginning of one of the main architectural orders. The items illustrated here demonstrate examples of some of the more imposing projects of the period.

GENERAL BIBLIOGRAPHY

W. B. Dinsmoor, *The Architecture of Ancient Greece* (London–Chicago, 1952); A. W. Lawrence, *Greek Architecture*[4] (Harmondsworth, 1983); H. Berve, G. Gruben and M. Hirmer, *Greek Temples, Theatres and Shrines* (London, 1963); J. J. Coulton, *Greek Architects at Work* (London, 1977).

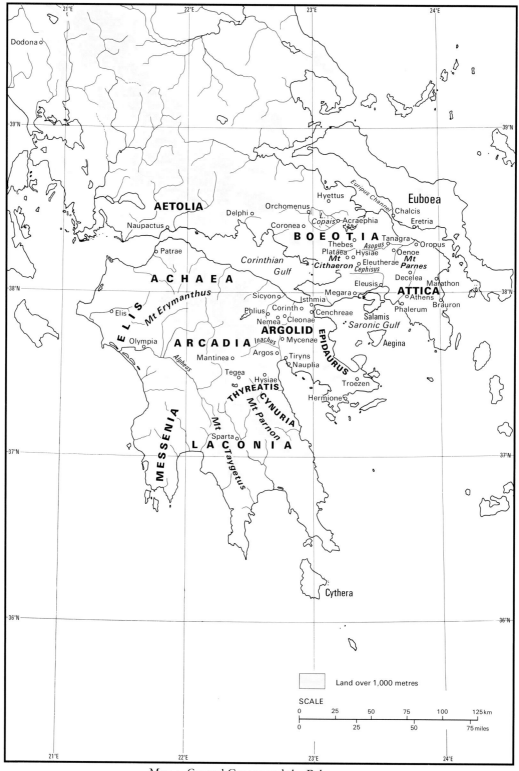

Map 5. Central Greece and the Peloponnese.

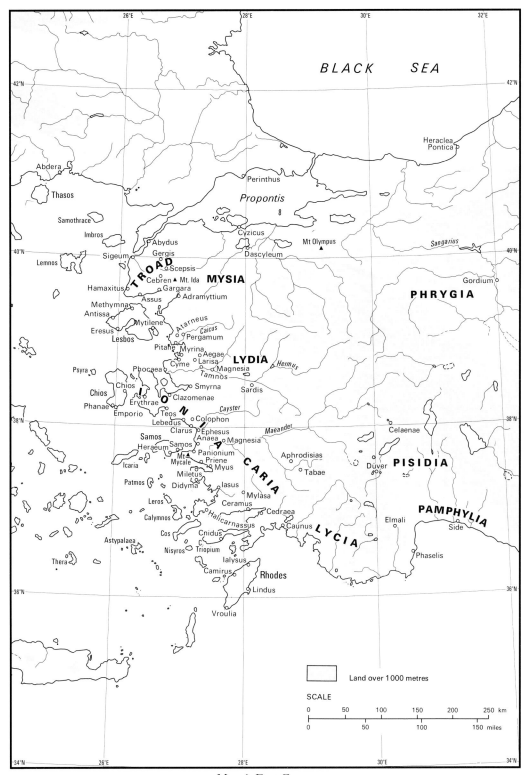

BLACK SEA

Abdera

Thasos

Samothrace

Imbros

Lemnos

Perinthus

Propontis

Cyzicus

Heraclea
Pontica

Sangarius

Abydus
Gergis
Sigeum
Scepsis
Cebren ▲ Mt. Ida
Hamaxitus
Gargara
Assus
Adramyttium
Methymna
Antissa
Mytilene
Eresus
Lesbos
Atarneus
Pergamum
Caicus
Pitane
Myrina
Cyme Aegae
Larisa
Magnesia
Hermus
Tamnos
Smyrna
Sardis
Dascyleum
Mt Olympus ▲

T R O A D
MYSIA

PHRYGIA

Gordium

LYDIA

Psyra

Chios
Chios
Phanae
Emporio
Erythrae
Clazomenae
Teos
Lebedus
Colophon
Cayster
Clarus
Ephesus
Anaea Magnesia
Maeander
Samos
Heraeum
Samos
Panionium
Mt Priene
Mycale
Myus
Icaria
Miletus
Patmos
Didyma
Iasus
Leros
Mylasa
Ceramus
Calymnos
Cedraea
Halicarnassus
Cos
Astypalaea
Cnidus
Thera
Nisyros Triopium
Ialysus
Camirus
Rhodes
Lindus
Vroulia

Phocaea

I O N I A

CARIA

Aphrodisias

Tabae

Düver

Celaenae

PISIDIA

PAMPHYLIA

Elmali

Side

Caunus

LYCIA

Phaselis

| | Land over 1000 metres |

SCALE

| 0 | 50 | 100 | 150 | 200 | 250 km |

| 0 | 50 | 100 | 150 miles |

Map 6. East Greece.

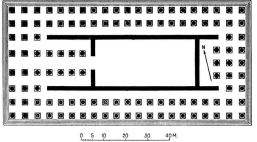

114a

114b

114. The Ionian cities were responsible for the major temple building of the Archaic period – at Ephesus, Didyma (near Miletus) and on Samos (see *Pls. to Vol. III*, pl. 315). These temples demonstrate early versions of the Ionic order, generally in a most elaborate form, and with double rows of columns along the flanks of the buildings and sometimes treble at the ends the structure took on the appearance more of a forest of columns enclosing a hall for the cult statue, than of a house for the god with pillar-supported eaves. Samos seems to have set the pattern, soon followed by Ephesus (**a, b**) with an enormous building. Most of the temples took long to build and the Ephesus temple received its sculpture over many years although the basic structure must have been in position within a generation. Herodotus (1.92) says that King Croesus of Lydia paid for some of the columns, which seems confirmed by incomplete inscriptions from column bases. The sculptured reliefs decorated the gutter (sima) and the lower (or upper?) drums of the columns. The plan measured 115.14 by 55.10 m, slightly larger than the Samos temple. The Ionic capitals show a variety of decorative features, but none as elaborate as an example from Samos (**c**) with its carved floral necking. This type of embellishment seems characteristic of Archaic Ionic architecture, in marked contrast with the comparative austerity of Doric. It is displayed in a near-bizarre form on smaller temples on Chios, where the by-now conventional egg-and-dart or leaf-and-dart mouldings were translated into floral interlaces (**d**) and where it was possible even for a lion-paw to be enlarged from its commoner role on furniture to serve as terminal for a temple wall (**e**).

114c

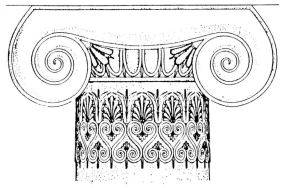

((d, e) Chios Museum. From Emporio and other Chian sites. (e) 38 cm high.)

For (a, b, c) Berve, Gruben and Hirmer, figs. 129, 130 (reconstruction by F. Krischen), 116; for (d, e) J. Boardman, *Antiquaries Journal* 39 (1959) 170–218.

115. Reconstruction (A. von Gerkan) of the altar of Poseidon at Cape Monodendri near Miletus, late sixth century B.C. Ionic altars tend to the monumental, with broad sacrifice platforms approached by flights of steps, and corners decorated with volutes and anthemia. In homeland Greece they are generally plain and block-like.

Berve, Gruben and Hirmer, figs. 111–12.

116. Doric temple of Aphaea (a minor local deity, apparently assimilated to Athena) on Aegina. The plan is conventional but for the two-tiered rows of columns within, and the size (28.815×13.77 m) is modest by comparison with the Ionian temples. It was built about 500 B.C. For the fortunes of its sculptures see below, **122**.

Berve, Gruben and Hirmer, figs. 42–3.

117. Two treasuries at Delphi. The Siphnian (a) was an ornate building in the Ionic order, with statues of women ('Caryatids') in place of columns in its front porch. For these see below, **124**, and for some of the very elaborate narrative sculpture in its friezes see *Pls. to Vol. III*, pl. 361. It was built around 525 B.C. The Athenian

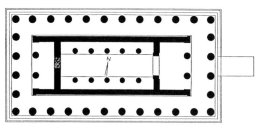

treasury (**b**) is Doric, its only sculptural decoration in its pediments and metopes (for these see
below, **125**). Pausanias (x.11.4) says that it was
built after the battle of Marathon, and this is
generally accepted now although for some time
scholars preferred an earlier date, on stylistic
grounds. For the placing of the treasuries at Delphi see *Pls. to Vol. III*, pl. 309.

Berve, Gruben and Hirmer, 134–8, fig. 26, pl. 72.

(b) Architectural sculpture

The placing of sculpture on temple buildings offers little chance for innovation. On Ionic buildings of the Archaic period advantage could be taken of the column drums themselves (see **114b, 127**) but the normal scheme was a frieze, in the entablature or, exceptionally, on the gutter. Pediments were left empty (the small, ornate treasury, **117a**, is an exception). On Doric buildings the pediments and the metopes (the rectangular panels in the entablature) could be filled, and there could be statuary at the gable corners (acroteria).

118. Limestone group from the pediment of the Athena temple on the Acropolis at Athens. A three-bodied, winged monster with snaky tail. Each human forepart carries an object: a water symbol, stalks of wheat and a bird. The symbolism is obscure and not repeated in Athenian art but the creature has been variously interpreted as a personification of the winds, or a variety of monster to be fought by Heracles (otherwise prominent in Acropolis pediments), even as a personification of the three political parties of the Attic state. There is a plethora of architectural sculpture from the Athenian Acropolis, sixth century, but not easily dated more closely. It has

118a

118b

119

been suggested that the figure can be combined with a group of lions attacking a bull, as centrepiece, with the left wing of the pediment occupied by a group of Heracles fighting Triton (**b**). The other pediment would then have a comparable animal group flanked by the Introduction of Heracles to Olympus and perhaps a Birth of Athena. Dates before and after 550 have been proposed, and this sculptural scheme could easily have been sponsored by Pisistratus although the temple building seems decidedly earlier and its pediments may at first have carried other animal groups, pieces of which have been found. A drawing of the pediment as restored by W.-H. Schuchhardt, is given.

(Athens, Acropolis Museum 35. Height 0·90 m.)
  Robertson *HGA* 93–4; *GSAP* 154–5, figs. 191–4 (fig. 190 for the earlier pediment); I. Beyer, *AA* 1974, 639–51; *CAH* III².3, 411.

119. Marble figure of a giant from the pediment of the Athena temple on the Athenian Acropolis. This is from a group showing the fight of gods and giants, from which other giant figures are preserved, and an Athena. It appears to have replaced the limestone group, described in the last plate, and its companion pediment had an animal group which recalls the earlier compositions. (We assume that there was only one major temple on the Acropolis in this period, not two, as has sometimes been argued.) It has generally been thought that the marble replacement was the work of the Pisistratids, answering the Alcmaeonid gift to Delphi of a marble pediment for the Apollo temple (apparently after 514). At Delphi there was also a gigantomachy, but for the other, limestone pediment. It is just as likely that the Athenian marble pediment is a post-tyrant creation, even Alcmaeonid-inspired; if so, little before 500 in date.

(Athens, Acropolis Museum 631c. Height 1.02 m.)
  Robertson, *HGA* 159–60; *GSAP* 155, fig. 199.

120. Marble group of Theseus carrying off the Amazon queen Antiope onto his chariot, from the pediment of the temple of Apollo Daphnephoros at Eretria. Probably of 500–490 B.C., commemorating Eretria's role with Athens in the Ionian Revolt, for which Eretria was sacked by the Persians in 490, on their way

to defeat at Marathon. The subject matter is Athenian (Theseus is the favourite of Athens' new democracy), and the story, a raid into Anatolia, matches the Athens/Eretria expedition which led to the Ionian burning of the lower town of the Persian capital at Sardis in 498. See also the next plate.

(Chalcis Museum 4. Height 1.10 m.)
  Robertson, *HGA* 163–4; E. Touloupa, *Ta enaetia glypta* (Ioannina, 1983); *GSAP* 156, fig. 205.

121. Marble figure of a kneeeling Amazon archer, from the same pediment at Eretria as the group in the last plate, but found in Rome, where it had been taken in antiquity. Livy (XXXII.16) speaks of the statuary plundered by L. Quinctius

Flamininus in 198. The figure may have been the only one (or one of the only ones) available in a fair state of preservation after the Persian burning of the city in 480, but it has been suggested that the second pediment had been filled later in the fifth century by a different Amazonomachy group which was also taken to Rome and which has recently been reassembled there; this attractive suggestion is at present unverifiable.

(Rome, Conservatori Museum 12. Height 0.69 m.)

See last plate. For controversy over the date, E. D. Francis and M. Vickers, *JHS* 103 (1983) 49–67, answered by J. Boardman, *JHS* 104 (1984) 161–3. For the Rome pediment, E. La Rocca, *Amazzonomachia* (Rome, 1985).

122. Part of the marble pedimental group from the temple of Aphaea on Aegina. This eastern

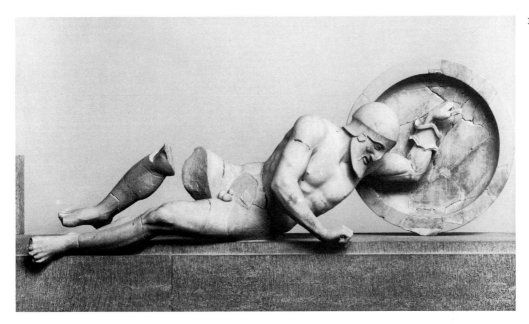

pediment seems somewhat later in style than the western pediment and is thought to be a replacement for sculptures which had been damaged. It is commonly dated to 490–480 B.C. Both pediments showed fighting at Troy; this one the attack by Heracles (the archer at the right) supported by Telamon (father of Ajax), an Aeginetan. Athena stood at the centre, and here (a) shows four figures from the right half of the pediment; (b) is a detail of the Heracles, wearing a helmet whose crown is fashioned as a lion-head, recalling his more usual dress; (c) is a collapsed warrior from the left corner of the same pediment.

(Munich, Glyptotek, East figures II, III, IV, V (Heracles); and figure XI (c); (b) height 0·79 m; (c) height 0·64 m.)

D. Ohly, *Die Aegineten* (Munich, 1976); Robertson, *HGA* 165–7; *GSAP* 156–7, fig. 206.

123. Frieze slabs from the temple of Athena at Assus (south of Troy), later sixth century B.C. (a) shows a feast, with a boy wine-pourer; (b) the struggle of Heracles and Triton, with alarmed water nymphs. The style is somewhat heavy and stiff in the coarse, hard stone (andesite). The Heracles subject recalls Athens, which was taking an active interest in this area and the approaches to the Black Sea in just these years. There may be a closer connexion, too, since this is the decoration for a Doric temple,

the only one of this date in the East Greek world, rather incongruously adorned with this Ionic frieze below its (also carved) metopes.

(Paris, Louvre. Height 82 cm.)

J. T. Clarke, et al., *Investigations at Assos* (Boston, 1902–21); *GSAP* 160, fig. 216; B. Wescoat, forthcoming.

124. Marble heads of Caryatids (casts) from Delphi. (a) belongs to the columnar façade of the Siphnian Treasury of about 525 B.C. (for its narrative friezes see *Pls. to Vol. III*, pl. 361; these are now better understood from newly read inscriptions which prove that the fight shown was over the body of Antilochos, and that Zeus was supervising the weighing of the fates of

123a

123b

Achilles and Memnon). See also **117a**. (**b**) used to be attributed to the Cnidian Treasury, then dissociated ('ex-Cnidian'), and now some French scholars believe that it may too be from the Siphnian Treasury despite the discrepancy in style (there were two artists for the friezes) and slight discrepancies in size.

(Delphi Museum; heights (**a**) 71 cm, (**b**) 66 cm; casts in Oxford, Ashmolean Museum.)

Robertson, *HGA* 152–9; *GSAP* figs. 209–10; frieze inscriptions, V. Brinkmann, *BCH* 109 (1985) 77–108.

125. Marble metopes from the Athenian Treasury at Delphi (see also **117b**). The metopes share the honours between the old favourite, Heracles, and the 'new' Theseus. On (**a**) Heracles fights Ares' son, Kyknos; the hero's helmet is in the form of a lion-head, as at Aegina – see **122b**. On (**b**) Athena confronts Theseus, a group very familiar for her with Heracles in the sixth century, and not forgotten in the fifth, but a unique honour for Theseus.

(Delphi Museum. Height 0.67 m.)
    Robertson, *HGA* 167–71; *GSAP* fig. 213.

126. Limestone pediment from the temple of Dionysus on Corcyra, end of the sixth century B.C. Dionysus, holding a drinking horn, reclines at a feast with a naked boy. A lion is crouching beneath the couch, a mastiff stands behind it, by a wine-mixing bowl. The boy is possibly Oinopion; the occasion, a feast with Hephaestus.

(Corfu Museum. 2.73 × 1.3 m.)
    A. Choremis, *Arch. Annals of Athens* 7 (1974) 183–6; *GSAP* fig. 207a; M. Crewer, *AA* 1981, 317–28.

127. Marble frieze from the temple of Apollo at Didyma (near Miletus), later sixth century B.C. At the corner is a Gorgon, beside her crouching lions. This style of frieze decoration is typical of the great Ionic temples in East Greece (exceptional on the Doric temple at Assus, **123**).

(Istanbul, Arch. Mus. 239. Height 0.91 m.)
    G. Gruben, *JDAI* 78 (1963) 78–182; *GSAP* fig. 218.

(c) Sculpture

The late Archaic period sees a revolution in sculptural style in Greece which was to have a profound effect on the future history of the representational arts in the west. At its simplest it may be described as a move away from a formulaic approach to the human figure towards a closer observation of the live model. The result was a degree of realism which went beyond superficial appearance and achieved a command of anatomical accuracy which enabled figures to be shown in real poses of repose or action. The figures were at last understood from within, in terms of balance, muscle and bone, and not simply as an assemblage of more-or-less life-like

parts. The concern with pattern and proportion, which had characterized the best of earlier sculpture was by no means abandoned, but continued to dictate sculptural styles for generations to come. The new style required far greater care in preparation for the figure, and direct carving into marble had to give place to working from modelled figures, probably of clay, in which the problems of movement and balance could be worked out. This shift from the carved to the plastic encouraged the use of bronze, which could be cast directly (or indirectly) from the model, and bronze is to be the favoured medium for the fifth century for all but architectural and grave sculpture. The stereotyped Archaic kouroi and korai (e.g., *Pls. to Vol. III*, pls. 330–1) change appearance and function, being less commonly used as grave monuments, more often as individual dedications, commonly of victors in games or war. The clearest record of this change is seen in Athens, though the finds are slight after the early fifth century, but the East Greek world had much also to contribute and had always been innovatory in the sculptural arts (e.g., *ibid.*, pl. 317). There too sculptural types and styles which we lack in Attica continued to flourish and they provide continuity in the record with the achievements of the early Classical and full Classical periods.

GENERAL BIBLIOGRAPHY

Robertson, *HGA* chapters 3, 4; Boardman, *GSAP* and *GSCP* for illustrated handbooks; W. Fuchs, *Die Skulptur der Griechen*[3] (Munich, 1983); B. S. Ridgway, *The Archaic Style in Greek Sculpture* (Princeton, 1977).

128. Marble kouros, the grave-marker of Aristodikos from near Mt Olympus in Attica, end of the sixth century B.C. This is one of the latest and most realistic of the Attic kouroi, but still basically composed as a four-square figure. Subtleties of stance which may deviate from the strictly frontal may be deliberate, and will predispose the artist to attempt other experiments in pose and balance, but they do not betoken any deeper understanding of anatomy, which is the essence of the imminent new style.

(Athens, National Museum 3938. Height 1.95 m.)
    Ch. Karousos, *Aristodikos* (Stuttgart, 1961); *GSAP* fig. 145; G. M. A. Richter, *Kouroi*[3] (London, 1970) no. 165.

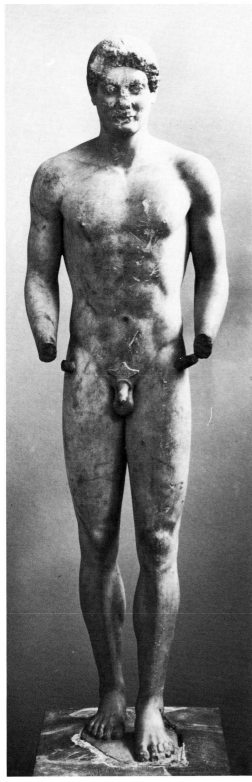

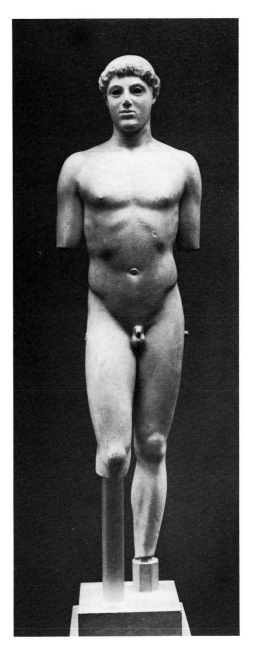

129. Marble youth from the Acropolis, Athens, about half life size, about 490–480 B.C. The so-called 'Kritian boy' for the similarity of his head to that of the young tyrannicide (see **141**) from the group made by Kritios and Nesiotes. This is the earliest figure well enough preserved to demonstrate the sculptor's new command of anatomical rendering for a figure in repose. The boy's weight is shifted on to his left leg, with

(Athens, Acropolis Museum 698. Height 86 cm.)

H. G. Payne and G. M. Young, *Archaic Marble Sculpture from the Acropolis* (London, 1936) pls. 110–12; Richter, *Kouroi* no. 190; *GSAP* fig. 147.

130. Marble head and hips of a youth from the Acropolis, Athens, about 490–480 B.C. This was a slightly larger figure than the Kritian boy (**129**) but apparently in the same pose and with the head more subtly inclined. It is known as the Blond Boy for the traces of yellow-brown paint preserved on his hair. The long back hair is shown plaited and bound round the head (beneath the front locks) in a manner which is to become typical of later figures. This, with the Kritian boy, must have been an individual dedication, perhaps of an athlete. The rather heavy, broad features also anticipate the early Classical.

(Athens, Acropolis Museum 689 +. Height of head 25 cm; of hips 34 cm.)

Payne–Young, *op. cit.*, pls. 113–15; Richter, *Kouroi* no. 191; *GSAP* fig. 148.

131. Bronze statuette of a youth from the Acropolis, Athens, about 510 B.C. He is probably an athlete, holding jumping weights (cf. **212**) in his outstretched hands. The style and pose are still those of the latest kouroi, as Aristodikos (**128**), but he is characterized as an athlete and stands at the head of a long series of athlete dedications, the new role for these 'standing male' figures.

(Athens, National Museum 6445. Height 27 cm.)

Richter, *Kouroi* no. 162; *GSAP* fig. 140.

132. Bronze head of a warrior (the helmet, made separately, is missing) from the Acropolis, Athens, about 490 B.C. This would have been a substantial standing figure of a warrior, over half life size, presumably the dedication of a victor in battle (it must be close to the date of the battle of Marathon) or in the race for armed runners (see **210**). The style is very close to that of the warriors in the pediments of the temple of Aphaea on Aegina (see **122**) and, in the light of Aegina's reputation in bronze sculpture in these years, scholars have not been slow to associate this head with the Aeginetan school.

(Athens, National Museum 6446. Height 25 cm.)

GSAP fig. 207.

the right leg realistically flexed and a correspondingly slight tilt of the shoulders indicated. This, with other marble sculptures on the Acropolis, had presumably been overthrown at the time of the Persian sack (480/479 B.C.), and afterwards (sooner or later) buried by the Athenians in pits on the Acropolis, mainly in terraces just within the new fortification walls at north and south.

complete major bronze from Greece. Some oddities in the treatment of hair and physique may be indications of the effect of the technique for such figures (see Introduction to this section).

(Piraeus Museum. Height 1.92 m.)
Richter, *Kouroi* no. 159bis; Robertson, *HGA* 175–6; *GSAP* fig. 150.

133. Bronze statue of Apollo, late sixth century B.C. The figure was found in the Piraeus in a cache of other bronzes and marbles which appear to have been awaiting shipment to Italy but were overtaken by Sulla's sack of the town in 86 B.C. The other pieces seem to come from Attica and Delos. The kouros pose has been adapted for the Apollo by bringing his arms forward, probably to hold a phiale and a bow. This is likely to have been a cult statue and is the earliest surviving,

134. Marble statue of a youth, inscribed 'I am Dionysermos, son of Antenor', about 520 B.C. The provenance of this statue is not known but its style – the rounded skull and set of hair – and the fact that it is dressed, as well as features of the inscription, place it in the East Greek world, where several other such dressed kouroi are known. The rather heavy, curving but unarticulated forms are also characteristic of sculpture from this area. Cf. *Pls to Vol. III*, pl. 318 for an even more spherical head, from Samos, and the Geneleos group (*ibid.*, pl. 317c) where there is another dressed male.

(Paris, Louvre MA 3600. Height 69 cm.)
P. Devambez, *Revue archéologique* 1966, 195–215; *GSAP* fig. 174.

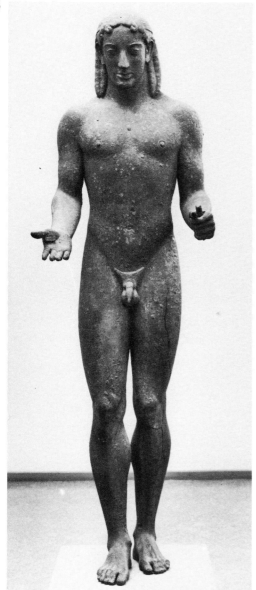

133

134

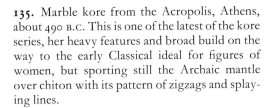

135. Marble kore from the Acropolis, Athens, about 490 B.C. This is one of the latest of the kore series, her heavy features and broad build on the way to the early Classical ideal for figures of women, but sporting still the Archaic mantle over chiton with its pattern of zigzags and splaying lines.

(Athens, Acropolis Museum 684. Height 1.19 m.)

G. M. A. Richter, *Korai* (London, 1968) no. 182; Payne–Young, *op. cit.* **129**, pls. 79, 80; *GSAP* fig. 159.

136. Marble statue of Athena by the sculptor Euenor, dedicated by Angelitos on the Acropolis, Athens, about 480 B.C. The figure had been set on a column, as were many of the smaller dedications on the Acropolis. She stands with spear in right hand (missing), hand on hip, in a pose which, though disguised by dress, is unmistakably the new, realistic one exemplified by the Kritian boy (**129**); the relaxed right leg presses out against the dress, which falls in straight folds over the left leg. This is very close to the typical early Classical, yet it probably antedates the Persian sacks of Athens.

(Athens, Acropolis Museum 140. Height 77 cm.)

B. S. Ridgway, *The Severe Style in Greek Sculpture* (Princeton, 1970) 29–31, fig. 39; *GSAP* fig. 173.

137. Marble stela from Athens, about 510–500 B.C. The finial can be restored with **S** volutes and an anthemion, but the shape is unusual for either a votive or a grave relief, both of which explanations have been proposed for the piece. The warrior is in the Archaic kneeling-running position. His bent head and arms seem, to a modern eye, to indicate imminent collapse, but in the conventions of Archaic art the pose has no such necessary connotations. It has been popularly, and erroneously, called 'the Marathon runner'. If from a grave it may not have been free-standing but applied to a block monument; if votive, it may commemorate success in the armed footrace (cf. **210**).

(Athens, National Museum 1959. Height 1.02 m.)
M. Andronikos, *Archaiologike Ephemeris* 1953/4.2, 317–26; Ridgway, *Archaic Style* 166, fig. 53; *GSAP* fig. 239.

138. Marble mask of a god, found at Marathon, about 500–480 B.C. The attachments at the forehead may be for horns, so this could be the earliest anthropomorphic representation of the god Pan. He becomes popular in Athenian cult and art from about this time, and the Marathonian association is explained in Herodotus' story (VI.105) of how the Athenian runner Pheidippides met him on his return from trying to summon the Spartans, and was promised the god's help. It is long before Pan is again shown with such an Olympian aspect. The mask might have been attached to a wooden body or post as an object of cult.

(Berlin (East), Staatliche Museen 100. Height 32 cm.)
A. Wrede, *Athenische Mitteilungen* 53 (1928) Beil.23; B. Ashmole, *Proceedings of the British Academy* 48 (1962) 215–16; *GSAP* fig. 171.

139. Marble base for a grave stela from Athens, about 510 B.C. The more elaborate grave stelae of Athens (see *Pls. to Vol. III*, pl. 332) were set into shallow bases decorated with reliefs on the front or front and sides. This one is decorated on three sides with scenes of young men at exercise or play (see also **215**). The shallow cutting comes very close to the linear styles of contemporary red-figure vase-painting (as **206–7**) with their display of unusual postures and interest in details of anatomy.

(Athens, National Museum 3476. Height 32 cm.)
F. Willemsen, *Athenische Mitteilungen* 78 (1963) 104–53; *GSAP* fig. 242.

140. Marble stela from Cos (Dodecanese), about 500 B.C. It is by no means clear whether this is a grave relief or a votive; in either case the subject is unexpected. In the foreground is a piper, at the left. Beyond is a symposium couch on which a man holding a lyre is clasping a naked girl (their heads are missing). Before and beneath the couch a small boy tries to lift to his feet a drunken but excited man. It is especially in East Greek art that the more exotic genre subjects appear to have been favoured for monumental expression such as this; in the Greek homeland they were generally shunned except in the minor arts.

(Cos Museum. Height 72 cm.)

Ch. Karousos, *Athenische Mitteilungen* 77 (1962) 121–9; *GSAP* fig. 249.

141. Marble group of the Tyrannicides (**a**), copy of the group by Kritios and Nesiotes set up in the Athenian Agora soon after 479 B.C., replacing the group by Antenor which had been carried off by the Persians (to be returned some two centuries later after the Persian empire had been overthrown by Alexander). It commemorates Harmodius and Aristogeiton, who had assassinated the Athenian tyrant Hipparchus in 514 B.C. (*CAH* IV² 299). This is an early example of an action group in the round, the viewer being placed in the position of the victim. The style is early Classical but there is much Archaic still in the poses and especially in the head of the young Harmodius (cf. the 'Kritian boy', **129**). Such a conspicuous and imposing group might be expected to be influential, but we can see from

an Athenian vase (**b**) of little later that straight copying is not to be expected, least of all in another medium, since the painter has added the victim and been very free in interpreting the poses and dress of the slayers. Groups such as (**a**) were made in studios in Italy for Roman homes, using as models, which could be almost mechanically copied, plaster casts taken from the originals. Finds from such a studio at Baiae on the Bay of Naples included part of the cast from the original head of the Aristogeiton from this group (**c**) and this provides us with an unusual opportunity to compare original (at least in cast) with copy and to judge the freedom of detail which the copyist allowed himself. The rather lumpy eyelashes on the cast show that on the original the lashes had been protected, probably with clay, before the mould was taken.

((**a**) Naples, Museo Nazionale G 103–4. Height 1.95 m. (**b**) Würzburg, Martin von Wagner Museum L 515. Height 34.2 cm. (**c**) Baiae Museum 174.479, copy in Oxford. Height 20 cm.)

S. Brunnsåker, *The Tyrant-Slayers of Kritios and Nesiotes* (Stockholm, 1971); Ridgway, *Severe Style* 79–83; *GSCP* 24–5 figs. 3–9; *ARV* 256, 5 – the Copenhagen Painter (the vase); C. von Hees-Landwehr, *Der Fund von Baia* (Frankfurt am Main, 1982).

(d) Painting

The incising, silhouette style of the so-called black-figure vases derived originally from the incising techniques of oriental and orientalizing metalwork and ivories. In Athens, about 530 B.C., a new, 'red-figure' technique was introduced, in which the linear element of the drawing was done with a brush, not a graver, and the figures were left in the clay ground colour of the vase, the background being filled in with the fine black gloss paint (often miscalled 'glaze'). The rather abrupt change in appearance probably denotes something which goes beyond technical innovation in a comparatively humble, though busy, craft such as clay pottery production. There is little evidence for painting on other or larger surfaces in earlier years, though there are indications of painted figures on walls at the Isthmian temple of Poseidon in the seventh century, and the large clay plaques, also Corinthian in inspiration, which appear for some seventh-century temple metopes (*Pls. to Vol. III*, pl. 351) give an idea of work probably more often executed on wood. In Anatolia finds at Gordium of the mid-century, and of later in the century in Lycia, suggest the existence of flourishing schools of wall-painting, and there is evidence from both Greece (near Corinth; *ibid.*, pl. 323) and the East Greek world (*ibid.*, pl. 299) for painted wooden panels (cf. also here, **234**). It is very likely that these induced the new technique on Athenian vases, and it may well be regarded as yet another symptom of that influx of artists from an East Greece beset by Persians which we observe in other arts of Athens.

Our knowledge of painting in the late Archaic period is derived almost wholly from vases, and especially Athenian vases, since other centres of production had by then mainly abdicated any attempt to compete in fine figure-decorated ware. The black-figure technique was still practised, and with some distinction, down to about 500 B.C. The vase scenes have been used freely in this volume to illustrate other subjects. The choice in this section is determined by what they can demonstrate of the quality of the technique and the intimations it offers of work in other media.

GENERAL BIBLIOGRAPHY

R. M. Cook, *Greek Painted Pottery* (London, 1972); Robertson, *HGA* esp. 214–39; Boardman, *ABFH* and *ARFH* for illustrated handbooks on Athenian black and red figure; J. D. Beazley, *The Development of Attic Black-figure* (Berkeley, 1951). Monographs on individual painters and other wares are cited in the following entries.

142. Athenian black-figure neck-amphora, by the Madrid Painter, about 520–510 B.C. This is the finest style of the late sixth century, still heavily dependent on ornament and added colour, as is most black figure, but showing influence of the new red-figure style in its attempt to vary the usually uniform and bold incised lines with lighter, barely scratched lines (as for Heracles' chest-hair) which resembles brushwork. The figures are also outlined by incision, which was not a regular practice before: the lines would have shown light beside the black paint and the artificially reddened background, and thus paralleled the use of relief-line contour (for

142

nysus and his rout of satyrs and maenads. The painter gives us just the young Hephaestus on his excited mule with satyr and maenad pairs: the satyr behind carries a wineskin, the one in front molests a maenad who holds a drinking horn. White ground is the natural medium for painting on wood or wall. It had been adopted for some vases in the seventh century (and in parts of Greece was preferred when the natural clay colour was dusky). It enjoys a new significance in Athenian vase-painting from the later sixth century and in the fifth century attracts a style of outline drawing which must be directly inspired by major painting. At this date and with the old technique it represents some problems: thus, the women's flesh cannot be distinguished by added white paint when the background is white, and the colour–sex distinction is lost.

(Oxford, Ashmolean Museum 1982.1097; formerly Hattatt Collection.)
　　D. C. Kurtz, *Oxford Journal of Archaeology* 1 (1982) 139–67.

144. Athenian bilingual (one side black figure, the other red figure) belly amphora, by the Andocides Painter, about 525 B.C. The artist is the first to practise the red-figure technique in Athens and is generally credited with being its inventor. It is almost impossible to believe that he did not also draw in black figure and he (in common with a few other artists) has left a number of vases decorated in both techniques. Beazley, the greatest connoisseur of Athenian vase-painters, changed his mind twice about whether both sides of these vases were by one hand and his last view was that they were not and that the black figure was the work of the Lysippides Painter. The debate continues and it is true that the criteria for painter attribution, attention to minor details that are drawn almost unconsciously (the 'handwriting', as it were), do not much support the identity of execution in the two techniques, though the techniques themselves impose notably different methods of drawing. Early red figure is very like a translation of black figure, with much added colour and incision still used around black outlines (here, hair and grapes). The scenes (for the subject see on 142) are the same but it is significant that the red-figure version is less cluttered and more emphasis is placed on the figures. The fine black lines stand in relief on the vase and are character-

which see text to **144**) in red figure. The scene is one of many which displays Heracles' special relationship with the city goddess, Athena (cf. *CAH* iv² 421). He reclines as a solitary mortal symposiast (gods sit at feast) in a setting which carries something of the air of a reception by a ruler, and which becomes especially associated with heroes and the heroized dead. For the decoration of the fine couch (*kline*) see **179**. Hermes attends. Heracles had a reputation as a glutton, hence the groaning side table, and it is not only the festive activity that suggests the presence of the vine since he has much in common with Dionysus and can sometimes recline with him in these years.

(New York, Callimanopoulos Collection; formerly at Castle Ashby, Northampton.)
　　ABV 329, 5; *CVA Castle Ashby* pl. 10. 3, 4.

143. Athenian black-figure neck-amphora, painted on a white ground, by the Hattatt Painter, about 510–500 B.C. The scene is probably an excerpt from a fuller version of the Return of Hephaestus to Olympus, accompanied by Dio-

144a

144b

istic of the technique, being used for outline and all major linear detail. The method of making these 'relief lines' is not altogether clear, but they had been invented by black-figure artists to render spears and decoration dividers, and so are not an innovation though they are used in a novel way. They lend a sparkle and hard definition to the drawing which is not easily captured by the camera.

(Munich, Antikensammlungen 2301.)
 ARV 4, 9; *ARV* 255, 4; *CVA Munich* 4 pls. 155–8; Simon–Hirmer, pl. 86–9; on the painter problem, *ARFH* 15–17.

145. Athenian red-figure 'eye-cup', by Oltos, about 520 B.C. Most of the red-figure vases made before about 500 B.C. were cups: there must have been a notable demand for them from Etruria where almost all have been found. The leading cup-painters were Oltos and Epiktetos (**146**). The use of eyes to decorate a cup was learned from East Greece in the mid-century: it turns the cup into something like a head, with handle-ears and an open foot-mouth. The shape is the one used in black figure and the interior is decorated still in the old technique. Between the eyes runs a sea-nymph (Nereid) holding two red dolphins. The demonstration example (**b**) is a cup in Oxford, Ashmolean Museum.

(Formerly at Castle Ashby, Northampton. Height 13.3 cm.)
 ARV 44, 77; *CVA Castle Ashby* pl. 32.

146. Athenian red-figure plate, by Epiktetos, about 520 B.C. Clay plates are not particularly common but the shape was favoured by some cup-painters, notably Epiktetos, one of the finest draughtsmen of his day. His signature can be seen in the field. The subject is two revellers; the boy plays the double pipes, the pipe-case (an animal skin) slung from his shoulder. Red-figure artists generally found it better not to let figures overlap since it was not always easy to distinguish them in a single contour, but Epiktetos has no difficulty.

(London, British Museum E 137. Width 18.7 cm.)
ARV 78, 95; *ABFH* fig. 78.

147. Fragmentary Athenian red-figure calyx-crater by Euphronios, about 510 B.C. Heracles has struck down Kyknos, and his patron Athena storms past him to drive off Kyknos' father, the god Ares. There is considerable refinement of the red-figure technique displayed here. Relief line is used freely to demonstrate a far better understanding of anatomy than was ever achieved, or looked for, in black figure. Beside it dilute lines are used for less emphatic anatomical detail and for the texture of dress, and a wash appears on the inside of Heracles' shield and for his lionskin. Euphronios was a leading member of the so-called Pioneer Group of artists who worked in red figure from around 520 to soon after 500 (for other works by them see **148–50**, **184**). They realize the full potential of the new technique, though still using minor incised detail (e.g. around hair) and their work has a truly monumental quality. They specialize in large vases and even their cups are generally outsize. They are free with inscriptions and repeatedly refer to each other on their vases giving the impression of being a conscious 'group' or 'movement' in their craft. They are the teachers of the great painters of the early fifth century, yet we may well believe that they devoted much of their careers to other media, perhaps painting on wood or wall (cf. **150**). Their overall production was far less numerous than that of their contemporary cup-painters.

(Fort Worth, Bunker Hunt Collection.)

M. Robertson, *J. Paul Getty Museum Journal* 9 (1981) 29–34; *Wealth of the ancient world* (Fort Worth, 1983) no. 6.

148. Athenian red-figure stamnos, by Smikros, about 510 B.C. A symposium. The artist, a 'Pioneer', names himself as the youth who seems enchanted by the music of the girl piper. Dilute lines are used freely here for minor details of anatomy and to render the soft texture of dress, which is also indicated by trebling the outline (the sleeve). 'Smikros' means 'tiny': several vase-painters sign with what must be nicknames (Epiktetos, cf. **146**, may be a slave name, 'acquired').

(Brussels, Musées Royaux A 717.)
    ARV 20, 1; *AK* 8 (1965) pls. 13–14; *ARFH* fig. 32.; Simon–Hirmer, pls. 110–11.

149. Athenian red-figure cup interior, by the Sosias Painter, about 500 B.C. Achilles binds a wound in Patroclus' arm; both figures are named. The artist has added white for the bandage and for Patroclus' teeth, bared in a grimace of pain. This is an unusually realistic expression of emotion for this period but, more remarkably, the eyes are drawn in a realistic profile view and not frontally, which had been the rule in black figure and remains the rule for red figure for some time. This is either an exceptional demonstration of how an artist may occasionally draw from life rather than from habit, or a trait taken from another medium which the artist also practised and which had admitted such details

earlier than vase-painting. Notice how Patroclus uses the border of the picture as a ground, and the fine detail on the top view of his foot. He has unfastened the shoulder-piece of his leather corselet above the wound.

(Berlin (West), Staatliche Museen F 2278.)
    ARV 21, 1; *ARFH* fig. 50; Simon–Hirmer, pls. 117–19.

150. Clay plaque from the Athenian Acropolis, probably by Euthymides, about 500 B.C. Euthymides was another 'Pioneer' of red figure and it is from comparison with his signed work in this technique, and with another, smaller Acropolis plaque which seems to be by him and shows Athena, that the attribution is made. Incising black figure is used for the warrior's dress but his body is drawn in outline and filled with a wash of paint. This must closely resemble paintings on wooden panels, which the artist must also have made. His Athena plaque was made for dedication by his father, the sculptor Pollias. The one shown here is as substantial as a metope and must have occupied a prominent position. The *kalos* inscription upon it praises the beauty of Megacles (such inscriptions praising youths are common on vases of this period, without reference to the scene they accompany). The name had been erased, probably when

Megacles was ostracized (see *CAH* IV² 337) and replaced by one Glaucytes.

(Athens, Acropolis Museum 1037. Width 52 cm.)
ARV 1598; J. Boardman, *JHS* 76 (1956) 20–2 and *ARFH* fig. 53.

151. Athenian red-figure amphora, by the Kleophrades Painter, about 480 B.C. The scenes show the exchange of gifts at Troy between Ajax and Hector, who have been separated by Phoenix and Priam(?). The inspiration is *Iliad* VII.303–5, which is quite closely followed, but the representation is unique. The artist, perhaps the greatest of the late Archaic period, shows a remarkable sympathy for unusual subjects, particularly Trojan ones which give the opportunity for what appears to be quiet comment on the effects of war on humanity (see **152**). His figures are heavy and confident, almost sculptural. Here, Ajax bears away the sword with which he will kill himself (see **154**), and Hector the belt with which his body will be bound to Achilles' chariot; the duel has been averted but the heroes carry the symbols of their ultimate deaths.

(Würzburg, Martin von Wagner Museum 508.)
ARV 182, 5; *CVA Würzburg* 2 pls. 12–13; J. Boardman, *AK* 19 (1976) 5.

152. Athenian red-figure hydria by the Kleophrades Painter, about 480 B.C. The shoulder bears five scenes from the Sack of Troy, composed symmetrically by theme. The centrepiece is the sacrilegious slaughter of old Priam who has taken refuge at an altar with the dead body of his grandson Astyanax (Hector's child) on his lap, at the hands of Achilles' son Neoptolemus. To left and right women provide the theme: Trojan Cassandra, the priestess, is raped from sanctuary at the statue of Athena by the Lesser Ajax, and to the right brave Andromache (Hector's wife) fights back against a Greek with a pestle. On the wings are messages of hope: at the left Trojan Aeneas escapes from Troy with his father Anchises and his son, and at the right Greek Aethra is rescued from long captivity at Troy (she had been taken there with Helen) by her grandsons Demophon and Acamas. The painter again (see **151**) takes an original view of a traditional subject and presents it almost as a poet might (he was a contemporary of Aeschylus). It is possible that this reflection on the sack of a great city was inspired by the artist's own experience of his home, sacked by the Persians in 480 and 479 B.C.

(Naples, Museo Nazionale 2422.)
ARV 189, 74; Boardman, *op. cit* **151**, 7–8, 14–15, fig. 3; Simon–Hirmer, pls. 128–9; J. D. Beazley, *The Kleophrades Painter* (Mainz, 1974).

153. Athenian red-figure amphora, by the Berlin Painter, about 490 B.C. The artist is a contemporary of the Kleophrades Painter (**151–2**) but a quite different personality, far more interested in quality of drawing (at least in his prime; he had a disappointing old age) than in subject, favouring therefore compositions such as this in which a single figure is, as it were, spotlighted on each side of the vase. The old Heracles–Athena association is expressed here by the goddess preparing to pour into the hero's cup, for a libation (an act of worship for mortals, but a gesture of close relationship between gods or god and hero). The drawing and attention to detail is exquisite without being merely fussy. Relief blobs are used to highlight the hero's forelocks and beard. The shape of his cup, a 'Sotadean kantharos', called a *karchesion* in antiquity, is often associated with him and may refer to the *karchesion* which Zeus gave Alcmene, to deceive her into thinking that she was lying with her husband Amphitryon, when Heracles was con-

ceived. The cup was supposed to be spoils from the expedition on which Amphitryon was engaged.

(Basel, Antikenmuseum BS 456. Height 79 cm.)

ARV 1634, 1bis; *Para* 342; J. D. Beazley, *AK* 4 (1961) 49–67 and, for the painter, *id.*, *The Berlin Painter* (Mainz, 1974) and D. C. Kurtz, *The Berlin Painter* (Oxford, 1983) which also presents Beazley's drawings from the painter's vases and explains the techniques of attribution and degree of anatomical knowledge displayed by the artist; J. Boardman, *JHS* 99 (1979) 149–51 (the cup).

154. Interior of an Athenian red-figure cup, by the Brygos Painter, about 480 B.C. The artist (see also **191**) is one of the liveliest and most imaginative of the late Archaic period. Here Tecmessa spreads a cloak over the body of Ajax at Troy. He has killed himself by falling on his sword, choosing his one vulnerable spot, beneath the left armpit (a detail not usually observed in ancient art). Maddened by disappointment at not

153a  153b

154

being awarded the armour of Achilles, he slew the Greek flocks believing them to be the Greek heroes. Restored to his senses and realizing his folly, he kills himself. He seems here to be lying on fleeces, which may refer to the precedent events. Tecmessa was a spoil of war, but devoted to him. Her attention to his body is recorded later in the century by Sophocles (*Ajax* 915–16), a detail which, but for this vase, might otherwise have been attributed to the poet's imagination.

(Malibu, Getty Museum 86. AE. 286.)
Para 367, 1bis; *AK* 16 (1973) pl. 10. 1; *ARFH* fig. 246.

155

155. Athenian white-ground alabastron, by the Pasiades Painter, about 500 B.C. The shape had been copied from an Egyptian stone vase (see *Pls. to Vol III*, pl. 301) and the background colour here was probably suggested by the stone models. The outline drawing is enhanced with more colour than we are used to seeing in black or red figure. For the technique, see **143** and the next vase. Two girls, one wearing a fancy headdress and animal skin, with a pet heron.

(London, British Museum B 668.)
ARV 98, 1; *ARFH* fig. 107.

156. Athenian white-ground lekythos, by Douris, about 490 B.C. Douris is best known for his many fine cups but he has also left a few very carefully drawn white lekythoi. The shape attracted the technique, and later in the century it monopolizes it for funerary vases. Atalanta, huntress and sportswoman, is shown here in her best clothes, as for a wedding, running in a swarm of Erotes, one of whom (behind her) is carrying a whip. She shunned marriage, and the message here seems to be that she cannot escape it; nor did she, being defeated in the footrace by Hippomenes, who distracted her with golden apples and so won her as his bride. This is one of the best demonstrations of late Archaic delight in dress patterning, with the mannered, flying edges of her cloak arranged in flat zigzags.

(Cleveland, Museum of Art 66.114.)
Para 376, 266bis; *CVA Cleveland* 1 pls. 32–5; J. Boardman in *Art Institute of Chicago Centennial Lectures* (1983) 3–19.

(e) Luxury arts

The luxury arts usually depend on the availability of precious materials. These seem to have been in relatively short supply, at least for the decorative arts, in late Archaic Greece. The gold and ivory statuettes and the silver bull at Delphi of earlier in the sixth century (*Pls. to Vol. III*, pl. 310) were probably the fruits of Anatolian patronage, and Persian domination in the East Greek world inhibited a continuing flow of such treasures to the homeland. Access to mineral wealth was absorbed by new coinage or payment for public works (e.g. the Siphnian Treasury at Delphi) rather than a distribution which provided the material for developing luxury crafts.

One new craft, however, began to flourish in the East Greek world, that of the engraving of precious stones (semi-precious to us: mainly quartzes such as carnelian). The inspiration was Phoenician, probably via Cyprus, and Greek studios were at work in this latest of the orientalizing arts of the mid-century (*ibid.*, pl. 303). By the end of the century major artists had emerged, masters of the miniaturist style on the scarab intaglios and already diffusing their skills into Italy and Etruria. The tiny scarabs and scaraboids were set on pendants or, less commonly, in finger-rings.

In finer metalwork we can judge only the bronze vessels, many with cast attachments, and figurines. The Vix crater (*ibid.*, pl. 373) is a prime example of what must have been not all that rare a type of prize or gift (cf. **233**), and there is plentiful evidence for high quality work on vases, mirrors and the like, without any clear indication that comparable work was available in any quantity in more precious materials, except for some Anatolian silverwork of limited distribution. The situation would change radically once the Persians were defeated and the loot from their armies was made available to a small but greedy Greek market.

156

GENERAL BIBLIOGRAPHY

J. Boardman, *Greek Gems and Finger Rings* (London, 1970) ch. 4, and *Archaic Greek Gems* (London, 1968); here, *GGFR* and *AGGems*. C. Rolley, *Greek Bronzes* (London–Stevenage, 1986).

157. Carnelian scarab, East Greek, about 530–520 B.C. A youth runs with jug and cup. The fine detailing of his head and hair is readily matched in the sculptural styles of Ionia, especially of Samos, in these years (cf. *Pls. to Vol. III*, pl. 318).

(Once Ionides Collection, London. Height 16.5 mm.) *AGGems* no. 97, pl. 7; *GGFR* PL. 302.

157

130

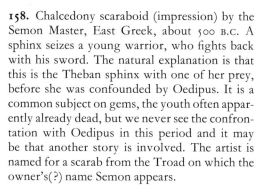

158. Chalcedony scaraboid (impression) by the Semon Master, East Greek, about 500 B.C. A sphinx seizes a young warrior, who fights back with his sword. The natural explanation is that this is the Theban sphinx with one of her prey, before she was confounded by Oedipus. It is a common subject on gems, the youth often apparently already dead, but we never see the confrontation with Oedipus in this period and it may be that another story is involved. The artist is named for a scarab from the Troad on which the owner's(?) name Semon appears.

(London, British Museum 1933.10–15.1. Width 8 mm.)
  AGGems no. 251, pl. 16; *GGFR* pl. 362.

159. Carnelian (cut down scarab or scaraboid) by the Semon Master, East Greek, about 500 B.C. A winged bull with human features. The iconographical repertory of the gem-engraver is markedly different from that familiar to us from, say, Attic vases, probably an indication of East

Greek styles not well recorded in other surviving media. The Greek river god Achelous may look like this, but is not winged, while winged man-bulls are familiar Mesopotamian monsters.

(London, British Museum Walters no. 498. Width 18 mm.)
  AGGems no. 253, pl. 17; *GGFR* pl. 364.

160. Carnelian scarab, probably by Epimenes, early fifth century B.C. A youth leans on his stick to adjust his sandal. A good example of a fine anatomical study, comparable with many on

Athenian vases of the period, but here executed in miniature.

(Malibu, J. Paul Getty Museum. Height 16 mm.)
  J. Boardman, *Intaglios and Rings* (London, 1975) no. 22.

161. Carnelian scaraboid from Athens, early fifth century B.C. A satyr stoops under the weight of a full wineskin on his back, held in place by a cord.

(London, British Museum Walters no. 516. Height 17 mm.)
  AGGems no. 337, pl. 24; *GGFR* pl. 377.

162. Bronze mirror support, probably Laconian, from Hermione (the Argolid), about 530 B.C. A naked girl holding a flower is standing on the back of a lion; tendrils from her headdress support sirens, and above rises the polished bronze mirror disk with a decorated border. The type derives from Egypt (for an example imported to Samos see *Pls. to Vol. III*, pl. 297). It is tempting to identify the girl as an Aphrodite but the goddess is not shown naked in these years, while ritual nudity for girls is attested for certain cults.

(Munich, Antikensammlungen Br.3482. Height of figure 19 cm.)
  Rolley, fig. 81.

163. Bronze statuette of Heracles, about 530 B.C., probably Peloponnesian work. It is unusual to find the hero wearing a corselet, and even

more to see his lionskin beneath it. There is a quiver at his back and he probably held a club and bow. A figure of a warrior in Berlin is very similar and both may have decorated the rim of one bowl.

(Kassel, Staatliche Kunstsammlungen Br. 17. Height 9.7 cm.)

U. Hockmann, *Antike Bronzen* (Kassel, 1972) no. 14, pl. 3.

164. Bronze statuette of a banqueter, cup in hand, perhaps from Dodona. This probably decorated the rim of a cauldron.

(London, British Museum 1954.10–18.1. Length 10.2 cm.)

Rolley, fig. 69.

165. Silver aryballos from Vani in the Caucasus, about 500 B.C. Late Archaic and fifth-century finds of silver work in Anatolia (with this unusual find from a group which travelled to the eastern shores of the Black Sea, and inland) are in a mixed Greek and Lydian style which is gradually superseded by one in which Persian styles are more dominant.

(Tbilisi Museum. Height 9.2 cm.)

J. Boardman, *Greeks Overseas* (London, 1980) 254, fig. 294; O. Lordkipanidze, *Vani* I (Tbilisi, 1972) fig. 210, and *BCH* 98 (1974) on finds in Georgia.

8. TRADE AND INDUSTRY

JOHN BOARDMAN
(**181** *by J. S. Morrison*)

See *CAH* III². 3 ch. 45*a* and IV² ch. 7*e*. Archaeological evidence for trade, within and outside the Greek world, is seriously restricted by the non-survival or the consumption in antiquity of most of the evidence. Trade in decorated pottery is the easiest to document but probably more useful as an indication of routes and of what might have accompanied trade in a comparatively cheap, though plentiful, commodity. Containers of fired clay are informative but we may only guess about the movement of raw materials. Cargoes were extremely varied, and the accidents of antiquity, shipwrecks, have much to teach us about this. We have come to know more about fighting ships (**181**) than merchant ships (cf. *CAH* III². 3, 455, fig. 61). Crafts are better documented since something can be learned from the artefacts themselves, while vase-painters were moved on occasion to record their own activities and those of their fellow craftsmen.

GENERAL BIBLIOGRAPHY

CAH locc.citt.; P. Cloche, *Les classes, les métiers, le trafic* (Paris, 1931); J. Ziomecki, *Les représentations d'artisans sur les vases attiques* (Wrocław, 1975); C. G. Starr, *The Economic and Social Growth of Early Greece* (New York, 1977).

166. Amphora for wine or oil, Athenian, sixth century B.C., from Vulci. The type is called 'SOS' for the pattern on the neck, and was manufactured in Athens and Euboea (this discovered as the result of clay analysis). The capacity is about 63 litres (this is a large specimen).

(London, British Museum 1848. 6–19.9. Height 68 cm.)
A. W. Johnston and R. Jones, *BSA* 73 (1978) 103–41.

167. Amphora for wine, Chian, from Old Smyrna, about 600 B.C. This is a typical early example of wine amphora, with the usual

pointed foot (it has to stand on a ring-tripod or the like; cf. the jar at the centre of *Pls. to Vol. III*, pl. 324). The origin of this can be determined by its fabric and decoration. Later amphorae from other sources are distinguishable by details of shape as well as clay but conform to the general type. Sixth-century Chian amphorae have a capacity of up to about 30 litres.

(Izmir Museum.)
V. Grace, *Amphoras and the Ancient Wine Trade* (Athens, 1961).

168. Athenian black-figure lekythos by the Gela Painter, early fifth century B.C. The sale of oil. The oil jars stand on the ground with dipsticks

166

in them, while a man demonstrates the contents
of a jar by the dipstick in his hand.

(Boston, Museum of Fine Arts 99.526. Height
24.6 cm.)
E. Haspels, *Attic black-figured lekythoi* (Paris, 1936)
pl. 24, 4; I. Scheibler, *Griechische Topferkunst* (Munich,
1983) fig. 123.

169. Athenian black-figure vase by the Amasis
Painter, about 540 B.C., showing a vintaging
scene with satyrs. One satyr, supporting himself
on the vine overhead, treads the grapes to the
sound of pipes. A satyr at the left pours into a
jar, perhaps watering the must. The wine-god's
servants are natural recruits for a demonstration
of the familiar activity.

(Würzburg, Martin von Wagner Museum 265.)
ABV 151, 22; Simon–Hirmer, pl. 68; B. A.
Sparkes, *Bulletin antieke Beschaving* 51 (1976) 47–56 for
these scenes.

170. Details from an Athenian black-figure lip-
cup, about 550 B.C. On one side the potter
centres his clay on the wheel, turned by a boy
squatting beside it. On the other side the completed and assembled vase is back on the wheel
for the last touches to be given, before a
customer.

(Karlsruhe, Badisches Landesmuseum 67/90.)
Scheibler, *op. cit.* **168**, figs. 68, 71; D. Metzler, *AA*
1969, 138–52.

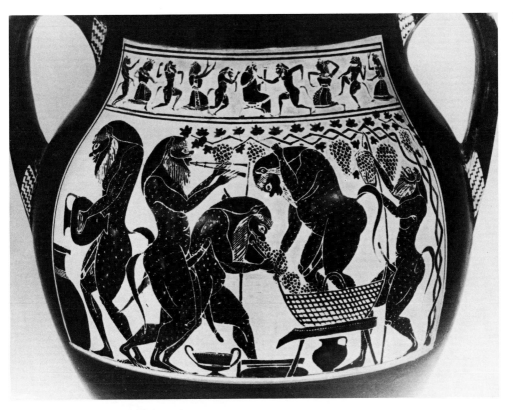

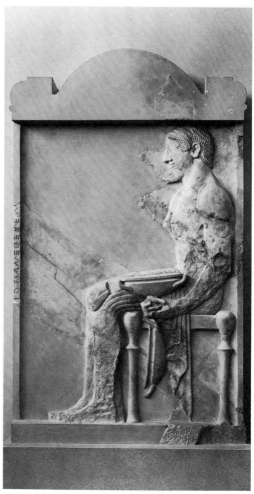

171. Interior of a red-figure cup in the manner of the Antiphon Painter, about 490–480 B.C. A boy is painting a cup using, it seems, a long thin-bristled brush. The cup is assembled, not yet fired but dried out sufficiently to be handled easily. The fine black line in the drawing, the so-called relief line, requires such an instrument. It has been suggested that it was produced, not by a brush, but by a syringe or even a dipped hair laid on the vase; neither suggestion seems plausible. The strigil and oil bottle hanging are for the after-work bath and rub down.

(Boston, Museum of Fine Arts 01.8073.)

ARV 342, 19; Scheibler, *op. cit.* **168**, fig. 82. For the other suggestions about the production of a relief line see J. V. Noble, *Techniques of Painted Attic Pottery* (New York, 1965) 56–8 and G. Seiterle, *Antike Welt* 7 (1976.2) 2–10; and Scheibler, *op. cit.*, 201–2.

172. Potter's signature on the edge of the foot of a red-figure cup painted by Douris about 490 B.C. The potter is Kleophrades, who names his father, Amasis, the potter/painter of the third quarter of the sixth century. Potter signatures are comparatively rare and not always so conspicuous. It is likely that the formula *epoiesen*, 'made', implies potting and sometimes painting rather than any looser involvement in the production, as by a foreman or owner.

(Malibu, J. Paul Getty Museum 83.AE.217. Diam. of foot 16.1 cm.)

D. von Bothmer, *The Amasis Painter and his World* (New York–London, 1985) 230–1.

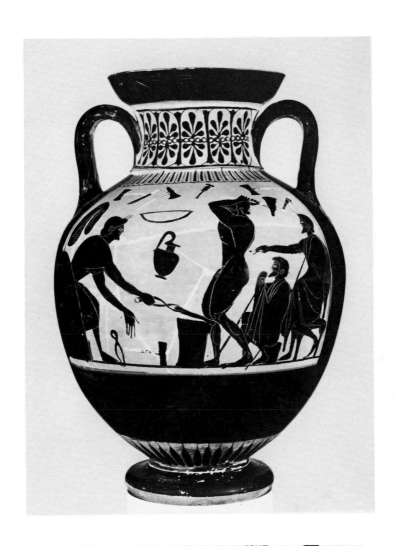

173. Marble relief dedicated on the Athenian Acropolis, late sixth century B.C. The man was a vase-maker, as we can judge from the cups he holds, though we cannot be certain whether he made clay or metal vessels. There are other craftsman dedications on the Acropolis. The giver's name here ends . . . ios and some have restored the sculptor's name En[doios on the right border.

(Athens, Acropolis Museum 1332. Height 1.22 m.)

GSAP fig. 137; J. D. Beazley, *Potter and Painter in Ancient Athens* (London, 1946) 22–3.

174. Athenian black-figure amphora, late sixth century B.C. Each side shows a workshop. (**a**) a smithy. Two men watch the smith working at his anvil on an ingot held by his assistant. We see tools on the floor and hanging up: tongs,

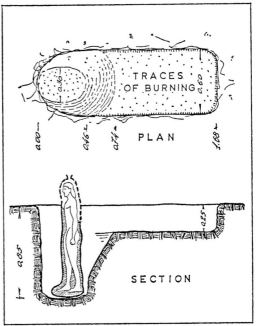

axes of various sorts, a saw, a bowdrill (centre top), a sheathed knife. (**b**) a shoemaker. The leather sole is drawn and cut around the foot of the girl standing on the cobbler's table, holding her purse. The boy at the right holds one completed sole. Beneath the table is the water pot (to soften the leather) and a sandal. Above hang pieces of leather and lasts.

(Boston, Museum of Fine Arts 01.8035. Height 36 cm.)

CVA 1 pl. 37.

175. Athenian red-figure cup by the Foundry Painter, about 480 B.C., from Vulci. Bronze sculptors' studio. On one side, at the left, a man sees to the furnace where the ore or scrap is melted while a boy behind works the bellows. Votive heads and plaques hang from horns above, to protect the operation, and a boy watches. At the right a man is adjusting the neck of a bronze statue (of a runner?) before affixing the head (between his feet). Hammers and a saw hang up, with two model feet. On the other side the completed statue of a warrior is being scraped down (to remove bloom and blemishes) by the two craftsmen recognizable from the front of the vase. Other scrapers hang, as well as the strigils and oil bottles of the workmen.

(Berlin (West), Staatliche Museen F 2294.)
ARV 400, 1; *ARFH* fig. 262; Simon–Hirmer, pl. 158.

176. Lower part of the clay mantle within which was cast a bronze statue (of Apollo?) in the sixth century B.C. Found in its casting pit (reconstructed in the drawing) just south of the temple of Apollo Patrous at the west side of the Athenian Agora. The core would have been the original

177

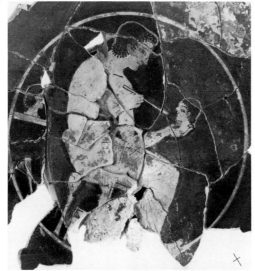

178

clay model, coated with wax which was melted out to admit the bronze (the '*cire perdue*' method).

(Athens, Agora Museum S741. Height 75 cm.)
   Agora Guide (Athens, 1976) 76, 235, figs. 29–30; H. A. Thompson and R. E. Wycherley, *Athenian Agora* XIV (Princeton, 1972) 188–9.

177. Athenian red-figure cup, about 500 B.C., by the Ambrosios Painter. A boy is painting (or modelling) a head; a completed head stands on the shelf behind him. This may be a rare illustration of a craftsman at work on a wooden figure, but if the head is being modelled rather than

painted, it may be a model for casting, in bronze or clay.

(Boston, Museum of Fine Arts 68.292.)

178. Athenian red-figure cup, about 480 B.C., in the manner of the Antiphon Painter (cf. **171**). A satyr sits fluting a column, apparently of stone, so presumably for a votive monument. His wine (or water) skin hangs behind. He lacks a tail but has animal ears. As in the vintage (**169**) a mortal activity is usurped by a semi-mortal but this is less readily explicable in terms of the satyr's main interests.

(Boston, Museum of Fine Arts 62.613.)
   ARV 1701, 19bis, C. C. Vermeule, *Classical Journal* 59 (1964) 205, fig. 17.

179. Ivory and amber revetments to the legs of an ornate couch (*kline*) found in a grave at Athens, late sixth century B.C. The type is easily recognized from vase representations of the couch at a symposium (cf. **144**), or for the laying out of a body (*prothesis*), which was the reason for the burial of this fine piece of furniture.

(Athens, Kerameikos Museum. Height of leg piece 45 cm.)
   I. Scheibler, *The Archaic Cemetery* (Athens, 1973) fig. 24; U. Knigge, *Kerameikos* IX (Berlin, 1976) 60–83, pls. 101–11.

180. Limestone relief showing the hull of a warship, perhaps western Greek, late sixth century B.C.

(Basel, Antikenmuseum BS 218. Length 2.2 m.)
   Führer durch das Antikenmuseum Basel (1969) 18–19.

181. (by J. S. Morrison) Drawing by J. F. Coates (**a**) of a *trieres*, trireme, manned and rigged, as it was reconstructed in 1987 by the Hellenic Navy in co-operation with the Trireme Trust; and (**b**) of a thranite oarsman's view in the reconstructed ship. The trireme, first mentioned by Hipponax (fr. 28 West) in about 540 B.C., a century later became the standard Mediterranean warship, remaining such for two centuries. She had a crew of two hundred and was built to ram. 'Fast' Athenian triremes were light and manoeuvrable with ten hoplites and four archers as secondary armament. As transports they carried thirty hoplites, or, after con-

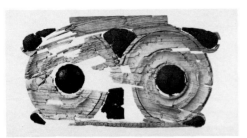

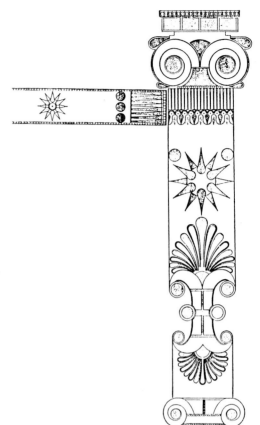

Trierarch	Helmsman	Soldiers					Soldiers	Bow Officer
	Two Seamen	Boatswain		Three Seamen		Seaman	Stowage for Spears	Seaman
Seamen			Thirty One Thranite Oarsmen on each Side of the Ship					

Twenty Seven Zygian Oars on each Side of the Ship

Twenty Seven Thalamian Oars on each Side of the Ship

version, thirty cavalry. Sails were used in favourable conditions, but left ashore before battle. Triremes went faster under oar, averaging seven to eight knots on a day's run. Crews disembarked for water, meals and sleep.

Maximum dimensions of Athenian triremes are determined by remains of the Zea ship-sheds (37 × 6 m). Athenian inventories give the numbers of oars in three categories: thranite 62, zygian 54, thalamian 54; also spare oars of 4 and 4.2 m in length. Literary evidence shows that the shorter oars were pulled at bow and stern where the hull narrowed, all three oars in any one unit of a thranite, a zygian and thalamian oar, although pulled at different levels *en echelon*, being of the same length.

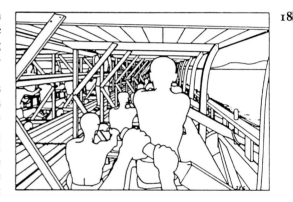

J. S. Morrison and J. F. Coates, *The Athenian Trireme* (Cambridge, 1986).

9. LIFE AND SOCIETY

JOHN BOARDMAN

In the late Archaic period contemporary life became a far more favoured subject for the vase-painter than hitherto, and this allows us a closer look at select activities, generally of the upper classes, or at least of the wealthy, metropolitan families, but not without some views of the life of artisans. The picture is by no means comprehensive and the scenes are presented with conventions closely comparable to those which informed scenes of myth-narrative (see *Pls. to Vol. III* 262, pls. 342–62) in earlier years. Generally, it is only in scenes of trade or craft that the painter seems to have looked about him for inspiration and included telling details of life, behaviour and furniture. An extension to this new interest is the number of scenes of religious life and sport which appear (and are surveyed in other sections here) and of contemporary entertainment (included in this section) which may offer some insight into the beginnings of the theatre. Earlier intimations of this in both Athenian and Corinthian art appear in the scenes on vases with komasts dancing, and sometimes apparently enacting a mythical occasion (see *CAH* III². 3, 459f, fig. 63).

It is to vase-painting, and to the vase-painting of Athens exclusively, that we have to turn for this pictorial information. These were not subjects for major media, or at least for any that have survived, although we may imagine that painting on wood, for objects to dedicate or to decorate a wall, may have shared the repertory.

GENERAL BIBLIOGRAPHY

Boardman, *ABFH, ARFH*; T. B. L. Webster, *Potter and Patron in Classical Athens* (London, 1972); *La cité des images* (Lausanne–Paris, 1984).

182. Details from a red-figure cup by Peithinos, about 500 B.C., from Vulci. Scenes of courting between youths, or between older men and boys,

182a

had acquired some popularity with vase-painters from the mid-century and suitable narrative conventions for them had been devised. One side (**b**) of the exterior of this cup is devoted to them. The exercise ground (*palaistra*) must have been a common meeting place for the establishment of such liaisons, and athletic equipment (the oil bottle, strigil and sponge; see **206**) is shown hanging in the background here. The depiction of comparable approaches to young women is extremely rare, unless they are naked and clearly courtesans (*hetairai*), but there are a few scenes of apparently respectable heterosexual encounters, and some appear on the other side of the cup (**a**).

(Berlin (West), Staatliche Museen F 2279.

ARV 115, 2; *ARFH* fig. 214; K. J. Dover, *Greek Homosexuality* (London, 1978).

182b

183

183. Red-figure stamnos, by the Siren Painter, about 480 B.C. The naked girls caught at their toilet beside a standed laver by an importunate youth are probably courtesans, though graced with elaborate headgear. The one at the right moves away with a sponge; what she is stepping over or into is not clear.

(Fort Worth, Hunt Collection. Height 36.5 cm.)
Wealth of the Ancient World (Fort Worth, 1983) no. 12.

184. Drawing of the figures on a red-figure psykter (wine cooler) by Euphronios, from Caere, about 510 B.C. The ladies are courtesans, reclining at a drinking party on cushions and mattresses. We should probably not imagine that they are raised on the usual symposium couches (*klinai*) unless they have usurped them for a private party before the men arrive. There is music from the double-pipes (the pipes case hangs behind the head of the piper, at the right). The second girl from the left (called Smikra) raises her cup in a gesture which shows that she is about to flick dregs from it – at whom or what, we do not know, but the gesture is one associated with the *kottabos* game, for which a target was offered at male symposia. Here it seems to take the place of a more formal libation of greeting, and the inscription shows that she is dedicating her throw to the handsome Leagros, much praised on cups in these years and identifiable in later years as an Athenian general.

(Leningrad, Hermitage Museum 644.)
ARV 16, 15; *ARFH* fig. 27, cf. fig. 38.1.

185. Red-figure cup, about 500 B.C. Two women are busy at solid tables, apparently making bread. But between them hovers an example of the Greek artist's unique essay in surrealism, a phallus-bird. The creature has no mythical history yet it appears as early as the seventh century in art, and often thereafter in scenes with satyrs, courtesans, or even in more mundane settings, as here. It is a 'symbol' and its content is clear enough, but its function in the range of scenes in which it is shown is not always apparent, nor certainly consistent.

(Berlin (West), Staatliche Museen 1966.21.)
A. Greifenhagen, *Die griechische Vase* (Wiss. Zeitschr., Univ. Rostock 16, 1967) 451–2, pl. 26.

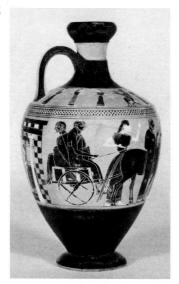

186. Black-figure lekythos by the Amasis Painter, about 540 B.C. To judge from vase-painting, a major element in the celebration of a marriage was the family procession from the bride's to the groom's house. Scenes of this sometimes assume a formal air (see **187**) but this is quite realistic, with the couple in a mule cart, the best man up behind, led by the bride's mother with torches to the bride's new home where the groom's mother, also with torches, awaits. Guests follow. The bride's gesture with her cloak implies a degree of veiling.

(New York, Metropolitan Museum of Art 56.11.1. Height 17.3 cm.)

Para 66; D. von Bothmer, *The Amasis Painter and his World* (New York–London, 1985) no. 47.

187. Black-figure amphora, from Vulci, about 550–540 B.C. The wedding procession is here conducted by chariot (compare **186**). Chariots were for racing and certain formal occasions such as this, rather than for fighting, in the Archaic period, and they carry a heroic connotation (cf. *Pls. to Vol. III* 254, pls. 340–1). Divine weddings and epiphanies feature chariots, but here the trappings are mortal although a Hermes is allowed to lead the procession. Household gifts are often carried by guests or servants. This scene is unusual in having two women carrying *likna* (winnowing fans) on their heads, objects associated with the fertility rites that inevitably accompanied such an occasion.

(London, British Museum B 174. Height 43 cm.)

ABV 141, 1, group of London B 174; *Cité des images* fig. 26.

188. Red-figure cup by Douris, from Vulci, about 480 B.C. The symposium. For the origins of this practice of lying at feast see *CAH* III². 3, 452–3. There are many late Archaic scenes of these all-male parties which played such an important role in Athenian social and probably political life. The eating is over and the side tables carry garlands only, while the cup-boys move in to fill cups. There is no music yet, it seems, only toasts. The couches (*klinai*) are of a lightweight type (contrast **142**) with moulded heads to hold the cushions; cups and jugs hang on the wall. The room for symposia, the *andron*, was designed to fit the appropriate number of couches set against the wall. The artist unusually here gives a realistic impression of a corner of the room with one couch seen from behind.

(London, British Museum E 49.)

ARV 432, 52; *ARFH* fig. 290; on symposia, P. S. Pantel, *MÉFRA* 97 (1985) 135–58.

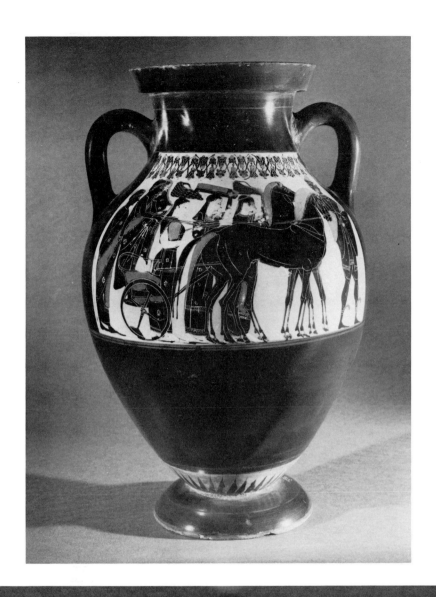

189. Red-figure cup by Douris, from Vulci, about 480 B.C. An accompaniment to the symposium was bouts of lively dancing, sometimes shown by vase-painters in the context of a group moving from one party to the next, accompanied by their music and liquor. The artist here concentrates on the dancing and its individuality of approach (note the central figure). These are the symposiasts themselves, not professional entertainers, such as we suspect in earlier scenes.

(London, British Museum E 54.)
   ARV 436, 96; *ARFH* fig. 291.

190. Red-figure amphora by the Andocides Painter, from Vulci, about 530–520 B.C. A recital by a rhapsode, standing on the performance plat-

form (*bema*) holding his kithara and accompanied by two casual admirers. Epic recitals had been admitted to the Panathenaic festival at the end of the sixth century and this may have prompted the number of such scenes that begin to appear on vases, but they do not generally carry any Panathenaic connotations and we may regard many as simply an indication of the more sober interests of those whose activity at the drinking party is also fully recorded in these years.

(Paris, Louvre G 1.)
   ARV 3, 2; on recitals in Athens, W. Burkert, *Papers on the Amasis Painter* (Malibu, 1987) 43–62.

191. Red-figure wine-cooler by the Brygos Painter, from Acragas, about 480 B.C. The shape is unusual, with an inner cavity (note the spout below) for coolant. Inscriptions indicate that the painter wishes us to take the figures for Alcaeus and Sappho, the famous poets of Lesbos of a century before, who already acquired some heroic status in the minds of Athenian literati, whether or not they had acquired cult at home. But identified recent mortals are rare subjects for the painter and this must be a special commission for a devotee of Lesbian lyric. They hold *barbiton* lyres, long-armed, and suitable for the accompaniment of male singing; unexpected, therefore, in the hands of Sappho (see also **192**).

(Munich, Antikensammlungen 2416. Height 25.3 cm.)
    ARV 385, 228; *ARFH* fig. 261.

192. Black-figure plate (painted unusually on a white ground) by Psiax, from Vulci, about 510 B.C. Dancing to the pipes. The elderly komast betrays by his headdress, boots and the early variety of *barbiton* lyre that he holds (with long wavy arms, see **191**) elements of Ionian/

Lydian komast behaviour that had been introduced to Athens in the later years of the tyranny. On the phenomenon, often associated with the Ionian poet Anacreon who had been brought to Athens by Hippias, son of Pisistratus, see *CAH* IV² 430, and see **193** for a later version with other foreign trappings.

(Basel, Antikenmuseum Käppeli 421. Diam. 21.5 cm.)
    ABV 294, 21; D. C. Kurtz and J. Boardman, *Greek Vases in the Getty Museum* 4 (1986) 35–70 for scenes of this type.

193. Detail from a red-figure column crater by the Pig Painter, about 470 B.C. See **192**. The headdress of these special, dressed komasts is more like the woman's *sakkos* now, less like the oriental turban. Ear-rings and parasol also give a transvestite air to the figures, although this was not the origin or intention of the dress, or of the behaviour; by this date, however, it may have taken on some such flavour.

(Cleveland Museum of Art 26.549.)
    ARV 563, 9; Kurtz–Boardman, *op. cit.* **192**, 62, fig. 25.

193

194. Red-figure cup by the Dokimasia Painter, from Orvieto, about 480 B.C. An Athenian youth parades with his horse before the recorder, seated at the right with a writing tablet on his lap. This inspection of horses is mentioned in [Aristotle]'s *Athenaion Politeia* 49.1, and this and similar vases are early evidence for the *dokimasia*. The recorder had to report on the condition of the horse to the *hipparchoi* and *phylarchoi*.

(Berlin (West), Staatliche Museen F 2296.)
    ARV 412, 1; H. A. Cahn, *Rev. Arch.* 1973, 3–22, and in *Festschrift Schauenburg* (Mainz, 1986) 91–3.

194

195. Black-figure hydria by the Priam Painter, from Vulci, about 520 B.C. An Athenian fountain-house scene with three Athenian women filling their hydriae at lion-head spouts. There are several such scenes on vases of these years, probably inspired by the work on Athens' water supply inaugurated by Pisistratus and involving the construction of several new fountain-houses and a system (or fountain-house) called Enneakrounos (see *CAH* III².3, 414). The Priam Painter is fond of such scenes, but this is unusual in showing Dionysus and Hermes at either side, presumably an indication of the location of the building that the painter had in mind.

(London, British Museum B 332. Height 59 cm.)

ABV 333, 27; on Athenian fountains see B. Dunkley, *BSA* 36 (1935/6) 142–204 and R. Tölle-Kastenbein, *JDAI* 101 (1986) 55–73.

196. Black-figure vase in the shape of a negro head, the lip decorated with Dionysus, satyrs and eyes, about 500 B.C. The negro is the first foreign type to be depicted realistically in Greek art, though this is probably used fairly indiscriminately at first for Africans in general. There seems to have been no serious colour-prejudice in Greek antiquity and Memnon, the Ethiopian king and son of Dawn (Eos), who fought for Priam, was regarded as a noble and handsome hero at Troy.

(Boston, Museum of Fine Arts 00.332. Height 17.7 cm.)
    ABV 614; F. M. Snowden, *Blacks in Antiquity* (Cambridge, Mass., 1970).

197. White ground alabastron from Tanagra, early fifth century B.C. The figure of a negro, dressed as an oriental and corseleted, holding a quiver and bowcase. Negroes may have served in eastern armies met by Greeks, and Amazons are the other common type seen on these small vases. The figures may also have been chosen for their appropriateness to the exotic contents of the vases, perfumed oil.

(London, British Museum B 674. Height 16.2 cm.)
    ARV 267, 1; *ARFH* fig. 208; cf. Snowden, *op. cit.* **196**, fig. 16.

198. Black-figure amphora by the Painter of Berlin 1686, from Caere, about 550–540 B.C. A piper plays for mummers, warrior cavaliers mounted on men dressed as horses (their basic garment being that of the 'komast dancers' of earlier years; cf. *CAH* III².3, 460, fig. 63). It is

perhaps unlikely that the dance (and song?) served the telling of any particular story, but this is possible if the figures acted as an accompanying chorus, in the manner of later Comedy; these figures in particular call to mind the chorus of Aristophanes' *Knights* more than a century later.

(Berlin (East), Staatliche Museen F 1697.)
    ABV 297, 17; *ABFH* fig. 137; A. D. Trendall and T. B. L. Webster, *Illustrations of Greek Drama* (London, 1971) 1,9 and ch.1 for such scenes.

199. Red-figure wine-cooler (psykter) by Oltos, about 510 B.C. Warriors ride dolphins. The creatures are shown realistically but it is likely that the scene, which appears on other vases, sometimes with a piper accompanist, is again of mummers. Each rider is singing *epi delphinos*, 'on a dolphin', perhaps a choral entry.

(New York, Schimmel Collection.)
    ARV 1622, 7bis; *Para* 80; Trendall–Webster, *op. cit.* **198**, 1, 15.

200. Red-figure hydria, about 465 B.C. A scene inspired by a satyr play, perhaps the *Sphinx* by Aeschylus, presented in 467 B.C. The chorus dressed as elderly satyrs are seated, apparently singing, before the Sphinx of Thebes, perched on a rock at the left to expound her riddle. Satyr plays are generally the easiest to recognize on vases since any scene with satyrs in a mythological situation are likely to be stage-inspired, and the satyrs themselves are sometimes shown

200

201

explicitly as actors, with shaggy trunks holding on their tails and erect phalli. The elderly satyrs here are unusual but the association with a stage presentation is clear.

(Tokyo, Fujita Collection.)

E. Simon in *The Eye of Greece* (edd. D. C. Kurtz and B. A. Sparkes, Cambridge, 1982) 141–2, pl. 37a–b.

201. Detail from a red-figure hydria by the Kleophrades Painter, about 480 B.C. The Mission to Achilles. The hero sits right of centre, muffled head on hand, a picture of dejection. Odysseus faces him, persuading him, unsuccessfully, to return to the battle field. To left and right, Phoenix and Patroclus. In the *Iliad* (IX.185–98) Achilles is talkative and forthcoming on this occasion, but here, and on several other vase scenes of the episode of this date, he is morose. Aeschylus' treatment of the scene was famous in antiquity for its 'silent Achilles' and this is surely the figure of the vase scenes rather than the Homeric; but the vases seem earlier than Aeschylus' production so both painter and poet (contemporaries in Athens) may be reflecting some other treatment of the story where this different attitude of the hero is prominent. The attendant personnel on the vases are also not

always those of the Homeric scene. It is not as easy to relate closely vase scenes with tragedy, as it is with satyr play (see **201**) and the inspiration, from stage to art or vice versa, may not always have been accurate in detail.

(Munich, Antikensammlung inv.8770.)

Para 341, 73bis; J. Boardman, *AK* 19 (1976) 4, 13–14, pl. 1.3; *LIMC* I s.v. 'Achilleus' XII.

202. Red-figure cup from Vulci, early fifth century B.C. The scenes seem to relate more to a fantasy world than to life, yet they may reflect other mumming dances of a less formal character. The satyr playing for the goats introduces the Pan-pipes, a rustic instrument that appears first in the Alpine area, then in Greek art, in the hands even of a Muse (on the François vase). Notice that the reeds are of equal length, not graduated as in later Pan-pipes. On the other side of the vase the human komasts have acquired monkey heads for their balancing trick on a see-saw, holding cup and drinking horn.

(Rome, Villa Giulia Museum 64224.)

G. Riccioni and M. T. F. Amoretti, *La Tomba della Panathenaica di Vulci* (Rome, 1968) 39–40, no. 24. On see-saws see R. Olmos in *Festschrift Schauenburg* (Mainz, 1986) 107–13.

10. SPORT

JOHN BOARDMAN

Athletic contests were a common accompaniment to religious festivals in Greece, and, at different dates and in appropriate societies, to major funerals (in the heroic manner, as in Homer). Success in the games in the sight of the deity brought unusual honour to the victor and a near-heroic status which was acknowledged in his home town, notably when he had achieved his success at one of the 'national' games: at Olympia, or in the new games organized in the sixth century and intended in some way to compete with Olympia, at Delphi, Nemea and Isthmia. The Panathenaic games at Athens, also a creation of the sixth century (see *CAH* III².3, 410–11) were never quite of this class but we learn more about them, as about all things Athenian, from written sources and from archaeology.

'Team games' were unknown in classical Greece and the individual events tested individual prowess, generally in activities which had some military potential, real or heroic (chariot races). In an age of casual measurement and with no possibility of accurate time-keeping, 'records' meant nothing and success on the day was all-important.

For the late Archaic period our principal sources are the figure scenes on Attic pottery, supplemented by the evidence of later authors and inscriptions recording rules of conduct and prizes.

GENERAL BIBLIOGRAPHY

E. N. Gardiner, *Athletics of the Ancient World* (Oxford, 1930); J. Jüthner, *Die athletischen Leibesübungen der Griechen* (Vienna, 1965–9); H. A. Harris, *Sport in Greece and Rome* (London, 1972); M. I. Finley and H. W. Pleket, *The Olympic Games* (London, 1976); J. Swaddling, *The Ancient Olympic Games* (London, 1980).

203. The starting area in the early stadium at the Isthmia sanctuary; a restored plan. The broad, paved triangle is about 20 m wide. The circle at the centre is a pit in which the starter stood. Radiating from it are deep grooves which carried cords running to each 'starting gate'. These were equipped with barriers of some sort which could be released or lowered simultaneously by the starter, who was in an ideal position to review the field of runners.

O. Broneer, *Hesperia* 27 (1958) 10–15, pl. 6a.

204. Panathenaic prize vase, from Athens, about 560 B.C. The prizes in the Panathenaic Games, from the time that they had been reorganized, with the festival, in the 560s B.C., were of olive oil, produced from a grove dedicated to the purpose. The oil was stored and eventually awarded in clay vases which had been specially commissioned and which retained a traditional style and technique (black-figure) of decoration from their earliest days into the Hellenistic period. This is

203

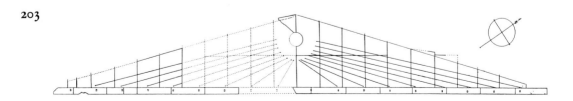

one of the earliest known and must belong to the early years of the reorganized festival. The decorative type is not yet wholly established (see **205**) but the front will always show the striding Athena with raised spear, perhaps reflecting a new statue of the goddess, and an inscription recording the source: 'I am from the games [or prizes] from Athens.' The reverse usually shows an event, in this case a racing two-horse cart. Some other early Panathenaic vases are more fully inscribed, naming the event.

(London, British Museum B 130. Height 61.3 cm.)
 ABV 69, 1; P. E. Corbett, *JHS* 80 (1960) 52–8; *ABFH* fig. 296.1,2. On Panathenaic vases see *ibid.*, ch. 7 and references on p. 237; R. Brandt, *ActaInstRomNorvegiae* 8 (1978) 1–23; J. Frel, *Panathenaic Prize Amphoras* (Athens, 1973).

205. Panathenaic prize vase by the Euphiletos Painter, from Vulci, about 520 B.C. This gives the classic form of decoration for these vases (compare the last item) with the Athena flanked by two columns on which stand cocks, and the usual inscription (without the 'I am . . .'). By this date we can see that individual painters are being commissioned to produce batches of vases for specific years (the games were quadrennial for the Great Panathenaea). On this example the shield of the goddess also carries, rather incongruously, a *kalos* inscription. The reverse shows four athletes practising: with jumping weights, javelin, discus, javelin.

(London, British Museum B 134. Height 62.5 cm.)
 ABV 322, 1; *ABFH* fig. 297.

206a

206b

206. Athenian calyx crater by Euphronios, from Capua, about 510 B.C. Scenes of preparation and practice in the exercise ground (*palaistra*) are almost as popular as scenes of contest. The figures on this vase offer several characteristic activities. A boy massages the ankle of his master. A youth pours from an oil bottle (*aryballos*) into his hand, preparing to oil his body after exercise; he will then scrape himself down with a strigil. The strigil, oil bottle and sponge are common items of athlete equipment. Another youth folds his cloak. On the other side of the vase a youth is preparing to tie up his foreskin ('infibulation'). (The Greeks found the *glans penis* ugly and despised the circumcised; since the *glans* can easily become exposed in violent exercise or while dancing, they commonly tied up the foreskin in this way: this explains the curled *penis* seen on many athletes and komast dancers on vases.) The youth with the discus is being

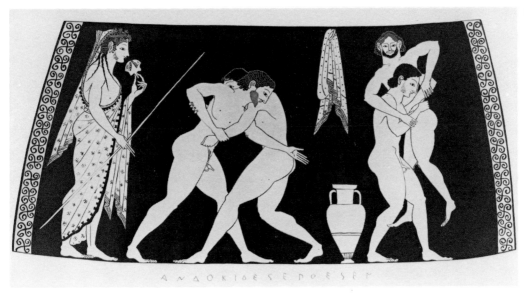

instructed by a young trainer, identified by his cloak and the cane (often forked) that he carries.

(Berlin (West), Staatliche Museen 2180.)
ARV 13, 1; *ARFH* fig. 24.

207. Athenian amphora by the Andocides Painter, from Vulci, about 520 B.C. Two wrestling moves are shown – preparing to engage, and the hoist – watched by a young trainer. In ordinary wrestling a win was registered by three falls.

(Berlin (West), Staatliche Museen 2159.)
ARV 3, 1; *ARFH* fig. 3: Simon–Hirmer, pl. 81.

208. Athenian cup by the Foundry Painter, from Vulci, about 480 B.C. In 'all-in wrestling' (*pankration*) the only moves not allowed were gouging and biting, and victory was proclaimed when one contestant submitted. In this scene both fighters are gouging and the trainer chastises them with his cane. Hanging above right is a discus in its carrying bag.

(London, British Museum E 78.)
ARV 401, 3; *ARFH* fig. 263.

209. Panathenaic prize vase by the Berlin Painter, from Vulci, about 480–470 B.C. The painter was one of the masters of red figure (cf. **153**) but could be commissioned to produce these prize vases in the black-figure technique. This reverse

shows the long-distance footrace (*dolichodromos*), with the runners approaching the turning post.

(New York, Callimanopoulos Collection; formerly at Castle Ashby, Northampton.)
ABV 408, 1; *CVA Castle Ashby* pl. 17, 3. Contrast the less realistic way in which the Euphiletos Painter portrays runners on a Panathenaic vase, *ABFH* fig. 298.

210. Athenian cup by the Antiphon Painter, from Tarquinia, about 490–480 B.C. A race for men in armour (*hoplitodromoi*) was introduced at Olympia in 520 B.C. and appears soon afterwards on Athenian vases, and so was presumably adopted then also in Athens. The runners wear helmets and carry the heavy hoplite shield. The one to the right here is practising his start, with one foot a little before the other. This was the regular starting position, marked on the race track by two close-set grooves on the stone starting line. His companion seems to be coaching him in the position.

(Berlin (East), Staatliche Museen 2307.)
ARV 341, 77.

211. Athenian black-figure stamnos by the Michigan Painter. About 500 B.C. Boxers. Soft leather thongs were wound around the wrists, in a later period strengthened and brutalized by metallic additions. Here the boxers wear loin cloths (*perizomata*) which are characteristic for

figures on this group of vases, both athletes and symposiasts. The vases seem to have been directed to the Etruscan market, where such dress was usual. In Greece athletes exercised and competed stark naked, a practice introduced, it was said, by the Olympic runner Orsippus in 720 B.C.

(Würzburg, Martin von Wagner Museum L 328.)

ABV 343, 2; E. Langlotz, *Griechische Vasen in Würzburg* (Munich, 1932) pl. 100.

212. Athenian cup by Onesimos, from Orvieto, about 490 B.C. On one side of the cup a jumper, supervised by a trainer, is in mid-leap. He is holding jumping-weights (*halteres*) of stone, against which he can pull in mid-air to gain extra length in the jump. These were a normal part of the jumper's equipment and several real examples have been found (cf. the inscribed example from Olympia illustrated in *CAH* III².3, 324 fig. 47, a dedication for victory). For the long jump the ground had to be loosened, for a softer landing, with a pickaxe, such as the one we see on the other side of the vase beside another jumper, practising his approach. (There was no high jump event.) At the centre on this side of the vase a youth prepares to throw the discus, balanced on his forearm, watched by a trainer. The interior of the vase shows the next move. In the background are two javelins and behind the youth hang his oil bottle, strigil and sponge.

(Boston, Museum of Fine Arts 01.8020.)
    ARV 321, 22.

212a

212b

212c

213. Bronze discus from Aegina, early fifth century B.C. The lightly incised figures on either side show a jumper, swinging forward his *halteres*, and a javelin-thrower. The javelin (*akontion*) was a light wooden lance, blunt-ended. It was thrown with the help of a throwing-thong (*ankyle*), seen here on the shaft and around the youth's fingers. This gave added leverage and direction, twisting the shaft; the device was also used for lances in battle (cf. *Pls. to Vol. III*, pl. 340).

(Berlin (West), Staatliche Museen Fr. 1273. Diameter 21 cm.)

P. Jacobsthal, *93. Berliner Winckelmannsprogramm 1933*).

214

214. The reverse of a silver tetradrachm minted at Syracuse, about 485 B.C. A charioteer with his team is being crowned by a small Nike (Victory). The most prestigious event at the national games was the chariot race and it afforded an opportunity for rich patrons to demonstrate their wealth at the same time as their piety. It therefore particularly attracted the rich tyrants of Magna Graecia, who won many of the chariot races in the homeland games and made expensive dedications there (e.g. the Delphi charioteer) to celebrate their victories. The Syracusan rulers were prominent in this and their coinage regularly alludes to such successes.

Kraay–Hirmer, fig. 76.

215. Marble base of a funeral monument, from Athens, about 500 B.C. The young dead are commonly portrayed as athletes on Archaic grave stelae (cf. *Pls. to Vol. III*, pl. 332 a, c) and athletic scenes decorate several bases for grave statues at the end of the fifth century (**139**). This unique and famous example is commonly called the 'hockey-players' base, but the name is misleading. No team event is shown, nor is this anything like 'bullying-off' in modern hockey. The players at the centre hold their hooked sticks by one hand only with the other hand, palm up, just beneath the ends of the sticks, apparently ready to flick them upwards, thereby lifting the ball, probably rather unpredictably, into the air to be caught. Vase scenes show ball-catching games for youths and this may be a more sophisticated version, alluded to in later literature as *keretizein*. This base had been built into the hurriedly constructed 'Themistoclean wall' of Athens, after the Persians had left the sacked city (cf. Thuc. I. 93.2).

(Athens, National Museum 3477. Height 27 cm.)

GSAP fig. 241 and p. 247 for references to studies on these bases. For the sport, L. Grundel, *AA* 1925, 80–7.

216. Spartan bronze statuette of a girl runner, from Dodona, about 550–525 B.C. Women were excluded from the Olympic games but enjoyed some athletic training and contests, notably in Sparta where the practice of exercising naked with youths was regarded by other Greeks as somewhat scandalous. It is by no means certain that this statuette represents a Spartan girl athlete but the style is Laconian and the subject suspiciously appropriate to the reputation of the city in this respect. The statuette was probably fixed to the rim of a cauldron, with others, possibly of the same subject.

(Athens, National Museum, Carapanos Collection 24. Height 12 cm.)

C. Rolley, *Greek Bronzes* (London–Stevenage, 1986) 108, fig. 79.

11. RELIGION

JOHN BOARDMAN

Vase scenes, especially from Athens, give us a far closer view of the practice of religion in the late Archaic period than hitherto and an insight into styles of sacrifice that contemporary documents usually ignore and that later sources may have overlaid with information about later customs. Votive monuments, in clay or stone, reveal the names and intentions of the dedicators, or by their subject matter indicate what was thought pleasing to the receiving deity or suitable for particular occasions. The nature and functions of the gods themselves may be made clearer from study of their images. But our evidence, in text or material, dwells rather on public religion and we are denied any close view of more private or even magic practices. It seems too that those private rites which relate most closely to the progress of a citizen in his society, rites of initiation or training for manhood, are also veiled from us, although determined attempts are made to read special significance into a wide range of scenes on vases which do no more than document everyday life.

GENERAL BIBLIOGRAPHY

W. Burkert, *Greek Religion: Archaic and Classical* (Oxford, Blackwell, 1985); *La cité des images* (Lausanne–Paris, 1984); H. W. Parke, *Festivals of the Athenians* (London, 1977); and see *Pls. to Vol. III* 227–53 on sanctuaries and burial customs.

217. Athenian black-figure plaque by the Sappho Painter, about 500 B.C. The scene is the laying out of a dead man on an ornate bier (*kline*) of the type familiar also in symposia. The ivory and amber fittings of such a bier, excavated in an Athenian grave, are shown in **179**. Women and children attend and mourn at the head of the bier, which is approached by men from the left, making a gesture, palm-out, which seems ritually appropriate in such scenes. The column at the left suggests that the *prothesis* takes place in the house porch; by law it had to be within the house but there were obvious advantages also in having it as exposed as possible to fresh air. (Contrast the busy Geometric burials, *Pls. to Vol. III*, pl. 327.) The Sappho Painter, who

specialized in funerary scenes, here carefully states the relationship to the dead of the mourners: aunt on the father's side, sister, father (greeting), mother and sister (by the dead youth's head), etc. These small plaques were nailed to grave markers, perhaps wooden stelae; earlier in the sixth century there are a series of larger plaques which could have been set as a frieze on a built tomb, some painted by major artists, such as Sophilos, Lydos and Exekias.

(Paris, Louvre MNB 905. Width 26.5 cm.)

E. Haspels, *Attic black-figured Lekythoi* (Paris, 1936) 229, 58; J. Boardman, *BSA* 50 (1955) 17–66; *ABFH* fig. 265; D. C. Kurtz and J. Boardman, *Greek Burial Customs* (London, 1971) 148–9, pl 33.

218. Athenian black-figure vessel by the Sappho Painter about 500 B.C. The preparation for a burial; a unique scene. At early morning – the time for burials, with the lamps still burning – mourners (and the coffin-maker shouldering his axe) assemble, already carrying or lifting their burdens of water-jars, baskets of food and a tray of oil flasks, while the dead man is lifted into his wooden coffin.

(Bowdoin College Museum of Art 1984. 23. Height 37.3 cm.)

ABFH fig. 266; Kurtz–Boardman, *op. cit.* **217**, pls. 37–8.

219. Painted marble disk, end of the sixth century B.C. The inscription records that this is the memorial (*mnema*) of the wisdom of a fine doctor, Aineas. This, and a few similar disks from Attica, might have been set on a burial mound or served

as covers to an ash urn (less probable, because invisible).

(Athens, National Museum 93. Diam. 27 cm.)
Kurtz–Boardman, *op. cit.* **217**, 87–8, fig. 16.

220. Marble votive relief from the Athenian Acropolis, about 500 B.C. A piper precedes three women and a child in a dance. The Graces (Charites) and Nymphs are often shown in threes, but we would expect the figures to relate to an Acropolis cult. The Aglaurids (Aglauros, Herse and Pandrosos) belong on the Acropolis but, so far as we know, enjoyed no common cult;

the boy might have a real function as the *pais amphithales* (with both parents living) who figures in various Athenian rituals. At about this date votive reliefs acquire this architectural frame of a pediment and corner anthemia (which would have been painted).

(Athens, Acropolis Museum 702. Height 39 cm.)
GSAP fig. 257; *LIMC* s.v. 'Aglauros' no. 25.

221. Marble votive relief from the Athenian Acropolis, about 490 B.C. Athena, in her finest dress but wearing a helmet (the crest painted on to the background), receives a worshipping family of a man, woman, two boys (one holding up a phiale) and a girl, accompanied by a sow for sacrifice. The mortals are shown at a smaller scale than the goddess, a regular feature later for these reliefs which commonly show such a confrontation.

(Athens, Acropolis Museum 581. Height 66 cm.)
GSAP fig. 258.

222. Athenian red-figure column crater (drawing) by the Pan Painter, about 460 B.C., from Cyme. Sacrifice before a herm, the garlanded head of Hermes on a pillar, embellished by an erect phallus (cf. *GSAP* fig. 169). A priest at the left pours a libation from a cup over the blazing altar (its sides daubed with blood) where the bones and fat (for the gods) burn. A boy uses

219

220

221

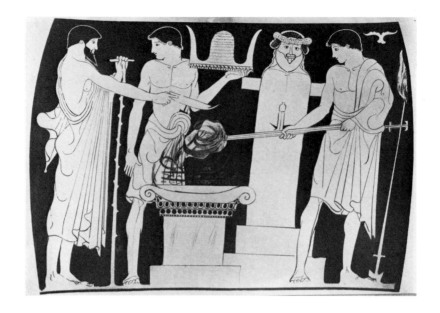

the flames to cook the edible meat from the sacrifice, on a spit (another spit is ready at the right). The boy at the centre holds a basket of a type common in such scenes; possibly the one which held the barley meal ritually scattered over the sacrificial animal. The scene brings home the point that a sacrifice was the usual if not the only occasion for a meat meal.

(Naples, Museo Nazionale 127929.)
ARV 551, 15; ARFH fig. 340; J. D. Beazley, The

Pan Painter (Mainz, 1974) pl. 30.1; F. Lissarrague, *Dialoghi di Archeologia* 1985, 77–88; on herms, H. Wrede, *Die antike Herme* (Mainz, 1986).

223. Athenian red-figure cup by Makron, about 490 B.C., from Vulci. Women dressed as maenads, piping and carrying the *thyrsos* (fennel branch wrapped with ivy, a Dionysiac wand), dancing before an altar and the pillar image of Dionysus. The dance continues on the other side

of the cup, with one of the maenads holding a small deer. The pillar has a mask for head and is richly dressed, with branches at the shoulders, decked with fruit (?). The rustic pillar image is often shown and is peculiar to Dionysus though related to the herm (see **222**). Many Dionysiac celebrations are shown on drinking cups and other vessels for the symposium, but it has not proved easy to identify the festivals accurately.

(Berlin (West), Staatliche Museen F 2290.)

ARV 462, 48; A. Pickard-Cambridge, *Dramatic Festivals of Athens*[2] (Oxford, 1968) fig. 17; Simon–Hirmer, pl. 169.

224. Athenian black-figure amphora, about 550 B.C., from Viterbo. Men have hoisted a bull on to their shoulders for sacrifice. One is cutting its throat while another is ready to collect the blood in a bowl. For sacrifices to Olympians the animal's head is normally raised to heaven, but this raising of the whole bull is an exceptional practice, barely recorded.

(Viterbo, Museo Civico.)

G. Barbieri and J. L. Durand, *Bollettino d'Arte* 29 (1985) 1–16.

225. Athenian black-figure lip-cup, about 550 B.C. A rustic procession for Dionysus. Youths hoist a 'float' in the form of a gigantic phallus, supported by the figure of a plump man. There is a similar scene on the other side of the cup, where the phallus is supported by the figure of a satyr. This recalls the countryside phallus processions for Dionysus described by Dikaiopolis in Aristophanes' *Acharnians* 241–79. The tyrants brought the worship of Dionysus into the city of Athens, making an Olympian of him and incidentally removing from Attic art any further representations of such country matters, preferring the better-regulated metropolitan festivals, or sacrifices and dances of a more formal character.

(Florence, Museo Nazionale 3897.)

L. Deubner, *Attische Feste* (Berlin, 1932) pl. 22; Pickard-Cambridge, *op. cit.* **223**, 42–5; E. Simon, *Festivals of Attica* (Madison, 1983) ch. 6.

226. Athenian black-figure amphora, about 530 B.C. A warrior studies the liver of a sacrificed animal (extispicy) to determine whether the

227

228

229

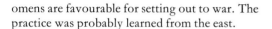

omens are favourable for setting out to war. The practice was probably learned from the east.

(London, British Museum B 171.)
   CVA 3, pl. 31.4; J. L. Durand and F. Lissarrague, *Hephaistos* 1 (1979) 92–108; W. Burkert, *Die orientalisierende Epoche* (Heidelberg, 1984) 48–54.

227. Athenian red-figure stamnos, about 470 B.C. Dionysos in ecstasy, tears in half a deer. The god worshipped as a pillar (see **223**) is seldom shown in other than a formal Olympian pose on Athenian vases, whatever his company and their behaviour, and this is exceptional in admitting a representation of activity normally exhibited by his maenads in their ecstatic dances. This too marks him off from the other Olympians in art as well as worship.

(London, British Museum E 439. Height 32.7 cm.)
   ARV 298; *CVA* 4, pl. 19.3.

228. Athenian black-figure amphora, about 510 B.C., from Vulci. Triptolemus prepares to leave Eleusis (Demeter, Kore, and two Eleusinian princes are in attendance). He holds the gift of agriculture (corn) for mankind, and travels on a wheeled chair which (as appears in other scenes) can fly. The tyrants had 'taken over' the Eleusinian Mysteries and given them an Athenian dimension. One result was the promotion of Triptolemus to this important role as missionary of the goddesses, and the first scenes of his journey are found on Athenian vases from the mid-century on.

(Würzburg, Martin von Wagner Museum L 197.)
   E. Langlotz, *Griechische Vasen in Würzburg* (Munich, 1932) pl. 51.

229. Agate scarab from Amathus, Cyprus, East Greek, about 500 B.C. A winged Athena. East Greek artists are freer than the mainland artists in attributing wings to deities and monsters, but the type was picked up for a while even in Athens, which had its own, very clearly defined view of the goddess' appearance. There were strong regional variations in conceptions of even the best known Olympians, although such influence from the crafts of other parts of Greece can affect the way deities are shown locally, even in Athens.

(London, British Museum Walters no. 437. Height 17 mm.)
   GGFR pl. 379; *AGGems* no. 237, pl. 15.

173

12. GREEKS AND PERSIANS

JOHN BOARDMAN

Material evidence for the Persian Wars, other than the geographical, is not easily identified. Persia itself has yielded evidence for the presence there of Greek guest-workers and of loot or presents from Greek cities. In Greece some of the results of the invasion can be documented, in terms of destructions and refortification. There are very few Persian spoils to look at rather than speculate about. On Athenian vases there are direct reflections of the conflict in fights of Greeks with Persians, with other scenes which may deal with contemporary military events allusively, through myth or personification. See also **76–82** for Greeks and Persians in Anatolia.

GENERAL BIBLIOGRAPHY

J. Boardman, *Greeks Overseas*[2] (London, 1980) 102–9; W. Raeck, *Zum Barbarenbild in der Kunst Athens* (Bonn, 1981) ch. 3.

230. Athenian red-figure amphora by Myson, early fifth century B.C. King Croesus of Lydia had been deposed by the Persians in about 545 B.C. He had been a philhellene and benefactor of several Greek sanctuaries. By the fifth century, in Greek eyes, he had acquired a semi-heroic status and stories were told of his rescue from the funeral pyre by Apollo. Bacchylides (3.15–62 Snell) and Herodotus (1.86–92) told the story in different ways, but this vase is the first evidence for it, with the king pouring a libation as the pyre is lit by one Euthymos (a reassuring name; 'of good heart'). The reverse shows Theseus and his companion Peirithoos carrying

230

230a

off the Amazon queen Antiope, a successful foray into Anatolia by the new hero-favourite of Athens which might seem to mirror Athens' part in the Ionian Revolt and the burning of the lower city of the Persian capital at Sardis (Croesus' old home) in 498 B.C. Theseus' later fights against Amazons in Attica were clearly invented to mirror the Athenian success in driving away the Persians.

(Paris, Louvre G 197. Height 60 cm.)
    ARV 238, 1; Simon–Hirmer, pls. 132–3; J. Boardman in *The Eye of Greece* (edd. D. C. Kurtz and B. A. Sparkes, Cambridge, 1982) 15–16.

231. Athenian red-figure amphora, by the Oreithyia Painter, about 475 B.C. Boreas, god of the North wind, icicle-whiskered, pursues Oreithyia. Scenes of this episode become popular on vases immediately after the Persian Wars. We are told by Herodotus (VII.189) that the Athenians had been told to invoke the help of 'their son-in-law' (interpreted as Boreas, for his seduction of the Attic princess). As a result the Persian fleet was wrecked by a storm off Artemisium, as it had been already off Mt Athos.

(Munich, Antikensammlungen 2345.)
    ARV 496, 2; *LIMC* III s.v. 'Boreas' no. 62b; S. Kaempf-Dimitriadou, *Die Liebe der Götter* (Bern, 1979) no. 393, pl. 31.3–4.

232. Bronze knucklebone from Susa in Persia. The inscription shows that it had been dedicated to Apollo at Didyma, whence it must have been taken by the Persians as loot.

(Paris, Louvre. Height 23 cm.)
    Boardman, *Greeks Overseas* 108; A. Rehm, *Didyma* II (Berlin, 1958) 6–7, no. 7.

232

231

233

234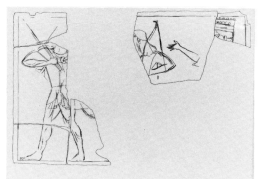

235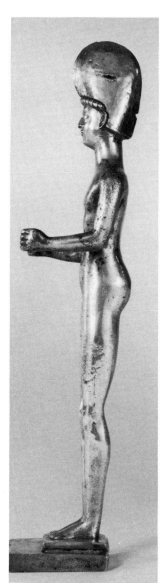

233. Two bronze horses from Persepolis; late sixth century B.C. They are from a team which had decorated the neck of a large volute crater, similar to the Vix crater (*Pls. to Vol. III*, pl.373). It was presumably either loot from Greece or a present from a Greek ruler.

(Tehran, Iran Bastan Museum. Length 26.2 cm.)
Schmidt, *Persepolis* II, pls. 38–9.

234. Fragments of a stone panel from Persepolis, about 500 B.C. Ionian Greeks are recorded as working on the buildings at Persepolis, and there are graffiti on some stone objects there which reveal a Greek hand. These are generally on objects being prepared for other uses; this is unusual in being a panel on its own, with a preliminary sketch for a scene of Heracles fighting Apollo (for the tripod, presumably) with Artemis to the right. The figures would have been painted and the panel must resemble many of wood made in Greece, which have not survived (cf. *Pls. to Vol. III*, pl.323).

(Persepolis storeroom. Height 18 cm.)
M. Roaf and J. Boardman, *JHS* 100 (1980) 204–6.

235. Silver statuette of a youth, from the Oxus treasure (see above, p. 52). Most of the objects from the treasure are of the finest Persian Court Style, some are provincial; this is the most unusual, presumably fifth century B.C. The nudity is quite un-Persian, yet the youth wears a Persian headdress (which is gilt) and has pierced ears. The stiff pose and stylized anatomy are quite un-Greek, yet the nudity is more in keeping with Greek portrayals and it may be that this is a provincial work heroizing a Persian prince in the Greek manner.

(London, British Museum WA 123905. Height 29.2 cm.)
Dalton, *Treasure*, no. 4.

236. Greeks fighting Persians on Athenian cups of around 480 B.C. (**a**) by the Triptolemos Painter. The Persian's patterned dress, with sleeves and trousers, is as that worn by other easterners, notably Scythians, but he wears a Persian leather cap and an odd overgarment. He has a quiver/

236b

236c

36a

bowcase at his waist. **(b)** by Douris. The collapsed Persian here is clutching a banner of a strange design, attested for the Persian army. **(c)** by the Painter of the Oxford Brygos. This Persian wears a corselet of Greek design over his patterned dress, and he carries a large rectangular shield, the *gerrhon*.

((**a**) Edinburgh, National Museum of Scotland 1887.213; *ARV* 364, 46. (**b**) Paris, Louvre G 117; *ARV* 433, 62. (**c**) Oxford, Ashmolean Museum 1911.615; *ARV* 399.)

A. Bovon, *BCH* 87 (1963) 579–602; A. A. Barrett and M. Vickers, *JHS* 98 (1978) 17–24, on (**c**); D. Williams, *Festschrift Schauenburg* (Mainz, 1986) 75–81.

237. A stretch of the town wall at Athens, excavated in the Kerameikos area (north west), showing successive periods of construction and repair: the lowest course is Themistoclean, the courses of larger blocks and the lower courses of mud-brick are Cononian, the upper courses of larger mud-brick are Demosthenic.

AA 1965, 366, fig. 51.

238

238. Oriental bronze helmet (Assyrian type) dedicated at Olympia from Persian spoils. Inscribed 'The Athenians, to Zeus, having taken it from the Medes'.

(Olympia Museum B 5100. Height 23.1 cm.)
E. Kunze, *Olympia Bericht* 7 (1961) 129–37.

THE WEST

13. THE WESTERN GREEKS

R. J. A. WILSON

By the end of the seventh century, with one or two exceptions (Acragas being the most notable) the Greek colonies of southern Italy and Sicily were already securely established. Nearly all had access to a fertile hinterland, principal source of their prosperity; some, such as Syracuse, Zancle and Taras, also possessed excellent harbours. The sixth century saw the tangible expression of the western Greeks' burgeoning prosperity and self-confidence, with the laying-out of ambitious street-systems and the construction of extravagant temples, some of gigantic proportions and striking originality. Most were in the Doric order, but western architects were not afraid to liven them up with colourful terracottas and other decorative details, including Ionic features; purists accustomed to mainland Doric no doubt looked askance. Architectural sculpture is also provincial by motherland standards, but vigorous and lively none the less. For work in the round, in the absence of suitable local marble, sculptors had largely to make do with the widely available limestones, but their work obviously lacks the polish and finesse of contemporary mainland products. The relative poverty of the sculptural tradition is partly compensated for by a prodigious terracotta industry, turning out a wide range of often eclectic votive offerings, some of remarkable power. Bronzework too produced in the West was not undistinguished, especially in some south Italian cities. Local attempts at pottery-making were sometimes showy but generally short-lived. Nothing except 'Chalcidian', emanating perhaps from Rhegium, rivalled the quality of imported wares, which comprised mostly Corinthian at first and then Athenian, with a scatter of East Greek as well; only from the later fifth century did the western Greek pottery industry become a force to be reckoned with. The native settlements of the interior both in Sicily and Italy were not unaffected by the more sophisticated life-style of their Greek colonial neighbours on or near the coasts, and Greeks themselves sometimes moved inland in small numbers with an eye to exploiting the potential for trade. The consequent hellenization of the interior, especially of Sicily, made rapid strides in the course of the sixth century; by the end of the fifth the process was largely complete. Scattered artefacts document contact as well with the Etruscans of central Italy; in western Sicily there was also limited interplay with the settlements there of Phoenician origin (Motya, Panormus and Soloeis). Apart from this, we know little archaeologically about the impact of Greek culture outside the colonies themselves – hardly anything, for example, with the shining exception of Metapontum, about the *chorai* of individual cities. A few rural sanctuaries have been located, but few Archaic farms.

GENERAL BIBLIOGRAPHY

T. J. Dunbabin, *The Western Greeks* (Oxford, 1948); E. Langlotz and M. Hirmer, *The Art of Magna Graecia* (London, 1965); E. Sjöqvist, *Sicily and the Greeks* (Ann Arbor, 1973); J. Boardman, *The Greeks Overseas*[2] (London, 1980), ch. 5; G. Pugliese Carratelli et al., *Megale Hellas: storia e civiltà della Magna Graecia* (Milan, 1983); id. et al., *Sikanie: storia e civiltà della Sicilia greca* (Milan, 1985).

Map 7. South Italy and Sicily.

239. Clay basin for purification water (*perirrhan-terion*), from the Greek emporion at Incoronata, between Metapontum and Siris (Policoro), about 640 B.C., decorated with mould-applied scenes in relief. The three registers on the stand, separated by bands of scroll pattern, show from top to bottom a couple (Zeus and Hera?) in a chariot drawn by winged horses, repeated eight times; warriors fighting over the body of a fallen comrade, repeated six times; and a group of unrelated scenes including two huge horned gorgons, a pair of heraldic lions, and mythologi-cal episodes mostly of uncertain interpretation. An outstanding South Italian product, probably made at Taras, where fragments of basins with sphinx and scroll pattern are also known. Relief jars with similar decoration from Taras' mother city, Sparta, are clearly close relations. Probably modelled on metal prototypes, the *perirrhanterion* also displays Corinthian influence in the recum-bent lions and panthers which decorate the rim, while the register arrangement and the multiplic-

ity of scenes recall the chest of the Corinthian tyrant, Cypselus, displayed at Olympia (Pausanias v.17.5–19.10).

(Metaponto, Antiquarium inv. 125064. Height 78 cm.)

P. Orlandini in *Scritti in onore di Dinu Adamesteanu* (Matera, 1980) 175–238; *id.* (ed.), *I Greci sul Basento: mostra degli Scavi archeologici all' Incoronata di Metaponto 1971–1984* (Como, 1986) no. 139 with pl. 56; *Arch.Rep.* 28 (1981–82) 78–9, figs. 29–33; *Megale Hellas* figs. 318–22. Taras fragments: M. Borda, *Arte dedalica a Taranto* (Pordenone, 1979) figs. 26–8. Laconian amphorae: Ch. A. Christou, *Arch.Delt.* 19 A (1964) 164–265.

240. Mixing bowl (*dinos*) found in the same building as **239** at Incoronata, about 650/30 B.C. This is a local product of Siris (Policoro), 20 km south, where kiln wasters are known as well as other examples of these characteristic dinoi with false ring-handles in relief and figured panels of horses (here winged) facing each other. The Siris potters also turned out hydriae, stamnoi and idiosyncratic shapes. The decoration, more commonly linear than figured, drew its inspiration mainly from Cycladic, East Greek, Argive and Corinthian models. Like much western Greek pottery in the seventh century (cf. **241–2**) it is spirited and eclectic but hardly outstanding; it was also shortlived (about 660–620). Incoronata,

originally native, was settled by Greeks for trading purposes at the end of the eighth century, and much of the pottery there, both the local ware and Chian and Corinthian imports, together with **239**, may have been intended for gift exchange with local native chiefs. The site was destroyed about 630, probably as a direct result of the foundation of Metapontum and her expansion inland at the expense of Siris.

(Metaponto, Antiquarium inv. 125073. Height 23.3 cm.)

D. Adamesteanu and H. Dilthey, *MÉFRA* 90 (1978) 515–20; P. Panzeri, *Festschrift B. Neutsch* (Innsbruck, 1980) 335–9; *Megale Hellas* 333–4, figs. 287–301; P. Orlandini, (ed.), *I Greci sul Basento* (see **239**), no. 96 with pl. 57. Incoronata in general: *ibid., passim*; D. Adamesteanu, *La Basilicata antica* (Cava dei Tirreni, 1974) 67–78; P. Orlandini, *AS Atene* 60 (1982) 315–26; *CAH* III^2.3, 175.

240

)a

;9b

241

241. Crater from the Fusco necropolis at Syracuse, first half of the seventh century, showing a sphinx confronting a stylized plant; the reverse depicts a lofty horse on spindly legs with a similar but smaller plant. Early pottery at Syracuse is dominated, not surprisingly, by imports from Corinth, the mother city, with only a modest scatter of other wares such as Rhodian and Euboean. Local potters were soon at work, concentrating on larger vessels such as craters which were absent in Corinthian at the time. Both the shape and the linear detail of this crater and others can be closely matched in Argive Sub-Geometric, but the fabric is distinct, and the Syracuse examples must have been made locally, very probably by immigrant Argive potters. The presence of Argives may explain the shadowy accounts of Pollis, an 'Argive' king of Syracuse,

242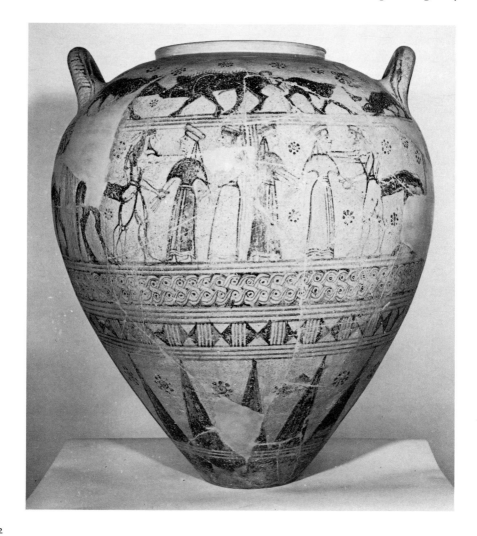

which crops up later in the literary record. Fragments of an almost identical crater (also with horse) were found in the heart of Ortygia in 1977–8, but most of this class does not bear figured scenes. A quite separate polychrome figured ware, however, was attempted by local potters about the same time, distinct too from that of Megara Hyblaea (242). The background was unslipped, unlike the Fusco craters, and the figures were mainly painted white and outlined in brown or red. Only scraps have so far come to light.

(Syracuse, Museo Archeologico Regionale. Height 50 cm.)

P. Orsi, *Not.Scav.* 1895, 185, fig. 86; P.E. Arias, *BCH* 60 (1936) 145, pl. 10; *Sikanie* fig. 114; P. Pelagatti, *ASAtene* 60 (1982) 140, fig. 35, with full discussion on 147–62. Painted ware: *ibid.*, 144–5. Argos in the literary tradition: T. J. Dunbabin, *The Western Greeks* 14–15, 93–4.

242. Two-handled stamnos of uncertain provenance (? Selinus), made at Megara Hyblaea about 650 B.C. The main figured scenes, arranged in six separate panels, depict sphinxes, centaurs seizing women, Theseus vanquishing the Minotaur, and perhaps the struggle for the Delphic tripod. Pottery was being made at Megara

Hyblaea from about 720. An early taste for Sub-Geometric spouted craters imitating Attic models gave way in the seventh century to a pictorial polychrome style with figures in outline, red, brown, yellow and white being freely employed. The inspiration came partly from Peloponnesian centres and partly from Cycladic and other island workshops. The Corinthian technique of incising detail (here used sparingly in the animal frieze of the top register) was not adopted wholeheartedly by Megara Hyblaean potters until later in the seventh century. Local orientalizing wares were also made in Sicily at Gela and Leontini, and at Selinus from about 580; but the vastly superior 'Chalcidian' ware in the sixth century (*Plates to Vol. III*, pl. 371), probably made at Rhegium, was the only western Greek archaic pottery to reach more than purely local markets.

(Paris, Louvre CA 3837. Height 51 cm.)

P. Devambez and F. Villard, *Fondation Piot, Monuments et Mémoires* 62 (1979) 13–41; *Arch.Rep.* 28 (1981–2) 89, fig. 3. Other Megara Hyblaean pottery: H. Tréziny, *MÉFRA* 91 (1979) 7–62 (craters); G. Vallet and F. Villard, *Megara Hyblaea* II: *La céramique archaïque* (Paris, 1964) 139–99; F. Villard, *Kokalos* 10–11 (1964–65) 603–8; *Sikanie* figs. 120–31 (polychrome ware).

243

243. Sixth-century remains of the city of Sybaris, founded about 720 and destroyed in 510. The site lies beneath four metres of alluvial soil and its discovery by magnetometer survey and test drilling in the 1960s was a triumph of modern archaeology. Total destruction of the entire city was allegedly effected by neighbouring Croton, who diverted the river Crathis after overwhelming the Sybarites in battle. This sounds like Crotoniate propaganda, archaic technology being not quite up to such comprehensively successful feats of ingenuity; a natural flooding disaster is more plausible. This 'Stombi' quarter, probably artisan, has a regular street grid and simple two- or three-roomed dwellings (pebble foundations, mud-brick superstructure), including some pottery kilns (one is under the shed, right of centre), but the flooding has taken its toll. Sybaris had a reputation for excessive wealth, derived from the fertility of the surrounding plain, and for extravagant living, but there is little sign of it here in the city's northern outskirts, and excavation further south is complicated by the overlay of Greek Thurii (founded 444/3 B.C.) and Roman Copia.

Not.Scav. 1970, 3rd Supplement, 74–113, 216–366; *Not.Scav.* 1972, Supplement, 19–163; P. G. Guzzo, *Parola del Passato* 28 (1973) 281–7. Destruction: Dio-dorus XII.9–10; Strabo VI.1.13 (263), cf. Hdt. v.44ff. Discovery: F. G. Rainey, C. M. Lerici, O. H. Bullitt, *The Search for Sybaris* (Rome, 1967); F. Rainey, *AJA* 73 (1969) 261–73; *CAH* III².3, 109–10, 182–4, 194–5.

244. The acropolis at Selinus, looking north from the fifth-century temple 'A' (foreground) towards the early non-peripteral 'megaron' (about 600: centre, right), with temple 'C' of unknown dedication beyond. The latter is an elongated building with six columns at the ends and seventeen along the sides. Some columns are monolithic, the rest made up of drums: the temple was probably long a-building, perhaps about 560–530. Irregularities in column spacing and in the number of flutes show carelessness, and the entablature, roughly half the height of the columns, is heavy by contemporary standards in mainland Greece, but western architects rarely concerned themselves with the elaborate precision aimed at elsewhere. The columns have a straight taper, entasis (see **247**) having not yet been thought of. The enclosed inner room (adyton) at the rear of the cella, instead of an opisthodomos, and a second row of columns behind the east façade, a borrowing from Ionic which occurs elsewhere at Selinus (in temple 'F', about 530) and at Syracuse (in the temples of

244

Apollo and Zeus, about 570–560), are typical of the individuality of sixth-century Sicilian Doric. By the end of the century Selinus could boast half-a-dozen impressive temples and an ambitious street layout, tangible evidence of the prosperity of this western megalopolis conceived on the grand scale. (See also **249, 253**.)

E. Gabrici, *Mon. Ant.* 35 (1933) 167–98; *ibid.*, 43 (1956) 257–71; W. B. Dinsmoor, *The Architecture of Ancient Greece*[3] (London, 1950) 80–3; G. Gruben, *Die Tempel der Griechen*[3] (Munich, 1980) 279–83; G. Gullini in *Sikanie* 442–3, 462–7, with new plan, pl. 7.1. Street plan: J. de la Genière and D. Theodorescu, *Rendiconti Accademia Lincei*[8] 34 (1979) 385–96; *ibid.*, 36 (1981) 211–17.

245. Limestone metope from the east façade of temple 'C' at Selinus, found in 1823 and recomposed from 32 fragments. Perseus, wearing a short tunic (chiton) and winged sandals, decapitates the Gorgon Medusa, from whose blood springs the winged horse Pegasus. An impassive Athena stands alongside. The two other reconstructable metopes from the same façade show a quadriga and Heracles carrying off trussed-up Cercopes. Selinus' architectural sculpture displays a vigorous and original provincial style. An earlier series of metopes from at least two unknown buildings (about 570/50 B.C.), with two-dimensional but lively scenes, gives way in temple 'C' to bold compositions in much higher relief, with a marked emphasis on frontality of head and chest even when, as here, the legs are in profile. Despite ungainly proportions and the rather static 'snapshot' poses, these robust metopes are not earlier than the mid-sixth century and were probably carved about 540/30. The suggestion that the folds of Perseus' chiton were recut then, but that the metope as a whole is earlier, does not convince.

(Palermo, Museo Archeologico Regionale. Height 1.47 m.)

Langlotz–Hirmer, pl. 15; Holloway, *GSSMG* fig. 113; *Sikanie* fig. 195; L. Giuliani, *Die archaischen Metopen von Selinunt* (Mainz, 1979) 15–22, pl. 4.1; V. Tusa, *La scultura in pietra di Selinunte* (Palermo, 1984) 115–16, pl. 5. Recutting theory: R. R. Holloway, *AJA* 75 (1971) 435–6.

246. Sandstone metope, probably depicting Heracles despatching a giant, from the small temple of Argive Hera at the mouth of the Sele (Silaris), 12 km north of Posidonia (Paestum). Over three dozen metopes in this remarkable early series (about 560/50) survive. Half feature Heracles' exploits, the rest show mostly scenes from the Trojan cycle or the Oresteia, but the iconography is sometimes unique and the sources used local; inspiration from Stesichorus' poetry has been claimed. In contrast to the slightly later Selinus metopes (**245**), the Sele figures are almost invariably in profile, and the relief is flat and shallow. Some are little more

45

246

than silhouettes, the details no doubt picked out in colour; others were probably never finished. They look like experimental works by Paestan artists more used to working clay than stone: the thick lips, bulging eyes and tubular rolls of hair are features matched in contemporary terracottas. For all their naivety these pioneering early metopes have a variety, a sense of dramatic urgency and a dynamism lacking in the technically more competent series from the later temple of Hera at the site (about 500: *Plates to Vol. III*, pl. 369).

(Paestum, Museo Archeologico. Height 78 cm.)

P. Zancani Montuoro, *Atti e Memorie della Società Magna Grecia* N.S. 5 (1964) 57–95; F. Croissant, *BCH* 89 (1965) 390–9; Holloway, *GSSMG* fig. 22. For the rest of the series, P. Zancani Montuoro and U. Zanotti Bianco, *Heraion alla foce del Sele* II (Rome, 1954).

247. Archaic temple of Hera at Posidonia (Paestum), dubbed 'the Basilica' by antiquarians who reckoned its unorthodoxy inappropriate to a religious building. The date is disputed but is probably about 530–520. Curiosities indeed abound. An odd column number on the façade (nine) is exceptional, setting a column rather than a space on the central axis. The close-set peristyle columns have a curving taper (entasis) to suggest vibrancy and resilience, the earliest and most exaggerated use of a feature that was to become commonplace. The cella has a single row of columns down the middle, a consciously archaizing feature in place of the normal double row; there may therefore have been two cult images, one on either side of it, presumably of Zeus and Hera. The triglyph frieze and the pediments are lost, but exuberant terracotta revetments have been found, and an exotic touch is provided by the rich decorative detail of some of the Doric capitals, their echini adorned with lotus, palmette, rosette and guilloche in a style unique to this temple.

F. Krauss, *Paestum. Die griechischen Tempel* (Berlin, 1976) 22–35, 67–8; Gruben, *op. cit.* **244**, 243–51 (both suggesting a mid-sixth-century date); G. Gullini in *Megale Hellas* 230–7 (about 570/60); J. de Waele, *AA* 1980, 369–81 (about 550/25); E. M. Stern, *Mededelingen Nederlandsch Instituut Rome* 42 (1980) 43–52 (about 515).

248. The temple of Athena ('Ceres') at Posidonia, about 510–500. Some influence from **247** is detectable – entasis is still marked and the capitals are comparable – but this is a more harmonious and disciplined temple, firmly guided in its layout by Pythagorean numerical principles. It also exemplifies the western architect's relish for novelty and his blatant disregard of standard Doric rules. The peristyle columns are six by thirteen in plan, soon to be the norm in mainland Greece. The distance they are set apart is the same as the column diameter at base, the only temple so designed. No concession is

247

made even at the corners: in the frieze the metope next to the corner is merely elongated, a solution rejected by Doric purists as aesthetically unacceptable. Above and below the frieze run Ionic mouldings (perhaps also present on **247**). Astonishingly, there is no horizontal cornice at either end and so no pediments; the sloping cornice opts for coffered decoration, continued along the side. The interior contains more surprises. The prostyle porch has six Ionic columns, a bold stroke repeated, it seems, in the Hera temple at the Sele sanctuary (about 500). These are the first temples to combine the two orders, an idea not taken up in the motherland for over half a century.

Krauss, *op. cit.* **247**, 36–45, 68; *id., Die Tempel von Paestum I.1 : Der Athenatempel* (Berlin, 1959); Gruben, *op. cit.* **244**, 251–6; de Waele, *op. cit.* **247**, 383–8; *Megale Hellas* 271–5. Pythagorean influence: R. R. Holloway, *Parola del Passato* 21 (1966) 60–4.

249. Painted terracotta revetment in black, purple, red and buff from the Treasury of Gela at Olympia, probably third quarter of the sixth century. An almost identical scheme, with rosettes substituted for the chevrons, is known from the temple of Athena at Gela. Clay fabric as well as style make it certain that the Olympia revetments were prepared in Sicily and exported ready-

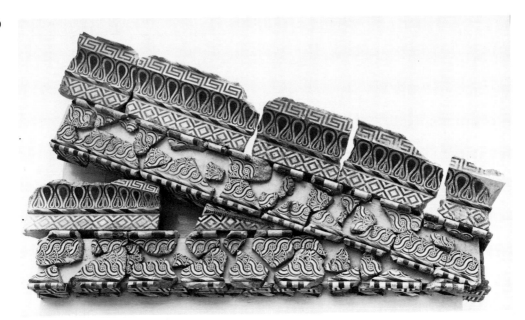

made. Both the repertoire of designs and the whole idea of decorative roof terracottas were derived from mainland Greece, but the polychromatic gaiety and variety of harmoniously blended designs lend to western Greek revetments a richness and exuberance all their own. Each major city doubtless had its own designers. Geloan creations were closely influenced by those of the Syracusan series; examples at Selinus, such as the well preserved revetments of temple 'C', are in a related but distinct style; those of South Italy, with a marked preference for lotus and palmette designs, are different again. A Sicilian peculiarity is the use, as here, of a gutter on the horizontal cornice of the pediment, its border diminishing in size and sloping downwards as it meets the raking cornice. In decline in mainland Greece from the second quarter of the sixth century, the use of terracotta revetments flourished in Sicily down to the early fifth century, and in South Italy even later.

(Olympia Museum. Original width of building 11.50 m.)

A. Mallwitz and H.-V. Herrmann, *Die Funde aus Olympia* (Athens, 1980) no. 99 (with references) and pl. 99; A. W. Lawrence, *Greek Architecture*[4] (Harmondsworth, 1983) fig. 117; C. Wikander, *Sicilian Architectural Terracottas: a reappraisal* (Stockholm, 1986) no. 88. Gela: L. Bernabò Brea, *AS Atene* 27–29 (1949–51) pls. 2–3. Selinus, temple 'C': E. Gabrici, *Mon. Ant.* 35 (1933) pl. 25. In general: E. D. van Buren, *Archaic Fictile Revetments in Sicily and Magna Graecia* (London, 1923); Dunbabin, *The Western Greeks* 269–75.

250. Limestone parapet with graceful Ionicizing volutes and palmettes (painted red), from the precinct of Athena at Syracuse, third quarter of the sixth century. It was one of a pair which stood on top of a rectangular stepped altar, the main body of which was surrounded by a Doric triglyph-and-metope frieze. Ionic influences became increasingly prevalent in eastern Sicily from 560 onwards, even in those colonies without formal links with the East Greek world, and this is one of a number of altars illustrating the trend. An overt mingling of Doric and Ionic side by side as here, however, appears to have been less common in Sicily than in South Italy, although it occurs at Megara Hyblaea, and the Ionic capitals from Gela might have come from a Doric temple with a similar arrangement to that of **248**.

(Syracuse, Museo Archeologico Regionale. Height 92.6 cm.)

P. Orsi, *Mon. Ant.* 25 (1918) 687–715, pl. 23; Langlotz–Hirmer, pl. 24; *Sikanie* fig. 177. Ionicizing altars: P. Auberson, *Mélanges Collart* (Lausanne, 1976) 21–9 (Megara Hyblaea), P. Pelagatti, *Kokalos* 22–23 (1976–77) pl. 85 (Naxos). In general: B. A. Barletta, *Ionic influence in Archaic Sicily* (Gothenburg, 1983).

251. Ionic temple in the sanctuary of Apollo Lykeios at Metapontum, first quarter of the fifth century. Now reduced to foundations, the temple had a peristyle of eight by twenty columns enclosing a long narrow cella without opisthodomos, as in other Metapontine temples. The

elevation, restorable from fragments, displays various idiosyncracies. The column bases, with bell-shaped lower part (*spira*) surmounted by horizontally-fluted *torus*, foreshadow later developments in mainland Greece, as does the combination of fasciated architrave in the Asiatic manner (here two bands instead of the usual three) with the continuous frieze of mainland Ionic. The decorative band at the top of the columns has a scroll pattern within meanders instead of the usual palmette and lotus, which is transferred to the frieze. The temple looks like another example of western Greek architectural originality (cf. **248**, **266**): certainly other Ionic temples in the West, at Syracuse (begun about 500) and Locri (about 480), show more dependence on the Heraeum at Samos. All represent the logical culmination of the trend towards Ionic which was increasingly manifest in the second half of the sixth century (see **250**).

D. Adamesteanu, D. Mertens and A. De Siena, *Bollettino d'Arte*[5] 60 (1975) 26–49; D. Mertens, *Architectura* 7 (1977) 152–62; *id.*, *Röm. Mitt.* 86 (1979) 103–39. Syracuse: P. Auberson, *Il tempio ionico di Siracusa* (Rome, 1988). Locri: G. Gullini, *La cultura architettonica di Locri Epizefirii* (Taranto, 1980) 11–110.

252. Fragmentary kouros from Megara Hyblaea, in Greek island marble (probably Naxian), around 550 B.C. The right thigh is inscribed 'for Som(b)rotidas the doctor, son of Mandrocles'. Sicily's lack of a decent marble does not automatically imply that this or the handful of other Sicilian kouroi were imported ready made from Greece. They were doubtless roughed out at source to save transport costs, but they were probably finished off in Sicily by itinerant Greek sculptors, or even by locals who had acquired the skills of working marble. The strength of the local sculptural tradition in sixth-century Megara Hyblaea is witnessed by several pieces, notably that of the woman suckling twins (*Plates to Vol. III*, pl. 368). Like the latter, this kouros marked a tomb, presumably that of Som(b)rotidas himself. Arguments have been advanced to show that his family was East Greek rather than Sicilian but these are not conclusive.

(Syracuse, Museo Archeologico Regionale. Height 1.19 m.)

L. Bernabò Brea, *AS Atene* 24–26 (1946–48) 59–66; G. M. A. Richter, *Kouroi*[3] (London, 1970) no. 134, figs. 388–90; Langlotz–Hirmer, pl. 7; Holloway, *GSSMG* figs. 196–8; Barletta, *op. cit.* **250**, 141–4;

Sikanie fig. 173. Origins: P. J. Bicknell, *Klearchos* 57–60 (1973) 96–100, with references.

253. Terracotta plaque depicting the Gorgon Medusa, found outside the temple of Athena at Syracuse (**265**), probably second quarter of the sixth century. The impressive winged monster, in conventional running pose (see **263**), wears a short-sleeved tunic and winged boots. Her off-spring Pegasus, tucked under one arm, may have been balanced by Chrysaor under the other (con-trast **245**). The polychromatic effect, making use of black, red and pale buff, is striking. Iconographically the figure is close to the series from Corinth, hardly surprising in view of Syracuse's Corinthian foundation. Nail holes show it was attached to a wooden frame, probably as a votive offering; suggestions that it belonged to an altar front or an architectural terracotta series of which this is the sole survivor are less plausible. Gorgoneia were very popular in the art of the West and appear in a variety of sizes and media (cf. **262**). The largest are the gigantic terracotta versions, sometimes three metres high, which formed pedimental centrepieces at Selinus (in temple 'C': **244**), Gela and elsewhere.

(Syracuse, Museo Archeologico Regionale. Height 56 cm.)

P. Orsi, *op. cit.* **250**, pl. 16; Langlotz–Hirmer, colour pl. 1; *Sikanie* fig. 179; S. Benton, *BSR* 22 (1954) 132–7. Corinthian gorgons: H. G. Payne, *Necrocorinthia* (Oxford, 1931) 79–89. Architectural gorgoneia in Sicily: P. Zancani Montuoro, *Memorie Accademia Lincei*[6] 1 (1925) 282–315; L. Bernabò Brea, *op. cit.* **249**, 71–5.

254. Terracotta statuette from Acragas of about 500 B.C., showing an enthroned goddess wearing a high polos, a necklace and an overgarment (*ependytes*) on top of a chiton. The large shoulder clasps are decorated with palmettes and the striking pectoral consists of three parallel ribbons with pendants in the form of bull- and ram-heads, circular disks, wine jars and acorns (?). This distinctively Sicilian creation, presumably reflecting a cult statue, occurs widely in eastern and southern Sicily and is especially common at Gela, Acragas and in the sanctuary of Demeter Malophoros ('Applebearer') at Selinus. An identification with that goddess or her daughter Persephone (Kore) is almost certain, and the pendants are appropriately suggestive of fecundity. An alternative view that it represents Athena Lindia at Gela is unlikely, the gorgon heads which appear very occasionally on the pectoral serving a general apotropaic purpose, not as a label of Athena (cf. **263**). The type was current from about 530 to the late fifth century, at the same time as another terracotta type, also widespread, representing a standing woman with a pig. Both document the popularity of the worship of Demeter and Kore in the island (cf. **256**).

252

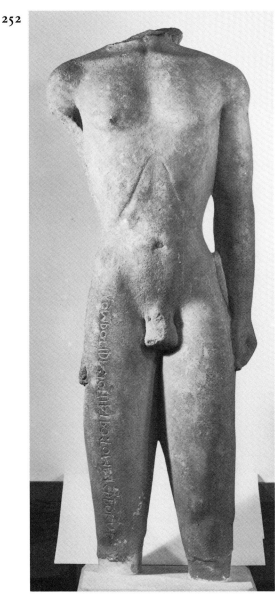

(Agrigento, Museo Archeologico Regionale. Height 29.9 cm.)

L. von Matt, *Ancient Sicily* (London, 1960) pl. 106; Langlotz–Hirmer, pl. 20; G. Zuntz, *Persephone* (Oxford, 1971) 114–41. For the type, see A. Q. van Ufford, *Les terre-cuites Siciliennes* (Assen, 1941) 54–5, 81–3; R.A. Higgins, *Catalogue of Terracottas in Department of Greek and Roman Antiquities, British Museum* (London, 1954) nos. 1099–1115; M. Bell, *Morgantina Studies* I: *The Terracottas* (Princeton, 1981) no. 15.

255. Fragmentary terracotta votive from a rural sanctuary at S. Biagio, 8 km west of Metapontum, about 530–510. The statuette depicts a winged female deity with flaring kalathos ('basket') on her head, on the edge of which are bud-shaped ornaments. Her hair falls in tresses on the shoulders, partly masked by large round disk-brooches. Her outstretched arms hold a springing animal, probably a kid. The lower part of the body, as other statuettes from the sanctuary reveal, was cylindrical and unadorned. Variants from the same site show the goddess wearing either polos with disks attached or pointed 'Phrygian' cap instead of kalathos, and some have animals or birds perched on the shoulders. There is also a quite distinct

unwinged version holding a lance. Such eclecticism poses problems of identification. There are marked elements here of the 'lady of the beasts' (*potnia theron*), usually identified as Artemis (so Homer, *Il.* XXI. 470); but the armed version makes identification with Athena more likely in her guise as both warrior goddess and protectress of nature and fecundity. This dual role she possessed in Mycenaean times but rarely later. The same or similar terracotta type recurs at Metapontum, Siris, Croton, Francavilla, Sybaris and Posidonia. As with **254** the model was doubtless a cult statue, possibly at Sybaris.

(Metaponto, Antiquarium. Height 26.5 cm.)

Adamesteanu, *Basilicata antica* (see **240**), 55–65; *Arch. Rep.* 23 (1976–77) 54, fig. 13; G. Olbrich, *Archaische Statuetten eines metapontiner Heiligtums* (Rome, 1979) 70–98 and pl. 29, A 122; *LIMC* II (1984) 628, no. 57 (Artemis). P. Zancani Montuoro, *Rendiconti della Accademia di Archeologia, Lettere e Belle Arti di Napoli* N.S. 50 (1975) 136–9; fig. 11; *Megale Hellas* fig. 406 (Athena).

256. Terracotta altar (*arula*) from Monte San Mauro, eastern Sicily, about 550 B.C., depicting a bearded, becapped man stealing a piglet from under a vast sow; there are further piglets on

254

the sides. The significance of this iconographically unusual scene is not certain, but the pig was
a favourite offering of Demeter, whose cult was
widespread in Sicily (cf. **254**), and the function
of such altars (a distinctively western Greek arte-
fact: see *Plates to Vol. III*, pl. 370) was frequently
votive. Two other altars from the same mould
are known from the site; they were probably
produced locally. Monte San Mauro was an indigenous hill-top settlement profoundly hellenized
in the course of the later seventh and sixth centuries. Greeks were living there then, perhaps
from a Chalcidian colony of eastern Sicily

255

256

(Catane or Leontini), as well as from Gela, but it was never a formal colony (cf. *CAH* III².3, 104).

(Syracuse, Museo Archeologico Regionale. Length 48 cm.)

U. Spigo, *Bollettino d'Arte*⁶ 4 (1979) 21–42, colour pl. II. Monte San Mauro: *Arch. Rep.* 28 (1981–82) 91, with references. Sicilian *arulae*: T. Fischer-Hansen, *Analecta Romana Instituti Danici* 8 (1977) 7–18.

257. Terracotta model of a small temple mounted on a pedestal, from Sabucina (Sicily), reconstructed from fragments; second half of the sixth century. The shrine is of Greek type with prostyle porch. Details such as roof-tiles and horsemen acroteria are shown with care but not skill. A gorgon is recognizable in the pediment from her protruding tongue; the other head is thought to be a satyr, an association unparalleled in temple architecture but perhaps here the result of artistic licence. The model is an eloquent document of the cultural intermingling of Greek and native deep in the heart of central Sicily, and must be the work of a Sicel craftsman aware of Greek architectural forms but lacking the relative sophistication and artistic ability of a contemporary Greek coroplast. The link some have seen with Cretan and Cypriot temple models of Mycenaean or Sub-Mycenaean date is neither likely nor relevant. Excavations at the spot where the votive was found have revealed two circular shrines of the seventh century, one with

257

added porch, which were replaced by a rectangular building about 550, presumably that depicted in the model. Pig bones suggest a chthonic cult. This and other work at Sabucina have documented with unusual clarity the progressive hellenization of a native centre (cf. **256**), a process which affected much of inland Sicily in the course of the sixth and fifth centuries.

(Caltanissetta, Museo Civico. Height 51.5 cm.)

P. Orlandini, *Kokalos* 8 (1962) 103–6, pls. 27–8; *id., Arch. Class.* 15 (1963) 88, pls. 27–8; E. Sjöqvist, *Sicily and the Greeks* (Ann Arbor, 1973) 72, figs. 43–6; M. Sedita Migliore, *Sabucina: studio sulla zona archeologica di Caltanissetta* (Caltanissetta, 1981) 91–5, fig. 58–9. Mycenaean 'survival': E. De Miro, *Bollettino d'Arte*[5] 60 (1975) 123–6; G. Castellana, *Rivista di Archeologia* 7 (1983) 5–11. Excavations: E. De Miro, *Kokalos* 26–7 (1980–81) 561–6.

258. Sunken limestone chamber, 3.85 m by 3.55 m externally, discovered at Posidonia (Paestum) in 1954. There is no access and the structure was walled up and covered by an earth mound on completion. Inside was a rudimentary couch (*kline*) consisting of five iron struts and remains of a mattress on a block base. Eight bronze vessels full of honey, and an Attic black-figure amphora made about 510, were ranged on either side. Interpretation is controversial. Though resembling an underground chamber-tomb it is not a burial, being within the city walls and lacking a body. In view of the date a link with the destruction of Sybaris (**243**), Posidonia's mother city, is plausible: it may have been a cenotaph for fallen Sybarites or the focus of a hero cult in honour of Sybaris' founder. More likely this is another shrine of Hera, who had demonstrated divine displeasure at Sybarite behaviour (Athenaeus 521D–F), and needed placating. The sacred couch is prominent elsewhere in her cult, and chthonic associations, while unusual, are also stressed in her sanctuary at the Sele mouth. The sherd found in the surrounding *temenos*, inscribed 'to the bride I am sacred', can be interpreted as additional supporting evidence, the epithet being used of Hera at Plataea and possibly Samos (Pausanias IX.3.1; Athenaeus 673B–C).

P. C. Sestieri, *Bollettino d'Arte*[4] 40 (1955) 53–64; B. Neutsch, *Tas numphas emi hieron* (Heidelberg, 1957); U. Kron, *JDAI* 86 (1971) 117–48; P. Zancani Montuoro, *Archivio storico per la Calabria e la Lucania* 23 (1954) 183–5; *ead., Rendiconti Accademia Lincei*[8] 35 (1980) 149–56; G. Säflund, *Opuscula romana* 13 (1981) 41–2.

259. Elaborate bronze hydria, one of eight bronze vessels (six hydriae and two amphorae) found inside **258**, about 530–510. The vertical handle is decorated with a lion head at the rim (not visible on this photograph) and recumbent sphinxes on the shoulder; the horizontal grips

258

have a double lion protome at each end. Opinion is divided between assigning the group to a mainland workshop, probably Laconian, or to a South Italian one (the claims of Rhegium, Taras and Sybaris have all been advanced). Not all the vessels, however, are equally accomplished and at least two production centres may be involved. The three best hydriae, decorated with female busts and recumbent lions and rams, are probably Spartan imports like the Vix crater (*Plates to Vol. III*, pl. 373); but the one shown here, along with two other hydriae, one of which has a vigorous but rather perfunctory lion serving as the handle (otherwise unparalleled), and the pair of amphorae (a shape, it seems, not attested in bronze in sixth-century mainland Greece), may very well be the products of a western workshop often closely imitating imported models. If so, Magna Graecian bronzesmiths were capable of nearly matching Peloponnesian standards. The question of the place of manufacture is, however, likely to remain open until metallurgical tests are developed which can help isolate individual workshops.

(Paestum, Museo Archeologico. Height 41.6 cm.)

P. C. Sestieri, *op. cit.* **258**, 58, fig. 10; E. Diehl, *Die Hydria* (Mainz, 1964) 217, B87; *Megale Hellas* fig. 373–4; C. Rolley, *Les vases de bronze de l'archaïsme récent en Grand-Grèce* (Naples, 1982) 20 and 24–6, with fig. 62–4 (cf. review in *JHS* 105 (1985) 238–40).

260. Elaborate bronze tripod from Metapontum, about 550 B.C. From the claw feet rise oblique supporting rods, three pairs forming high arcs and three further straight rods terminating in palmettes. Horizontal struts link the back of the feet to a central base ring for stability. The animal decoration comprises horse protomes and recumbent lions on the upper circle, standing cows inside the arcs, and snakes and further recumbent lions on the lower circle. No traditional cauldron could have sat comfortably on this ornate tripod, probably a specially manufactured votive offering. The complicated support arrangement and the decorative richness mark this out as an exuberant western Greek product, and the style of the angular horse heads recalls that of **261**, but our knowledge is too flimsy to attribute the piece confidently to any one workshop. Taras has been suggested on no firm grounds; Sybaris or Metapontum itself are other possibilities. The type was copied later in the sixth century in a series of rich tripods at Vulci, either by immigrant Greek craftsmen working there or by Etruscans copying imported south Italian models.

(Berlin (West), Staatliche Museen, Fr. 768. Height 73.5 cm.)

L. Savignoni, *Mon. Ant.* 7 (1897) 305, pl. 8; W. Lamb, *Greek and Roman bronzes* (London, 1929) pl. 45a; C. Rolley, *The Bronzes* (Monumenta Graeca et Romana 5.1) (Leyden, 1967) pl. 46, no. 136; *id., Greek Bronzes* (London, 1986) fig. 106; *Megale Hellas* fig. 372. Ascription to Taras: U. Jantzen, *Bronzewerkstätten in Grossgriechenland und Sizilien* (Berlin, 1937) 27, no. 14; 32. Vulci tripods: K. A. Neugebauer, *JDAI* 58 (1943) 210–33.

261. Bronze horse and rider from the Lucanian city of Grumentum, probably second quarter of the sixth century. Both are cast solid but separate from each other. The rider wears a short tunic and 'Corinthian' helmet decorated with a pair of lotus buds and with a transverse crest, now missing. The appealing horse, technically well finished, is somewhat stiff and angular, and the ill-judged proportions, with elongated body and small head, evidently betray the hand of a Greek provincial workshop in South Italy. Strikingly similar, and also bearing helmeted riders, are the elongated horses on the terracotta reliefs of about 580–570 from Serra di Vaglio, in the hinterland of Metapontum. The friezes might point to that city as the most likely origin of the Grumentum bronze, but on present evidence confident attributions are hazardous (see **260**).

(London, British Museum, 1904.7–3.1. Height 25.2 cm.)

H. B. Walters, *Select bronzes . . . in the Departments of Antiquities* (London, 1915) pl. 1; Lamb, *op. cit.* **260**, pl. 39b; Jantzen, *op. cit.* **260**, 26, no. 5 and 36 (ascribed to Taras); Langlotz–Hirmer, pl. 26 (possibly Rhegium); *Megale Hellas* fig. 366; W. Fuchs, *Die Skulptur der Griechen*[3] (Munich, 1983) fig. 369; C. Rolley, *Greek Bronzes*, fig. 110. Serra di Vaglio: E. Fabricotti, *Atti e Memorie della Società Magna Grecia* N.S. 18–20 (1977–79) 151–7.

262

261

262. Bronze mirror handle, said to have been found near Rome, about 500 B.C. The stand attached to the feet, and the mirror disk itself, are missing. The handle takes the form of a female figure wearing diadem and the Ionic dress of mantle and undergarment (chiton); as in contemporary marble korai in Attica and elsewhere (**135**), the chiton is clutched by the hand to one side. The right hand holds a seated sphinx, and there are further sphinxes rampant on the shoulders. The type is modelled on Peloponnesian mirror handles featuring Aphrodite, but the sphinx rather than a dove in the outstretched hand is a western idea, and the harsh overall treatment and slender profile view also point to a South Italian workshop: Taras is suggested by the sharp features and pointed nose (cf. **264**). South Italy and Sicily had a prolific mirror production at a number of different centres in the sixth and fifth centuries, but unlike in Greece it was the kouros that proved a far more popular choice for handle ornament than the kore.

(London, British Museum. Height 23.6 cm.)

H. B. Walters, *Catalogue of the Bronzes in the Department of Greek and Roman antiquities, British Museum* (London, 1899) no. 548; Jantzen, *op. cit.* **260**, 27, no. 21 and 41–2, pl. 13.53–4; Langlotz–Hirmer, pl. 27; *Megale Hellas* fig. 389; Fuchs, *op. cit.* **261**, fig. 171; Rolley, *Greek Bronzes*, 241, no. 256; I. Caruso, *Röm. Mitt.* 88 (1981) 41, no. D18 and 80–83 (advocating a Crotoniate workshop).

263. Detail of a bronze greave from Ruvo, southern Italy, second half of the sixth century. A lively winged Gorgon, partly engraved and partly repoussé, is shown in conventional archaic running pose, with left leg almost kneeling and the right flung out sideways (cf. **253**). She wears a short chiton and holds a pair of snakes; there is a further pair below the figure. The eyes would have been inlaid with glass or stones; teeth and protruding tongue are of ivory. The holes round the edge were for attachment to a leather or tunic lining. While finds of armour, and especially decorated armour, are rare in the West, the area must have helped in the transmission of the hoplite panoply to the Etruscans, who were using it by the late seventh century. Gorgon heads (but not the full-length figure, which is exceptional) are found decorating other armour thought to be of western Greek manufacture, as at Caulonia and Olympia, but were only occasionally used elsewhere, despite their obvious

apotropaic value in protecting a vulnerable part of the body. Also from South Italy comes a bronze statue-leg wearing a similar greave with gorgoneion decoration on the kneecap.

(London, British Museum, one of a pair of greaves 40.6 cm long. Height of Gorgon figure 19.4 cm.)

H. B. Walters, *op. cit.* **262**, no. 249; *id., op. cit.* **261**, pl. 5. South Italian statue: *ibid.*, pl. 12. Olympia: A. Mallwitz and H.-V. Herrmann (edd.), *Die Funde aus Olympia* (Athens, 1980) no. 65, with references. Caulonia: G. Foti, *Il Museo nazionale di Reggio Calabria* (Cava dei Tirreni, 1972) pl. 22. Elsewhere: S. Reinach (ed.), *Antiquités du Bosphore Cimmérien* (Paris, 1892) pl. 28.7.

264. Bronze statue of Zeus, rather less than half life size, from the Messapian city of Uzentum (Ugento). It presumably stood in a sanctuary there but had been concealed in a cave, where it was found in 1961. Carrying a thunderbolt in his right hand and probably an eagle in his left, the god wears a laurel wreath and a rosette-studded diadem, carefully engraved, as are the hair and beard. The meticulous ringlets framing the forehead and other stylistic features such as the angular shape of the head and the prominent pointed nose find close parallels in some terracottas of about 530–520 from Taras, and the Ugento Zeus must be a contemporary product of a bronze workshop there. It is also an early example for a bronze of this size of hollow casting by the 'lost wax' method. Rendering of the anatomy is not yet perfect, but is no worse than mid-sixth-century kouroi in mainland Greece, and the action pose, frozen rather than fluent, is more adventurous than surviving large-scale

freestanding sculpture anywhere at this date, although it must have been not uncommon (cf. **267d**). The Ugento Zeus provides both a rare glimpse of the quality of western Greek Archaic bronze sculpture and a salutary reminder of how much is lost.

(Taranto, Museo Nazionale. Height 74 cm.)
  N. Degrassi, *Lo Zeus stilita di Ugento* (Rome 1981); Holloway, *GSSMG* figs. 67–8; *Megale Hellas* figs. 367–9.

265. South peristyle of the temple of Athena at Syracuse, incorporated into the fabric of the present cathedral. This is a rare example of a well-preserved ancient temple still the focus of active worship: 25 out of the original 40 columns remain visible in whole or in part. Intended as the showpiece of the Deinomenid tyrant Gelon after he moved his seat to Syracuse in 485, this 6 × 14 column Doric temple may not have been started until after the great victory over the Carthaginians at Himera in 480. One of a rash of edifices put up between 490 and 460 at a time of understandable Sicilian self-confidence, the Syracuse temple abandoned most of the idiosyncrasies of archaic Sicilian Doric (cf. **244**): the opisthodomos behind the cella, long current in

264

26

mainland Greece, is now introduced, and this and a very similar temple at Himera built to commemorate the victory are the first to place the two columns nearest the corner closer together to avoid elongated metopes in the frieze (see **248**). The horizontal cornice with its lion-head gutter-spouts and the roof tiles were, exceptionally for Sicily, of imported Cycladic marble; the rest was of local limestone originally stuccoed. The door to the cella with ivory figured reliefs and gold nails was much admired, and the gilded shield above the east pediment was a prominent landmark. Later the temple doubled as a noted art gallery, with a range of panel paintings on display.

B. Pace, *Arte e Civiltà della Sicilia antica* II (Milan, 1938) 230–6; Dinsmoor, *op. cit.* **244**, 108–9; Gruben,

op. cit. **244**, 270–3. Shield: Athenaeus 462c. Doors and paintings: Cicero, *Verr.* II. 4.55.122–56.125.

266. Part of a cork model suggesting how the Temple of Olympian Zeus at Acragas may have appeared. Most revolutionary of the western temples, this extravagant display of Sicilian megalomania, the biggest of all Doric buildings, measured some 110 × 53 m and stood nearly 40 m high. Probably started when Theron came to power in 488, construction was in full swing when Carthaginian captives from Himera were put to work on it in 480 (Diodorus XIII.82.1–4). Unlike temple 'G' at Selinus (about 520 onwards), nearly as big but planned as a conventional temple merely magnified in scale, the Olympieum at Acragas broke every rule in the

a

b

c

d

Doric book. On a platform with five (not three) steps rose a solid exterior wall with 14 gigantic engaged semi-columns along each side and seven across front and back. That number ruled out an axial entrance (cf. **247**); it seems there were two doorways, at either end of the east façade. The columns (and intervening wall) have Ionic-inspired base-mouldings, unique for Doric. Unique too were the Atlas figures nearly 8 m high on the upper part of the wall between the columns. The tripartite interior was no less unconventional. Part of the centre was open to the sky (there are rainwater cisterns in the 'cella' wall), making it one of Vitruvius' hypaethral temples (III.2.8) and misleading Diodorus into thinking it unfinished: pedimental sculptures (which he describes) and evidence of roofing over the north and south aisles belie him. Relatively small blocks were used throughout, no doubt aiding its construction but also its subsequent despoliation. This bold architectural experiment had no imitators, and later Agrigentine temples were by and large conventional, even dull.

(Agrigento, Museo Archeologico Regionale.)

von Matt, *op. cit.* **254**, pl. 115; Dinsmoor, *op. cit.* **244**, 101–5; Gruben, *op. cit.* **244**, 305–9; M. Bell, *AJA* 84 (1980) 359–72; J. de Waele, *op. cit.* **247**, 190–209. Atlas figures (legs together, not apart): *id., Cronache di Archeologia e Storia d'Arte* 18 (1979) 163–6. Pedimental sculpture: *id.,* in *Aparchai. Nuove ricerche e studi . . . in onore di P. Arias* (Pisa, 1982) 271–8; cf. also P. Griffo, *ibid.,* 253–70 (arguing for windows beside the Atlas figures rather than a solid wall).

267. Coinage was not adopted in the West until the third quarter of the sixth century, and then initially only by a few cities. The idea of minting silver coins came from mainland Greece, but by and large the form they took shows a marked independence of models in the motherland. In Sicily Naxus, one of the earliest cities to coin, was alone at the time to use a fully developed die on both obverse and reverse (**a**), a feature soon followed by Himera ('day' or 'daybreak'), whose symbol was appropriately the cockerel. In South Italy the Achaean colonies (Sybaris, Croton, Metapontum) and their daughter foundations adopted a type of coin, not found elsewhere, in which the obverse type is reproduced on the reverse, sometimes simplified, in incuse (i.e. intaglio). Such issues also use a common standard, apart from Posidonia, which lay much further west and had a separate sphere of commercial interest. See also **318** and **319** below.

Kraay–Hirmer, 279–317; C. M. Kraay, *Archaic and Classical Greek Coins* (London, 1976) 161–238; A. Stazio, in *Megale Hellas* 105–69; *id.,* in *Sikanie* 81–122. The coins are shown at twice life size.

(**a**) Coin (drachma) of Naxus, about 530–510. Obverse: head of a bearded Dionysus, wearing ivy wreath. Reverse: grape cluster flanked by vine leaves, with legend *NAXION*. Naxus controlled only a small coastal plain which afforded little scope for arable, but the hills around including the fertile slopes of Mount Etna were ideal for vines; the wine of the region was later well known to the Romans. Kraay–Hirmer, fig. 1.

(**b**) Coin (stater) of Metapontum, about 520–510: ear of barley, with cicada, and city name abbreviated. The incuse reverse repeats the barley ear and adds a dolphin, but such subsidiary symbols are rare, occurring on staters only in this issue. Metapontum has, by contrast with Naxus, a rich and extensive plain in its immediate hinterland, and the coin alludes to its principal agricultural produce, confirmed archaeologically by carbonized seeds from Incoronata and other sites in Metapontine territory. Kraay–Hirmer, fig. 229.

(**c**) Coin (stater) of Croton, about 510: ring-handled tripod with pair of snakes at its feet; city name abbreviated. The tripod is Apollo's at Delphi, where the oracle had given explicit instruction for the colony's foundation (Strabo VI.1.12 (262); Diodorus VIII.17). There is no need to see Pythagoras' influence in the choice of type, even though the philosopher, who stressed his connections with Delphic Apollo, settled at Croton around the time of the first coin issues (about 530). Some Crotoniate coins, while retaining the obverse tripod, have incuse reverses with a different type (eagle, helmet, bull). That with the bull, symbol of Sybaris, postdates 510 and alludes to Croton's defeat and incorporation of that city (see **243**). Kraay–Hirmer, fig. 264.

(**d**) Coin (stater) of Posidonia, about 510–500: the god Poseidon in a short cloak strides forward brandishing a trident; city name abbreviated on the left. Obverse dies always feature the god after whom the city was named, and the image may well have been based on a cult statue (cf. **264**), but his temple has not been located. Kraay–Hirmer, fig. 220.

14. ITALY

DAVID RIDGWAY

The millennium between about 1400 and 400 B.C. saw a variety of crucial developments in the Italian peninsula, which provides an effective land-bridge from Epirus (visible on a clear day from Otranto) to central Europe. While it would be unduly simplistic to propose that change was invariably stimulated by external forces, the fact remains that from the Middle Bronze Age onwards Italian (and Sardinian and Sicilian) natural resources – agricultural land, minerals and navigational convenience – attracted the interest of the outside world. At no stage, however, is there much evidence for the foreign exploitation of purely passive indigenous communities. On the contrary, there is abundant reason to believe that by the Archaic period (about 580–480) many of the Etruscan coastal cities had long been major centres of consumption no less than of production. Outside Etruria, the pace of change was slower – though not, perhaps, as slow as that suggested by the geographically uneven accumulation of archaeological evidence over the past two centuries. It is becoming increasingly clear, in fact, that the Etruscans and their Italic neighbours should not be considered as separate entities. Just as their ancestors were all affected in one way or another by Mycenaean enterprise between the sixteenth and the twelfth centuries, so the differing local reactions to later external phenomena – colonization from Greece, the growing power first of Carthage and then of Rome – can profitably be combined into a single Italian story of Mediterranean significance. It amounts to more than a rustic and occasionally eccentric prelude to the awesome vicissitudes of Republican and Imperial Rome.

GENERAL BIBLIOGRAPHY

L. Bonfante (ed.), *Etruscan Life and Afterlife: A Handbook of Etruscan Studies* (Detroit, Warminster, 1986); M. Gras, *Trafics tyrrhéniens archaïques* (Bibliothèque des Écoles françaises d'Athènes et de Rome, fasc. 258, Paris, 1985); M. Pallottino, *Storia della prima Italia* (Milan, 1984); M. Pallottino, G. Mansuelli, A. Prosdocimi, O. Parlangeli (eds.), *Popoli e Civiltà dell'Italia Antica* I-VII (Rome, 1974–8); D. and F. R. Ridgway (eds.), *Italy before the Romans* (London, New York, San Francisco, 1979) = *IBR*; J. Swaddling (ed.), *Italian Iron Age Artefacts in the British Museum* (London, 1986).

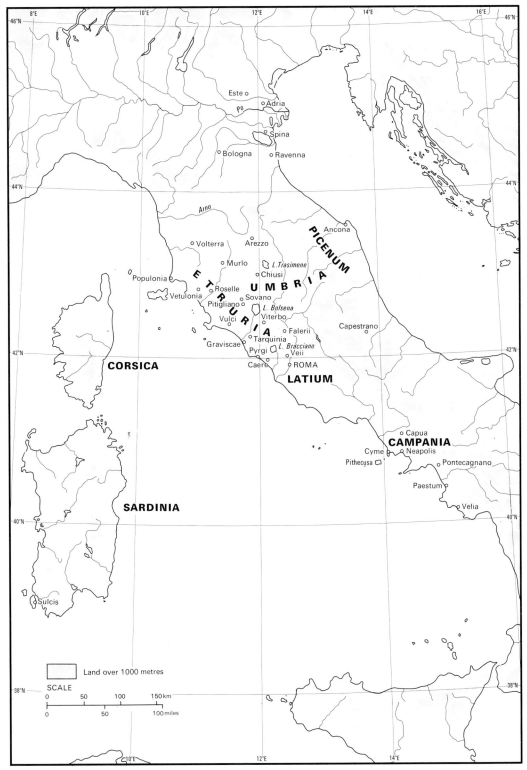

Map 8. North Italy.

LEVEL 1	
LEVEL 2	
LEVEL 3	
LEVEL 4	
LEVEL 5	
LEVEL 6	

(a) Italy and the Mediterranean

268. Five painted Mycenaean sherds found in successive levels of the Bronze Age Apennine Culture sunken 'long houses' investigated (1960–1963) at Luni sul Mignone (prov. Viterbo) by the Swedish Institute in Rome. They were originally identified by the excavator, C. E. Östenberg, as follows: Level 2, LH III C and (?) III B–C; Level 4, LH III B; Level 6, LH III A:2–III B. It has since become apparent that these attributions are no more than generally acceptable: the size of the sherds precludes detailed diagnosis, and the larger piece from Level 2 is frankly unclassifiable.

(Civitavecchia, Museo Archeologico.)

C. E. Östenberg, *Luni sul Mignone e problemi della preistoria d'Italia* (Lund, 1967) 128–51, 245–54; L. Vagnetti in E. Peruzzi, *Mycenaeans in early Latium* (Rome, 1980) 151–4, fig. 10 and pl. 1; *ead.*, in *Enea nel Lazio* (exhibition catalogue: Rome, 1981) 106–7, nos. B80–84. On indigenous Recent (Proto-Villanovan) and Final Bronze Age associations and chronology see M. A. Fugazzola Delpino, *IBR* 42–5; general survey by A. F. Harding, *The Mycenaeans and Europe* (London, 1984) 244–61.

269. Miniature tripod-stand from the bronze hoard said to have been excavated in 1925 at Santa Maria in Paulis, near Ittiri (prov. Sassari), Sardinia. Physical analysis has demonstrated Sardinian manufacture; typology points unequivocally to the Late Cypriot III (about 1230–1050) tradition of bronze-casting by the investment or 'lost-wax' technique. The Santa Maria stand is one of many indications that the originally Levantine technology used to make the famous series of Sardinian figurines was available locally from the Late Bronze Age, significantly earlier than the *terminus ante quem* in the late ninth century suggested by the contexts of some Sardinian exports to Etruria.

(London, British Museum 1926.5–11.2. Max. height 7.1 cm.)

E. Macnamara, D. and F. R. Ridgway, *The Bronze Hoard from S. Maria in Paulis, Sardinia* (London, British Museum Occasional Paper 45, 1984) 2–7, pl. 2 and fig. 2; F. Lo Schiavo, E. Macnamara, L. Vagnetti, *BSR* 53 (1985) 43, fig. 15, pl. 3 and *passim* on Late Cypriot imports to Italy and their influence on local bronzework; F. R. Serra Ridgway, *SSA* 2 (1986) 85–101.

270. Pottery from tomb 944 in the San Montano cemetery, Pithecusa (Ischia, prov. Naples); about 750–725. (**a**) local Late Geometric oinochoe. (**b**) Corinthian Late Geometric skyphos (a 'Thapsos cup'). (**c**) Levantine aryballos, with close parallels on Rhodes (Lindus, Exochi) and attested in the West only at Pithecusa by this specimen and others from con-

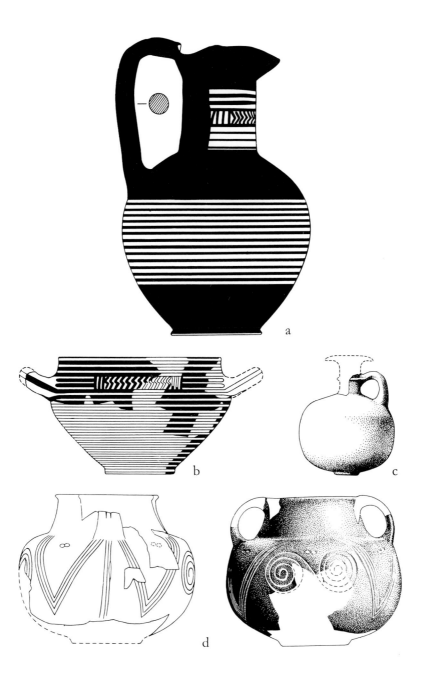

a

b

c

d

temporary tombs of the third quarter of the eighth century. (**d**) small spiral amphora of impasto, with close parallels in Etruria (Veii) and Latium (Castel di Decima). The personal ornaments in tomb 944 are all of silver, and indicate a female deposition in an upper middle class family plot. The association, which is not unique at Pithecusa, of an Etrusco-Latial piece (**d**) with one from the Levant (**c**) suggests that by the time of their deposition the Bay of Naples had acquired the status of a Euboean way-station on the route that conveyed the Orientalizing phenomenon from the Near East to Campania, Latium vetus and Etruria. In addition there is food for thought in the fact that the only aryballoi deposited in Pithecusan tombs at this early stage were Levantine imports as (**c**). It is at least conceivable that the ritual implications of their presence may extend to ethnic identity – 'resident orientals' in other words, for which there is epigraphic evidence in the form of Semitic inscriptions on local pottery.

(Naples, Soprintendenza Archeologica; store, Lacco Ameno d'Ischia. Heights 19.8 cm (**a**), 7.8 cm (**b**), 7 cm (**c**), 9.2 cm (**d**).)

G. Buchner and D. Ridgway, *AION* 5 (1983) 1–9 on these pieces. Background: G. Buchner, *IBR* 129–44; papers by *id.*, P. J. Riis and J. N. Coldstream, *Madrider Beiträge* 8 (1982) 237–306.

271. Painted jar (**a**: stamnoid olla) and lid (**b**) from Sulcis, island of Sant'Antioco (prov. Cagliari, Sardinia); about 730–700. The form of the jar is not without parallels in the native Sub-Geometric repertoire of the Italian peninsula (as

271a

271b

272 from Etruria), and may also be more or less distantly related to that of certain Corinthian Late Geometric pyxides with similarly facing birds in the handle zone attested in Sicily (Syracuse, Naxus) and Calabria (Francavilla Marittima). Both the main motif and the ancillary decoration have long been recognized as having affinities with Euboean Late Geometric and particularly with the version of it that was developed in the second half of the eighth century at Euboean Pithecusa, Ischia (whence **270**) – which is in any case the nearest source to Sardinia of Euboean characteristics. These are if anything even more apparent in the shape and decoration of the fragmentary lid: and there is no reason to doubt that both pieces were actually made at Pithecusa.

The archaeological context of the jar and its lid is informative. Writing in the second century A.D., the Greek traveller and geographer Pausanias (X.17) attributed the foundation of Sulcis to Carthage; in fact, the Punic city was preceded by a Phoenician establishment, probably founded in the ninth or eighth century. The *tophet*, or sacred place required for the ritual sacrifice of the first-born (Book of Jeremiah 7:31), was excavated in the 1960s and is one of the largest and best preserved of its kind in the West: the painted jar imported from Pithecusa contained infant remains, and is the only receptacle – out of hundreds – used for this purpose at Sulcis that is not wholly Phoenicio-Punic (plain red) in appearance. The presence of Pithecusan products in a Phoenician context in Sardinia is presumably explicable in terms of the Levantine connexions (see **270**) of the first western Greeks: there are grounds for believing that these may have extended to the Phoenician or Phoenicianizing community of silver miners at Riotinto in Spain, the route to which cannot possibly have bypassed Sardinia.

The 'Pithecusan connexion' appears to be confirmed by the reported discovery in the 1980s of imported Corinthian Late Geometric, Early Protocorinthian, Phoenician and Pithecusan sherds in a stratified domestic context elsewhere at Sulcis.

(Cagliari, Museo Nazionale. Jar height 16.3 cm. Lid maximum preserved width 11 cm.)

J. N. Coldstream, *Greek Geometric Pottery* (London, 1968) 388, 429; C. Tronchetti, *Rivista di Studi Fenici* 7–2 (1979) 201–5, pls. 67, 68. On Spain, Sardinia and the first western Greeks see B. B. Shefton, *Madrider*

Beiträge 8 (1982) 337–70; P. Bernardini and C. Tronchetti, *Sardegna preistorica* (exhibition catalogue: Milan, 1985) 285–92; D. Ridgway, *SSA* 2 (1986) 173–85.

272. Painted jar (stamnoid olla) of the Sub-Geometric Heron Class typical of southern Etruria during the late eighth and early seventh centuries; no provenance. The production of this class (which also includes plates, amphorae, craters and oinochoai) appears to be centred on Caere, where it is immediately followed by the first bucchero in the second quarter of the seventh century. The 'heron' itself is a popular motif in the Iron Age repertoire: its characteristically elongated bill and body appear on

impasto amphorae, and seem to be echoed in the incised decoration of Villanovan sheet bronze belts like **286**. On painted pottery, the birds are further related to those depicted on certain locally made plates at Euboean Pithecusa, of a form that closely resembles that of imported Phoenician Red Slip plates at the same site. Etruscan plates of the Heron Class have in fact been defined as an amalgam of Phoenician-derived shape and a Euboean-derived decorative motif. In the circumstances, it is hardly surprising that the Heron Class is the earliest category of Etruscan painted pottery to travel beyond the confines of Etruria. Ollae similar to that illustrated have been found in Latium (Castel di Decima, Marino) and Campania (Pontecagnano), suggesting that during the Orientalizing period Caere took the lead in the commercial exploitation of the well-established pre-existing contacts between the three areas.

(London, British Museum 1921.11–29.1. Height 20.3 cm.)

S. Leach in J. Swaddling (ed.), *Italian Iron Age Artefacts* (1986) 305–8; on the Heron Class generally, see ead., *Subgeometric Pottery from Southern Etruria* (Stockholm, 1987).

273. Figured scene in low relief on a small situla of faience (the 'Bocchoris vase'). Found in a chamber tomb excavated in 1895 in the Monterozzi cemetery, Tarquinia, it bears the cartouche of the Egyptian Pharaoh Bakenrenef (Bocchoris in Greek), of the Saïte dynasty. His brief reign (about 720–715) provides a *terminus*

post quem for the contents of the 'Bocchoris Tomb', now generally assigned to the first quarter of the seventh century, and for contemporary material in the local indigenous sequences established at Tarquinia and elsewhere.

(Tarquinia, Museo Nazionale RC 2010. Height 23 cm.)

E. Schiaparelli, *Mon. Ant.* 8 (1898) 89–100, whence the drawing reproduced here; E. Hall Dohan, *Italic Tomb-Groups in the University Museum* (Philadelphia, 1942) 106–7; A. Rathje, *IBR* 150–2. On the Bocchoris Tomb and its contents see: W. Helbig, *Not. Scav.* 1896, 15ff; Hencken, *Tarquinia* 364–78; I. Strøm, *Problems Concerning the Origin and Early Development of the Etruscan Orientalizing Style* (Odense, 1971) 149–50; *CVA Tarquinia* III 23; Cat. Florence 1985, 93–95. Cf. *CAH* III².3, 32–3 (Bocchoris).

274. Incised decoration on an ostrich egg from a rich Orientalizing tomb excavated in 1972 near Pitino, San Severino Marche (prov. Macerata) in Picenum. The associations of the evidently male deposition included a two-wheeled chariot with iron fittings, two pairs of local cuirass disks, two bronze shields, a number of bronze vessels, carved ivory, decorated bone and ivory plaques and an Ionic cup in silver which suggests a date in the late seventh or early sixth century. The egg forms the body of an oinochoe, the neck and handle being of ivory; the decoration has been identified as the work of a school at Vulci (represented in the Isis Tomb there, whence **298**, and in the Tomba della Montagnola at Sesto Fiorentino). Though decorated in the West, the egg itself will most probably have been laid in the upper valley of the Nile, and been despatched to Italy from the Phoenician coast; the development of the egg-incising technique has reasonably been traced to Naucratis. Earlier eggs in Etruria are painted, notably the fine unprovenanced example in the Tarquinia Museum, assigned by Torelli to the early seventh century.

(Soprintendenza Archeologica delle Marche/Città di San Severino, Museo Archeologico.)

G. Colonna, *Stud. Etr.* 41 (1973) 515–17, no. 18; D. Ridgway, *Arch. Rep.* 1973–74, 53f; A. Rathje, *IBR* 171–6. Distribution of ostrich eggs in Italy: M. Torelli, *Stud. Etr.* 33 (1965) 329–65.

275. Anthropomorphic funerary stela of sandstone from Saletto di Bentivoglio (prov. Bologna); second half of the seventh century.

The decoration, in low relief, is thoroughly oriental in character: a winged sphinx in the upper disk; below, a pair of rampant goats eating from the topmost branches of a (sacred) tree. The latter motif recalls that in the central panels of the well-known krater by the Euboean Cesnola Painter (third quarter of the eighth century: *Plates to Vol. III*, pl. 280); it could have reached the West via Pithecusa, and followed the same path across the Apennines as the Etruscan elements that surfaced in Situla Art (**288a–b, 293**). At the same time, the possibility of direct contacts in the Orientalizing period between the Near East and the head of the Adriatic need not be ruled out.

(Bologna, Museo Civico Archeologico 25677. Height 65 cm.)

Cat. Bologna 1960, 143 no. 524 with pl. 23. Another stela with similar iconography from San Varano (prov. Forlì): G. Bermond Montanari, *Stud. Etr.* 35 (1967) 655–8.

276. Small inscribed bucchero amphora said to have been found in 1882 in the Late Orientalizing chamber tomb at Formello (Veii) that yielded the well-known Protocorinthian olpe by the Macmillan Painter (the 'Chigi Vase'); early in the last quarter of the seventh century. An Etruscan model alphabet is incised round the neck; it is demonstrably derived from its Euboean counterpart, which reached the West via Pithecusa.

(Rome, Villa Giulia 22678. Height 17.8 cm.)

T. Mommsen, *Bull. Inst.* 1882, 91–6, ('Chigi Vase': *ibid.*, 98f); G. Buonamici, *Epigrafia etrusca* (Florence, 1932) 107–8; M. Pallottino, *Testimonia Linguae Etruscae*[2] (Florence, 1968) 30, no. 49; M. Verzar, *AK* 16 (1973) 47f and fig. 3 (dating *c.* 630–625); Rasmussen, *Bucchero* 71–2 (amphora type 1d). On the introduction of the Greek alphabet into Etruria see M. W. Frederiksen, *IBR* 287–94; M. Cristofani, *ibid.*, 377–9; and more generally G. and L. Bonfante, *The Etruscan Language* (Manchester, 1983). Cf. *Plates to Vol. III*, pls. 376–8.

277. Attic black-figure neck amphora signed Νικοσθενες εποιεσεν by the potter Nicosthenes, active about 540–510; this example, decorated (apparently like all others of its kind) by Beazley's Painter N, falls midway in the development from a broader to a more slender body and may accordingly be dated about 530–520. Nicosthenes' signature is the commonest in Attic black

276

a   b   c

figure, and many examples of his other shapes were exported to Vulci. In sharp contrast, most of the provenanced Attic 'Nicosthenic' amphorae come from Caere, which also seems to be the source of what can only be described as their bucchero model (as **290a**, top row). In Etruria, the shape is directly descended from Iron Age impasto amphorae with broad flat handles (as **270d**), and reached its final form in the second quarter of the sixth century via earlier bucchero types (as **276**). In Athens, the shape is

exclusive to the enterprising workshop of Nicosthenes and his younger partner Pamphaios, who were clearly aiming an Etruscan shape (with the novel addition of painted decoration, often figured) at the promising Etruscan market of Caere – which was on particularly good political terms with Athens in the years following 540. Production of the bucchero shape was past its peak when the Attic versions began to appear, and the latter did not survive the last decade of the sixth century. By then, Caere was returning to its traditional allegiance with Carthage against the Greeks (cf. **297e**): and Nicosthenes and Pamphaios were making cups for the early red-figure Nicosthenes Painter.

(Melbourne, National Gallery of Victoria D392/1980, Felton Bequest. Height 30.6 cm.)
  ABV 221, 40; *CVA Castle Ashby* 11, no. 17, pl. 19; I. McPhee, *Art Bulletin of Victoria* 21 (1980) 8–12. On Nicosthenes' bucchero models see M. Verzar, *AK* 16 (1973) 45–56; Rasmussen, *Bucchero* 74f, type 1g; *id.*, *AK* 28 (1985) 34f. Nicosthenes: *ABFH* 64f; *CAH* III².3, 454.

278. Caeretan hydria from tomb 1 in the Banditaccia cemetery, Caere, showing the blinding of Polyphemus; about 520. Hydriae like this were produced in a single workshop, in existence at Caere for around twenty years after 530/525. Their shape and decoration set them apart from other hydriae, and Hemelrijk has suggested that the two masters involved, though undoubtedly from East Greece (most probably Phocaea), may have emigrated to Etruria with a family background in a craft other than vase-painting such as architectural decoration. It is possible that they were involved in the painting of tombs at Tarquinia, where similarities with the Tomba degli Auguri are particularly striking.

(Rome, Villa Giulia. Height 40 cm.)

J. M. Hemelrijk, *Caeretan Hydriae* (Mainz, 1984) 36ff, no. 20; Cat. Florence 1985, 219. Cf. *Plates to Vol. III*, pl. 362.

279. Etruscan black-figure hydria by the Micali Painter, said to be from Vulci; about 510–500. The scene shows a warship on active service, and has been identified with the landing of the Greeks at Troy. But it is by no means certain that an Etruscan painter would possess this degree of mythological knowledge. His picture is more likely to be intended as a general comment on Etruscan prowess at sea – an appropriate subject in the decades following the naval battle fought and won by the Carthaginian and Caeretan fleets against the Phocaeans of Alalia (540).

(London, British Museum B60. Height 40 cm.)

J. D. Beazley and F. Magi, *La raccolta Benedetto Guglielmi nel Museo Gregoriano Etrusco* 1 (Vatican City, 1939) 79, no. 49; J. S. Morrison and R. T. Williams, *Greek Oared Ships 900–322 BC* (Cambridge, 1968) 112, pl. 22b; Cat. Florence 1985, 227. In general: N. J. Spivey, *The Micali Painter and his Followers* (Oxford, 1987).

280. Attic black-figure belly amphora by the Priam Painter, from tomb 610 (the Tomba Martini Marescotti) in the Monte Abatone cemetery, Caere; about 510. Dionysus seated, and satyrs making wine.

(Rome, Villa Giulia. Height 53.9 cm.)

M. Moretti, *Tomba Martini Marescotti* (Milan, 1966), several unnumbered illustrations; *Para* 146, 8ter.

281. Inscribed bronze helmet of an Etruscan form related to the Negau type in central Europe; found at the sanctuary of Olympia in 1817 (and presented to the British Museum by King George IV in 1823). This rather battered piece was presumably taken from an Etruscan sailor after victory won by Hieron's Greeks off Cyme in 474 (Diod. Sic. 11.51–2; Pindar, *Pyth.* 1.71–5). The dedication reads 'Hieron the Deinomenid and the Syracusans, to Zeus, the Etruscan [booty] from Cyme'.

(London, British Museum 1928.6–10.1. Height 20.5 cm.)

L. H. Jeffery, *The Local Scripts of Archaic Greece* (Oxford, 1961) 275, no. 7, pl. 51; M. Guarducci, *Epigrafia greca* 1 (Rome, 1967) 344; Cat. Florence 1985, 256.

(b) Life and death

282. Foundation trenches and post-holes of an Early Iron Age hut, one of a number encountered by R. E. Linington of the Lerici Foundation beneath later (Etruscan) tumuli in the Calvario locality of the Monterozzi cemetery at Tarquinia. On present evidence, the area involved is as much as two hectares; to date, traces of at least thirty structures have been defined, of various sizes, shapes (mainly oval, but some rectangular and perhaps long) – and presumably functions. This unexpected discovery provides evidence for the existence, long suspected, of the Iron Age settlement agglomeration that preceded the late urban concentration on the Civita, and corresponds chronologically to the vast Villanovan cemeteries at Tarquinia (whence **284–5**), Veii (**283**) and elsewhere.

R. E. Linington, F. Delpino, M. Pallottino, *Stud. Etr.* 46 (1978) 3–23; Cat. Florence 1985, 47.

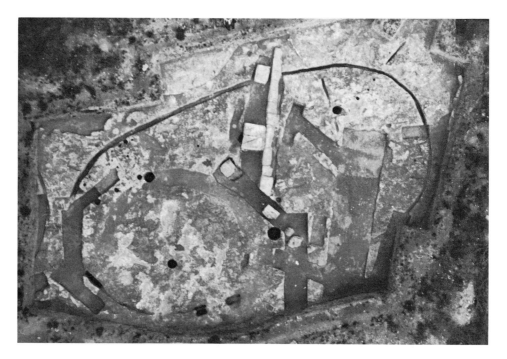

yielded by the 651 cremation and inhumation graves excavated, mostly intact and all published by 1976, has formed the basis of a concerted attack on local relative chronology between the ninth and seventh centuries. The absolute dating of the native Iron Age phases was greatly assisted by the presence in context of painted Geometric pottery of Greek type. Connexions with events on the Bay of Naples (Pithecusa, **270**) are self-evident; the principal shape involved at Quattro Fontanili is the Euboean Middle Geometric drinking cup (skyphos), which was both imported and imitated locally on an appreciable scale.

Quattro Fontanili excavation reports (catalogues): *Not. Scav.* 1963, 1965, 1967, 1970, 1972, 1975, 1976. Chronological schemes: J. Close-Brooks, *Not. Scav.* 1965, 53–64 with *Stud. Etr.* 35 (1967) 323–9 = *IBR* 95–113; J. Toms, *AION* 8 (1986) 41–97. Greek Geometric imports and imitations: D. Ridgway, *Stud. Etr.* 35 (1967) 311–21 = *IBR* 113–27; *id.* and O. T. P. K. Dickinson, *BSA* 68 (1973) 191f; J.-P. Descoeudres and R. Kearsley, *BSA* 78 (1983) 9–53; A. Deriu, F. Boitani, D. Ridgway, *BSA* 80 (1985) 139–50.

283. Part of the Villanovan cemetery of Quattro Fontanili, Veii, showing a selection of fossa (trench) graves cut into the tufa bedrock, which is perilously close to the present ground level and visibly scarred by a modern deep plough. The deleterious effect of the latter led to the major rescue operation mounted jointly by the Rome University Institute of Etruscology and the British School at Rome between 1961 and 1972. The massive corpus of associated artefacts

284. Biconical ossuary of impasto with comb-incised decoration from tomb 179 in the Selci-atello di Sopra cemetery, Tarquinia; second half of the ninth century. The classic container for

early cremations of the indigenous Early Iron Age Villanovan culture.

(Florence, Museo Archeologico 83681/A. Height 33.8 cm.)
  Hencken, *Tarquinia* 81; Cat. Florence 1985, 54f.

285. Crested bronze helmet from tomb 1 in the Poggio dell' Impiccato cemetery, Tarquinia; first half of the eighth century. Helmets like these are common in Villanovan cemeteries, where they succeed their pottery counterparts as frequent ossuary-covers in cremation tombs.

(Florence, Museo Archeologico 83379. Height 35.7 cm.)
  Hencken, *Tarquinia* 115–23; Cat. Florence 1985, 57–9.

286. Villanovan belt of sheet bronze, with rich repoussé and incised decoration, from tomb 543 in the Benacci cemetery, Bologna; first half of the eighth century. Belts of this type are relatively common in southern Etruria, where Veii provides a good parallel for a specimen that found its way to Euboea. At Bologna, they are limited to three upper-class female depositions in the Benacci cemetery. Like the horse-bits in

certain contemporary male graves there (and the axe-shaped pendant from a later female grave, **288a–b**), they should probably be seen as symbols of rank. The decoration of this belt, like that of similar pieces elsewhere, incorporates stylized birds' heads and 'sun disks'; these have been compared with elements in the central European Urnfield repertoire.

(Bologna, Museo Civico Archeologico 15014. Length 47.5 cm.)
  Cat. Bologna 1960, 71f, no. 89, pl. 5. On the decoration and its affinities see Hencken, *Tarquinia* 551 (s.v. 'broad bronze girdles'); and, for the Euboean connexion, J. Close-Brooks, *BICS* 14 (1967) 22–4.

287. Askos of impasto from tomb 525 in the Benacci cemetery, Bologna; a rare example of Villanovan plastic art, probably made locally and datable between the late eighth and early seventh centuries. The basic horned quadruped is one of a number of surreal combinations of animal and bird found in Italy; available sources of inspiration include Greece, Cyprus and eastern Europe. The defensive armour worn by the cavalryman finds no parallel in the contemporary Bolognese cemeteries, where the absence of helmets and

shields contrasts strikingly with the situation south of the Apennines.

(Bologna, Museo Civico Archeologico 12791. Height 17.7 cm.)

Cat. Bologna 1960, 87, no. 179, p. 6. On the type, Hencken, *Tarquinia* 519–30.

288. Material from the 'Tomba degli Ori' (tomb 5) in the Arsenale Militare cemetery, Bologna, excavated in 1874; late seventh century.

Bronze rattle, with scenes in low relief (revealed by modern restoration) of wool-working: cleaning and carding (**a**), spinning and weaving (**b**). The loom, a large structure with a woman sitting on a substantial chair in the top storey, is the most elaborate example known from antiquity; and this unique set of illustrations bears witness to the importance of heavy woollen fabrics in northern Italy in all periods (cf. Pliny, *NH* VIII. 191). Stylistically, the piece bears all the hallmarks of the 'Situla Art' that flourished in the Po Valley, the Veneto (Este), the Alpine regions, Austria and Yugoslavia in the late seventh and more particularly the sixth centuries (cf. **293**). A significant Etruscan contribution to Situla Art reached the north via the region of Chiusi, where the terracotta figures and relief-decorated frieze-plaques from Poggio Civitate (Murlo: **292**) illustrate the immediate source of various items of dress and furniture that were subsequently fossilized in the northern representations.

(**c**) The associations of the rattle include typically Orientalizing personal ornaments of gold (fibulae; head-bands) and amber (necklaces); they are clearly the grave-goods of a woman of high social class. In this respect, it may not be entirely coincidental that the rattle is actually a pendant in the shape of an axe – a symbol of rank and power also seen on the Certosa Situla (**293**) and widely attested in Etruria (**295b**) and later in the Roman world.

(Bologna, Museo Civico Archeologico 25676. Rattle height 11.5 cm.)

O. Montelius, *La civilisation primitive en Italie* I (Stockholm, 1895) pl. 87; C. Morigi Govi, *Arch. Class.* 23 (1971) 211–35; L. Bonfante, *Etruscan Dress* (Baltimore, London, 1975) 157, fig. 2; Cat. Florence 1985, 172.

289. The fine sixth-century bronzes encountered since 1965 in the cemetery at Campovalano, near Campli (prov. Teramo), contrast sharply with the image of backward mountain folk traditionally conferred on the eastern Italic peoples who descended on the coastal plains a century later. Arms and armour abound, and recall those worn by the Warrior of Capestrano (**299**); they are accompanied by bronze vessels in quantities (and of a quality) that recall the richer cemeteries

289a

289b

in contemporary Etruria. The emphasis on the mixing, straining and drinking of wine is somewhat reminiscent of Celtic preferences; the analogy may be the result of a similar impact made by luxury goods exported from Etruria.

(**a**, **b**) Bronze oinochoe of the so-called Rhodian type from Campovalano, tomb 97; first quarter of the sixth century.

(**c**, **d**) Bronze strainer (*infundibulum*) from Campovalano, tomb 2; first half of the sixth century.

(Chieti, Museo Nazionale 7514, 5146. Oinochoe, height 28.5 cm. Strainer, total length 32.2 cm.)

O. Zanco, *Bronzi arcaici da Campovalano* (Rome, 1974) nos. 2, 18; Cat. Florence 1985, 234–6; and in general B. B. Shefton, *Die 'Rhodischen' Bronzekannen* (Mainz, 1979).

290. Material from an intact chamber tomb excavated in 1965 at Trevignano Romano on the shores of Lake Bracciano in southern Etruria;

first half of the sixth century, with nearly 200 items divided between six depositions in two rooms. The categories illustrated here, all made in Etruria, were also appreciated abroad from the end of the seventh century. Bucchero (**a**), rightly defined by H. B. Walters as 'the national pottery of Etruria', has been found as far afield as Catalonia and Carthage, and often accompanied Etruscan wine exported (notably to France) in Etrusco-Corinthian wine amphorae (**b**). Less predictably, Etruscan footware (**c**) seems to have been renowned throughout the classical world (Pollux VII.22.92f, writing about A.D. 180): and although a jocular reference (Cratinus fr. 131) to *Tyrrhenia sandalia* in connexion with Pheidias' statue of Athena need not mean that Etruscan sandals were imported by Athens in any great quantity, it clearly implies fame – and quite possibly 'Etruscan primacy of invention' (Bonfante).

The Trevignano tomb also contained two other amphorae, with figures reserved on a red

ground, depicting an aristocratic wedding procession with a biga, and sphinxes, panther, lion, eagles, etc., in the Orientalizing tradition. This interesting pair (one by a master, the other a less accomplished copy) is attributed by G. Colonna to a Veientine workshop of the end of the seventh century: Cat. Florence 1985, 245, colour ill. 247.

(a) A selection of bucchero shapes (with height). Top row, from left to right: oinochoe (type 7a; 26 cm); amphora (type 1g; 34.5 cm); oinochoe (type 8a; 23.5 cm); oinochoe (type 7g; 24.5 cm). Middle row: kantharos (20.5 cm); pyxis (with lid: 19.5 cm); oinochoe (20 cm); 'skyphos' (21.5 cm). Bottom row: chalice (type 1b; 17.5 cm); face-cup (11 cm); kyathos (type 4c; 14 cm); jug (15.5 cm). The amphora in the top row is of the Caeretan type copied by the Athenian potter Nicosthenes for the Etruscan market (277).

(b) Etrusco-Corinthian amphorae. Heights 66 cm, 67 cm. The influence of Corinth is seen to good effect in the confident zoomorphic and vegetable friezes on the bodies and necks of these local products; volutes on the shoulders.

(c) Sandals. Restored; original dimensions no longer available. One each of two pairs: male, with only iron frame surviving; female, with fragmentary components of leather, wood and bronze.

(Rome, Villa Giulia.)

M. Moretti in *Arte e civiltà degli Etruschi* (exhibition catalogue: Turin, 1967) 45–77, nos. 59–230 *passim*, with unnumbered illustrations. Type nos. from Rasmussen, *Bucchero*. On Etrusco-Corinthian generally, see J. G. Szilágyi, *Etruszko-korinthosi vázafestészet* (Budapest, 1975). Etruscan footwear: L. Bonfante, *op. cit.* 288, 59–66.

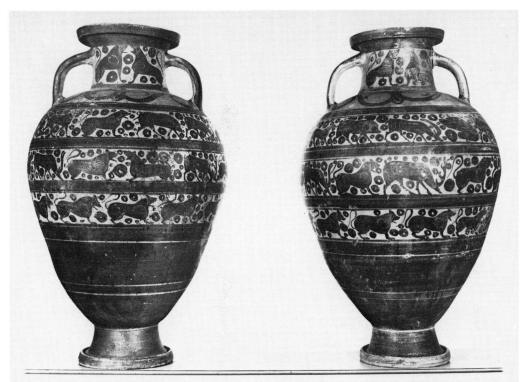

291. Stand or vase-carrier of impasto; sixth century or slightly earlier. No context or provenance is recorded for this piece; similar items are known from Sovana and Pitigliano, which may also be the source of the thirty cooking pots, identical in fabric with the stand, in the same collection. The vents in the lower box and the funnel-shaped openings on the top have ensured interpretation of this type (and of functionally related items) as some sort of cooking stand,

portable stove, 'hot-plate' or incense burner. But it has been well observed that not every hole is a ventilation hole, and not every perforated pottery object is necessarily connected with fire. 'The most likely theory is that the stands were just stands; on them were placed pots that were probably often round-bottomed and needed something to stand on' (Scheffer).

(Toronto, Royal Ontario Museum 920×92.111. Maximum height 20.7 cm.)

J. W. Hayes, *Stud. Etr.* 43 (1975) 96, no. 45, pl. 24; id., *Etruscan and Italic Pottery in the Royal Ontario Museum* (Toronto, 1985) 58, B68. On the type see C. Scheffer, *Acquarossa* II.1: *Cooking and cooking stands in Italy, 1400–400 BC* (Stockholm, 1981) 58–61.

292. Architectural decorations from the anonymous Etruscan centre at Poggio Civitate, near Murlo (prov. Siena), where excavations by Bryn Mawr College began in 1966; first quarter of the sixth century.

The building complex at Poggio Civitate has two phases. The first (i.e., lower: Orientalizing) seems to have been built about 650 and accidentally burnt down about 610/600. The second (i.e., upper: Archaic) was superimposed on the first about 600/590, and had a central court (about 60 × 60 m) surrounded by rooms and on three sides by rows of columns: this was deliberately (ritually ?) dismantled and interred about 550/530. The precise function – religious, political or civil – of the complex during either phase has been hotly debated for many years. The excavators' original cautious identification as a religious sanctuary has been succeeded by their equally cautious proposal at a later stage in the excavation that the Archaic complex could have been the seat of a northern league, political with inevitable religious overtones. Although Poggio Civitate is indeed more or less equidistant from Volterra, Arezzo, Chiusi, Roselle and Vetulonia, it is perhaps more realistic to think in terms of links with smaller and nearer centres. These could well have rendered Poggio Civitate

nique) of the cow-boy owes nothing to the tastes and skills imported to the more southerly part of Etruria in the circumstances traditionally associated with the arrival of Demaratus of Corinth at Tarquinia in the mid-seventh century. The quantity and quality of the frieze-plaques and acroteria recovered at Poggio Civitate bear witness to the presence of a capable and well-informed school of local terracotta workers in the territory of Chiusi. There, however, architectural decoration of this early date has not been found.

(a) Mass-produced frieze-plaque, showing a horse-race: the trophy is a bronze cauldron (left), resting on an Etruscan version of a Doric column. (b) Mass-produced frieze-plaque, showing the earliest representation of a reclining banquet known in Etruria: four men on two couches, waited on by female servants. (c) Acroterion: bearded figure, wearing a broad-brimmed hat of the type that appears later on the Certosa Situla (293).

(Florence, Museo Archeologico. Plaques, *c.* 24 × 54 cm. Acroterion, preserved height 85 cm.)

The latest account of Poggio Civitate, and of the types illustrated here, is provided by the excavators, E. O. Nielsen, K. M. Phillips Jr *et al.* in *Case e palazzi d'Etruria* (exhibition catalogue: Siena, 1985) 64–154, with extensive illustrations and previous bibliography.

locally powerful – and hence liable to the remarkable act of deliberate destruction, presumably by Chiusi, that is attested beyond doubt by the archaeological evidence.

The three pieces illustrated are frieze plaques (**a**, **b**) and an acroterion (**c**), all recovered from the dismantled remains of the upper building. The frieze plaques both belong to series mass-produced in local terracotta. Their subjects – a horse-race (**a**) and an all-male banquet (**b**) – are not incompatible with local federal meetings, and neither are those of the other two series: an assembly of (divine ?) personages and a procession. The 'cow-boy' (**c**) is one of a number of nearly life-size seated- and standing-figure acroteria, hand-made and originally painted. While the makers of the frieze-plaques were well acquainted with contemporary Greek art, notably Early and Middle Corinthian, it has to be said that the style (as distinct from the tech-

293. Situla of sheet-bronze, with repoussé decoration, used as an ossuary in tomb 68 in the Certosa cemetery, Bologna. A date about 490–480 for the deposition of the 'Certosa Situla' is indicated by an Attic black-figure lekythos, one of the few associated grave-goods. The Etruscan component in the 'Situla Art' (cf. **288a, b**) of northern Italy and the transalpine regions is stylistically closest to the territory of Chiusi, where the discoveries at Poggio Civitate (**292**) provide an archaeological reflection of the traditional account of the long journey to the north made by Arruns (Livy v.33,2–3).

(Bologna, Museo Civico Archeologico 17169. Height 32 cm.)

Cat. Bologna 1960, 190, no. 642, pl. 49; *Mostra dell'arte delle situle dal Po al Danubio* (Florence, 1961) 87–9, no. 17; J. V. S. Megaw, *Art of the European Iron Age* (Bath, 1970) 52f, no. 24.

294. The painted chamber tombs of Etruria constitute the largest complex of pre-Roman painting that has survived anywhere in the classical world. They range in date from the seventh to the second century, with the great Tarquinian series beginning in the sixth. Whether the scenes depicted show the everyday world (pleasant situations – banquets, hunting – in which the deceased may be supposed to have taken part) or the ceremonies (mourning, games) that surrounded the funeral itself, Etruscan painting prior to the middle of the fourth century has an interest in direct observation that contrasts sharply with the idealization of Greek funerary art – not least in its attention to amusing and occasionally earthy details, like the mouse in the Tomba del Topolino or the scenes of group sex in the Tombe della Fustigazione and dei Tori. After the mid-fourth century, the focus changes under Greek influence from the real world to the imaginary and frequently terrifying world of the hereafter, with the emphasis on events such as leave-taking from loved ones, the journey to the underworld (escorted by demons), and reception by the ancestors. The following three examples are from single-chamber tombs in the Monterozzi cemetery at Tarquinia; the paintings in the Tomba della Nave (**b**) were detached on dis-

covery and restored for display in the Tarquinia Museum.

(a) The Tomba del Cacciatore (Hunter), discovered in 1962 in the Calvario area; about 510–500. The painted decoration in this tomb is evidently intended to simulate a hunting pavilion, and as such is redolent of the luxurious life-style of the Etruscan upper classes. It is possible that the representation of patterned cloth was inspired by contemporary textiles imported from the Levant.

(b) Banquet scene on the rear wall of the Tomba della Nave (Ship), discovered in 1958 in the Secondi Archi area; end of the fifth century. The tomb takes its name from the detailed representation (unique in Etruscan tomb-painting) on the left wall of a seascape featuring a large two-masted merchant ship; it probably alludes to the source of the deceased's wealth. The conventional banquet shown here is made up of three couches, on each of which recline a man and a woman of equal rank. Unlike the all-male banquet shown on **292b**, this is a basically un-Greek situation: and one that was accordingly taken to indicate a distasteful degree of sexual freedom by Theopompus, writing in the fourth century (in Athenaeus 517D–518L).

(c) Musical and athletic scene (presumably funeral contests) on the left wall of the Tomba del Guerriero (Warrior), discovered in 1961 in the Calvario area. A date in the second quarter of the fourth century is suggested by Attic and Italiote parallels for the calyx-krater on the *kylikeion* (far right), and supported by the perspective attempted in the representation of the naked *discobolos* next to it.

S. Steingräber (ed.), *Etruskische Wandmalerei* (Stuttgart, Zurich, 1985) / *Pittura Etrusca* (Milan, 1985) / *Etruscan Painting* (New York, 1988) catalogue nos. 51, 91, 73.

(c) Religion

295. These three bronzes were found during the 1982–5 excavations conducted by the University of Milan on the Pian di Civita (site of the ancient city) at Tarquinia. Of local Etruscan manufacture, they may be dated to the first quarter of the seventh century. Their immediate context is a votive trench apparently associated with the erection of a religious building and with the isolated inhumation burial, effected at the end of the ninth century, of a boy aged about eight years and clearly the object of uninterrupted veneration since his deposition. The cult implications are complex, and await further study (and excavation); a connexion with the legendary figure of Tages has been suggested.

(a) Trumpet-lituus. Full length 1.35 m.

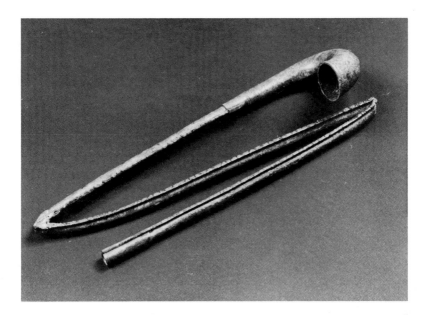

(**b**) Axe. Length 16 cm. (**c**) Folded shield. Estimated diam. 96/100 cm.

(Tarquinia, Museo Nazionale.)
M. Bonghi Jovino (ed.), *Gli Etruschi di Tarquinia* (exhibition catalogue: Milan, 1986) nos. 197–9.

296. Evidence of a resident Greek community at Graviscae (modern Porto Clementino), the port of Tarquinia, goes back to the early sixth century and provides a modest context for a coarse East Greek amphora (**a**, diam. neck 10.7 cm) with the inscription ὑδρίη μετρίη. In the Greeks' sanctuary, the range of votive material is illustrated by a fragment of an Ionic cup of Vallet–Villard type B₃ (**b**, about 550), inscribed [. . .] ἠφροδίτηι, and by a rim-fragment of a Laconian crater (**c**, about 560) with a dedication in Etruscan (*mit[u]runs*; *Corpus Inscriptionum Etruscarum* 10335) to Turan, the Etruscan equivalent of Aphrodite – which affords interesting evidence of the early local assimilation of foreign divinities. An Attic band-cup with an erotic scene (**d**, height 8 cm; maenads and satyrs) is appropriately inscribed on the inside: [. . .] ιχλεος ἀφροδί[τηι].

(Tarquinia, Museo Nazionale.)
CAH IV², 669. On these pieces, see Cat. Florence 1985, 181–3; on Graviscae generally, Cat. Arezzo 1985, 141–4.

297. (**a**) Plans showing reconstructions of the two phases in the development of the Etruscan sanctuary at Pyrgi (modern Santa Severa), the main port of Caere; based on the University of Rome excavations (1957 onwards). *Left*, about 500, Temple B (**b**, **c**); *right*, about 450, Temple B (**b**, **c**), Area C, which contained three inscribed gold tablets (**e**, **f**, **g**), and Temple A (**d**).

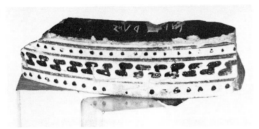

The sanctuary was founded about 510, with Temple B facing south west (towards the sea), the sacred Area C and, along the southern temenos wall, a long line of rooms (seventeen to date: D). Fully contextual with Temple B, the latter feature has been variously interpreted as a shelter for pilgrims and as a series of cubicles connected with sacred prostitution – a hypothesis that is supported both by Lucilius' reference to *scorta pyrgensia* (fr. 1271 Marx) and by the evidence for this rite in sanctuaries (e.g. that at Eryx in Sicily) dedicated to Astarte, as Pyrgi was (cf. tablet **e**). However this may be, Temple B illustrates the tendency to increase public rather than private expenditure at the end of the sixth century. The process continued: notwithstanding the slow decline of the Tyrrhenian cities that resulted from the Etruscan defeat off Cyme (474), Pyrgi witnessed the foundation of a second and larger temple around 460: Temple A. At the

0 30 60 90 ATTIC FEET

0 10 20 30 METRES

same time, the road from Caere was diverted to enter the sanctuary at its north corner as a true *via sacra*. Temple A appears to have been dedicated to the Etruscan goddess Thesan (= Eos, Dawn), whose powers can be considered as special aspects of those of the Mother Goddess Uni/Astarte.

As late as 384, the sanctuary was still so wealthy that Dionysius of Syracuse was moved to plunder it (Diod. Sic. xv.14.3): his prize was a thousand talents in coin, plus statues and offerings. This has led to the suggestion that Pyrgi was the repository of at least part of Caere's public treasury – a situation not unknown in Greece, but so far without parallel in Etruria. If so, the blow came at the worst possible time: following the fall of Veii (396), Caere was inevitably the next target of Rome's inexorable advance northwards into Etruria and Umbria.

(**b, c**) Two views of Temple B (reconstruction by G. Foglia and F. Melis), a *peripteros* on a raised platform, about 20 × 30 m (= 63 × 96 Attic feet) with a small cella in antis close to the back row of four columns, six columns along each side and a double row of four at the front. This plan is a modified version of the basically Greek type already employed at Selinus in Sicily and at Satricum in Latium. The gabled roof is typically Tyrrhenian, made of wood and covered with terracotta tiles and ornaments, recovered in quantity and amounting to the earliest and most

complete example known of the so-called second phase of Etruscan architectural decoration. Walls and columns were made of tufa blocks covered with white plaster.

(**d**) View of Temple A (reconstruction by G. Foglia and F. Melis), resting on a raised platform, about 24 × 34 m (= 81 × 116 Attic feet). The plan is Tuscan (in Vitruvius' nomenclature), with one central and two smaller lateral cellae at the back; the side walls were prolonged in front, with four columns placed two by two in line with the inner walls and a row of four columns across the front. The altars were situated on the broad terrace (now much eroded by the sea) that precedes the temple; the two wells there (W on plan **a**) were filled with pottery and architectural decorations. Like those of Temple B, the outside walls were made of tufa blocks covered with white plaster.

The most striking feature of Temple A was undoubtedly the well-known central picture on a terracotta square (about 140 × 130 cm) mounted in the back gable. Technically and artistically, it is the finest surviving example of late Archaic sculpture in the west Mediterranean. Six figures in high relief arranged at different heights and levels are drawn from two separate episodes in the mythical siege of the Seven against Thebes: Capaneus struck by the bolt of Zeus; and the death of Tydeus and Melanippus. Neither scene is commonly represented in Greek art: but it is interest-

297b

297c

297d

ing to note that whereas in Attic vase-painting the *athanasia* brought to Tydeus appears as a female figure, it is shown at Pyrgi as a *pharmakon* carried in a jug by Athena – which conforms more closely to the Greek literary tradition.

(**e**, **f**, **g**) Three inscribed gold tablets, each about 10 × 20 cm, with nail holes implying public display. They were deliberately hidden in Area C, probably on the eve of the Syracusan depredations of 384. Translations (cf. J. Heurgon, *JRS* 56 [1966] 1–15): (**e**) (Phoenician text) 'To the lady Astarte. Here is the holy place which has made and given Tibèrie Vèlianas, king over Kisry, in the month of the sacrifice of the Sun, as a gift in the temple and its holy place (?), because Astarte raised him with her hand (?) in the third year of his reign in the month of Karar on the day of the burying of the God. And may the years of the statue of the Goddess in her temple last as long as these stars (?).' (**f**) (long Etruscan text) 'This is the shrine and this is the place of the image dedicated to Uni: Thefàrie Vèlianas gave it, as a thank offering, because he had been raised to be king for three years . . . stars . . . (?).' (**g**) (short Etruscan text) 'Thus Thefàrie Vèlianas founded the shrine and made the offering in the month of Masan; and this was the annual ceremony in the temple.'

(**e**) is the only Phoenicio-Punic text so far known from the Italian peninsula, and refers to the same event as (**f**), which is further confirmed by (**g**): the dedication at the end of the sixth century by the Etruscan ruler of Caere (Kisry) of Temple B to the oriental goddess Astarte. This presumably means that the ruler in question, Thefàrie Vèlianas, was guiding Caere back to its earlier allegiance with Carthage, whence help had been forthcoming at the end of the battle in the Sardinian Sea (540: off Alalia). The policy had clearly been reversed by the time of Temple A.

The Pyrgi tablets provide unique contemporary documentation of the nature of Mediterranean relationships at the time of the first treaty between Rome and Carthage. They show too that treaties could be written at this early date.

(Models: University of Rome. The finds from Pyrgi are displayed in the Villa Giulia, Rome and in the Antiquarium at the site itself, near Santa Severa.)

Excavation reports: G. Colonna et al., *Not. Scav.* 1959, 143–263; *ibid.*, 1970, Suppl. II; *ibid.*, in press since 1979. Conferences: *Le lamine di Pyrgi: Tavola rotonda internazionale, Roma 1968* = *Quaderni Lincei* 147 (1970); F. Prayon (ed.), *Akten des Kolloquiums zum Thema Die Göttin von Pyrgi, Tübingen 1979* (Florence, 1981); Cat. Arezzo 1985, 127–41.

e	f	g

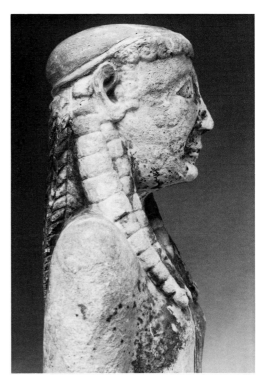

274. Many of the associations are imported, and the same may be true of this statuette – or of the sculptor who made it: the stylistic dilemma is produced by the status of Vulci as one of the foremost artistic cities of Etruria.

(London, British Museum D1. Height with base 89 cm.)
 S. Haynes, *Antike Plastik* 4 (1965) 13ff; on the tomb-group, *ead.* in *La civiltà arcaica di Vulci e la sua espansione = Atti X Convegno Studi Etruschi* (Florence, 1977) 17–29.

298. Votive statuette of gypsum, wearing chiton, himation (gilt belt) and sandals; from the Isis Tomb in the Polledrara cemetery at Vulci. Comparisons with Peloponnesian sculpture have suggested a date about 570, which makes this one of the earliest examples of sculpture in the round from Etruria. The date accords well with the associated Late Orientalizing luxury objects, which include decorated ostrich eggs related to

299. The limestone cult image known as the Warrior of Capestrano (prov. L'Aquila, in Samnite territory), discovered in 1934; late sixth century, and the most impressive of a number of large stone statues from the Middle Adriatic region, characterized by the same frontality and presumably ritual gesture of arms and hands. The Warrior's panoply (*kardiophylax*, belt, sword and spearhead) finds parallels in the cemeteries of his area – notably that of Campovalano (**289**), where many of his real-life contemporaries and peers are interred.

(Chieti, Museo Nazionale. Height 2.09 m.)
 G. Moretti, *Il guerriero italico di Capestrano* (Rome,

1936). In general: V. Cianfarani in *Popoli e Civiltà dell'
Italia Antica* v (1976) 61–3, 71–92; P. Orlandini, *ibid.*,
VII (1978) 252, 259; E. T. Salmon, *Samnium and the
Samnites* (Cambridge, 1967).

300. Votive statuettes were produced in considerable quantities by Etruscan bronzesmiths from
the seventh century onwards. Though doubtless
originally inspired by Greek models, the products of the Archaic Etruscan workshops have a
degree of freedom and originality that sets them
apart from the inimitable perfection of their
Greek counterparts. References below are to E.
Richardson, *Etruscan Votive Bronzes: Geometric,
Orientalizing, Archaic* (Mainz, 1983).

(a) One of the first Etruscan bronze warriors
to wear complete hoplite armour; third quarter
of the sixth century, and so apparently the
earliest hollow-cast bronze from Etruria. No
provenance.

(London, British Museum 453. Preserved height
43.2 cm.)

Richardson, 168 with fig. 385: Middle Archaic
Warriors, Series A no. 4.

(b) Walking kore, said to have been found at Falterona near the source of the Arno; in the range 520–450, and one of 'the first small bronze ladies to step forward with any determination; they have no counterparts in Greece' (Richardson). She has been identified with Artemis and compared with representations of Minerva and Juno Sospita.

(London, British Museum 450. Height 14.3 cm.)
    Richardson, 292ff with fig. 692: Late Archaic Korai, Series A, Group 4 no. 2.

(c) Turms, the Etruscan Mercury / Hermes, identified by his petasus and winged boots. Ploughed up at Uffington in Oxfordshire; late

Archaic, fifth century. Although Turms is frequently represented (and named) on Etruscan mirrors, there is no evidence for a cult nearer to Etruria than Rome (where an *aedes Mercurii* was dedicated in 495 : Livy II.21.7). It is not clear when this piece reached its English findspot.

(Oxford, Ashmolean Museum 1943.38. Height 22 cm.)
    P. J. Riis, *JRS* 36 (1946) 43–7. Richardson, 359f with fig. 863: Divinities, Type VII, Mercury no. 2.

301. From the mid-sixth century onwards, high-quality Etruscan bronzework was exported to Umbria, with the result that the votive types produced in Umbrian workshops from the end of

the century were borrowed from the Etruscan repertoire. But the tendency towards geometric or even abstract elongation, seen to good effect in (a) and (b), is wholly Umbrian and rooted in an indigenous tradition that is much older than the helmet, cuirass and greaves worn by (a). Further south, some Sabellian figures like (c) seem to be influenced by Greek at least as much as Etruscan types. The following three examples, all unprovenanced, are in the range 525–375. References below are to G. Colonna, *Bronzi votivi umbro-sabellici a figura umana* I: *periodo 'arcaico'* (Florence, 1970).

(a) Mars, by Colonna's North Umbrian 'Calgi-Londra' master; another example by the same hand comes from Cagli (prov. Pesaro).

(London, British Museum 1905.10–27.1. Height 29 cm.)
Colonna, no. 6.

(**b**) Minerva; South Umbrian (the lance is modern).

(London, British Museum 443. Height 20.9 cm.)
Colonna, no. 139.

(**c**) Hercules; Sabellian.

(London, British Museum 604. Height 13.5 cm.)
Colonna, no. 478.

15. COINAGE

M. JESSOP PRICE

The late Archaic period saw the blossoming of coinage in Western Asia Minor, Greece and Magna Graecia. The existence of these little objects of precious metal which we recognize as coins did not suddenly change the manner of using money that had existed for two thousand years previously. The earliest coins came from the western area of Asia Minor, centred on Sardis, the capital of the kingdom of Lydia, and were made of the gold/silver alloy, electrum. Even the smallest denomination of this white gold coinage had a considerable purchasing power, and would have been a good day's wages. The earliest coinage was not, therefore, a response, as Aristotle supposed, to a need for a simple currency in the market place, but, far more probably, coins were created to meet a need to standardize more major payments and valuations of all sorts – payments made by the issuing authority by way of salaries, and payments by the people in taxes.

Profits accrued both in valuing the coins higher than the intrinsic value of the metal, and in charging commissions whenever any form of exchange took place. Coinage was a source of profit to the issuer, and [Aristotle]'s *Oeconomica* Book II reflects the awareness of this on the part of statesmen in the fourth century. The quantity of gold in the electrum alloy varied considerably in different issues. Since it may safely be assumed that electrum pieces of the same denomination circulated at the same accepted value, the possibility of profit to be made through turning metal into coinage existed from the very beginning, and may have been the primary reason why electrum alone, and not pure gold or silver, was apparently thought to be the most suitable metal for coinage.

The increasing use in the fifth century of fractional coins in silver, and ultimately of bronze coins, brought about changes in social patterns. Plato (*Gorgias* 515e) complained that Pericles, in encouraging the payment of coinage in recompense for state service in the assembly and jury courts, was responsible for making the Athenians lazy. In fact it was the existence of coins of small purchasing value and of payments in coin rather than in kind for services and labour that led along the path towards democracy.

Through the study of hoards and other contexts in which coins have been found, and through the detailed inspection of the designs and inscriptions of the coins themselves, the general development of coinage is well documented. The last twenty-five years, however, have been exciting times for numismatists. New evidence and a thorough re-inspection of traditional assumptions have resulted in radical changes in the dates to be given to particular coinages. Historians are asked to accept, for example, that the law of Solon altering the weights and measures to be used at Athens, cannot, as Aristotle had thought, have affected coinage, since no coinage existed in the city at that time. In the fourth century B.C. a change in weight standards would certainly have changed the weight of the coinage, and in this way misconception of the situation in the sixth century must have arisen. Solon may certainly have gained experience of the use of coinage during his famous visit to Croesus, but it can be shown that the famous 'owl' tetradrachms were only introduced in the last quarter of the sixth century, and are most plausibly to be linked with the machinations of Hippias, who recalled for restriking all previous coinage ([Aristotle] *Oeconomica* II, 1347a). There can be no question that the brief coinage that preceded the 'owls' could have been instituted as early as the time of Solon.

The reverberations created by this revolution are not yet over, but recent attempts to lower the date of the introduction of coinage to the time of Croesus, and consequently radically to revise the dates of all later artefacts, have met with little acceptance. The delicate network of interlinking evidence from hoards, overstrikes, influences of design, and die patterns must be treated as a whole, and the temptation to impose preconceived views on issues of particular states or areas must be resisted at all costs. Although fixed points in the chronology are difficult to establish in the sixth century, there is fairly reliable evidence in the first decades of the fifth century, and from this and the relative chronology a clear pattern of development emerges.

GENERAL BIBLIOGRAPHY

C. M. Kraay, *Archaic and Classical Greek Coins* (London, 1976); M. J. Price and N. M. Waggoner, *Archaic Greek Silver Coinage: The Asyut Hoard* (London, 1975); L. Weidauer, *Probleme der frühen Elektronprägung* (Fribourg, 1975); R. Carson *et. al.* (eds.), *A Survey of Numismatic Research 1972–1977* (Berne, 1979); J. H. Kroll and N. M. Waggoner, 'Dating the earliest coins of Athens, Corinth, and Aegina', *AJA* 88 (1984) 325–40; M. Price *et. al.* (eds.), *A Survey of Numismatic Research 1978–84* (London, 1986). For a controversial late dating of coinage, but with good bibliography, see: M. Vickers, 'Early Greek coinage, a reassessment', *Numismatic Chronicle* 145 (1985) 1–44; *id.*, 'Persepolis, Athènes et Sybaris: Questions de monnayage et de chronologie', *Revue des Études Grecques* (1986) 239–70.

302. Money before coinage. Precious metals had been regularly used in financial transactions for two thousand years before the introduction of coinage.

(a) Electrum nugget from a tomb at Enkomi, Cyprus, about 1300 BC. (b) Silver ingot from Zincirli, North Syria, eighth century B.C., marked with the name of the owner, Bar-rakib, son of Panammu.

((a–b) British Museum.)

J. E. Cribb, *Money: From cowrie shells to credit cards* (London, 1986).

303. The foundations of the temple of Artemis at Ephesus, with the building of which King Croesus of Lydia is believed to have been connected, provide the earliest context in which

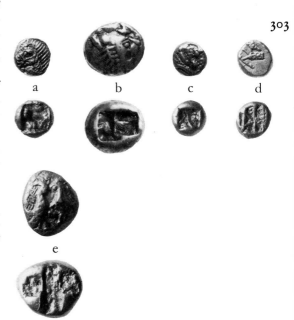

coins have been found. The three small fractions of electrum coinage (a–c) come from the earliest phase of the buildings, the foundation deposit to be dated at the end of the seventh century or even later. This earliest deposit included one of the rare varieties signed with the name of the issuer in Lydian script, Walwel (c). The coins of this deposit display every stage of development of this early electrum coinage.

(a) Horse head. Twelfth stater. (b) Lion head. Third stater. (c) Lion head, inscribed with the name of Walwel in Lydian script (cf. **305c**). (d) Stag forepart. Twelfth stater. This piece also comes from the excavations of the earliest phase of the temple of Artemis at Ephesus, from the West Basis, and the treatment of the stag's head and skin, and of the pattern in the reverse, indicate that it is probably a fraction of the stater inscribed with the name of Phanes (**305a**). This, added to the evidence of the inscribed piece (**c**), emphasizes that the earliest phase of building of the Artemisium comes towards the end of the early electrum coinage. (e) Two cocks. Half stater. This and several other pieces of the same issue were found with other varieties in a pot hoard in the foundations of the Artemisium, but in a level that must be later than the original foundation deposit. The containing vase has been dated to the third quarter of the seventh century.

((**a–e**) Istanbul Museum.)

M. J. Price, 'Thoughts on the beginnings of coinage', in C. N. L. Brooke *et. al.* (eds.), *Studies . . . Grierson* (Cambridge, 1983) 1–10.

304. A recent hoard from Colophon confirms the evidence of the Artemisium deposits that the earliest phase of coinage consisted of many small issues of different designs, and that these coins circulated together. The conclusion that this phase was fairly short is inescapable. Since no other coinage was found in the various phases of the foundations of the Artemisium, it should follow that the period of time over which these were constructed was also fairly short, and if the

tradition is correct that the final phase should be placed during the reign of Croesus, a date not long before 600 B.C. for the making of the first coins must follow.

(a) Simple lines, an early form of design. Twelfth stater. (b) Horse head. Twenty-fourth stater, from the same series as **303a** from the Artemisium. (c) Facing bull head. Forty-eighth stater.

((**a–c**) British Museum.)

305. Although a coin inscribed with the name Walwel appears in the earliest context from the Artemisium (**303c**), there are not many of the early electrum issues from the area of the kingdom of Lydia so signed. The derivation of coin types from personal seals is however clear from these examples.

(a) ΦΑΕΝΟΣ ΕΜΙ ΣΕΜΑ 'I am the seal of Phanes.' Stater.

(b) Third stater, of the same issue as (a). An attempt has been made recently to link this issue with the town of Phanai in Chios, by suggesting that the final letter of the name is N, not Σ, which would give the genitive plural of a people, rather than the singular of a person. This seems most unlikely since the letter form would differ significantly from that of the first N, both on the stater and on the third, It has also been suggested that

305

a

b

c

d

e

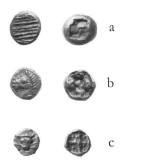

304

a

b

c

the name should be linked with that of a known Phanes, of Halicarnassus (Hdt. III.4) of the time of Amasis and Cambyses. The connexion with Halicarnassus is attractive since the stater here illustrated was acquired at Bodrum, but other signed electrum issues cannot be linked to persons whose names happened to have survived in other historical sources. Since this Phanes' grandfather or other members of the family may have had the same name, it would be dangerous to use this connexion to date the coins.

(c) Two lion heads facing inwards. Third stater, inscribed down the centre with the name Walwel. This issue is linked by the use of the very same reverse punch with an issue in the name of Kalil. Since neither of these figures can be equated with known royal personages, they offer the possibility that rich landlords might have issued their own coins at this time, before coinage became the monopoly of the state.

(d) Goat forepart. Stater. Though unsigned, such a device would have been recognizable to the users of the coins as representing the issuer's seal.

(e) Stater of electrum, plated on a copper core, with double volute pattern design. Similar pieces come from Samos, and this coin recalls a story reported incredulously by Herodotus (III.56.2) that in 525/4 B.C. Polycrates of Samos managed to bribe a besieging force of Spartans by paying them with specially minted coins of lead plated with gold. No pure gold issues have survived which could have been struck by Polycrates, and the importance of the anecdote is that the issue in question must in fact have been of white gold, electrum, and that c. 525/4 B.C. electrum was still a regular coinage medium in the area, acceptable even by foreigners.

((a,b, d,e) British Museum. (c) Fogg Museum, Cambridge, Mass. Dewing Collection 2420.)

(a,b) W. Krastner, '"Phanes" oder "Phano"?', *Schweizerische Numismatische Rundschau* 65 (1986) 5–11; M. Vickers, *Numismatic Chronicle* 145 (1985) 19–20. (e) J. P. Barron, *The Silver Coins of Samos* (London, 1966) 17.

306. It is unlikely that the earliest phase of coinage, using electrum alone as the medium, lasted more than two generations. There is also no evidence to suggest that coinage in pure gold and silver should precede the reign of Croesus (560–547 B.C.). Indeed, the evidence of hoards is mounting to demand that much of the coinage

normally attributed to Croesus, with the lion and bull forepart design, should belong in fact to the Persian period at Sardis, after 547 B.C. There is no evidence to link this coinage with Croesus.

(a) The earliest gold issue, with a style that closely parallels the lion heads in electrum such as those signed by Walwel (**303c,305c**). Gold of these types continued to be struck at Sardis, with one reduction in the weight standard, until the introduction of bowman Darics at the very end of the sixth century or in the early fifth century B.C. (**307b**).

(b) Recently discovered stater in silver, said to have come from a hoard found at Ödemiş, and the earliest coin in the hoard. The design is comparable with that on an electrum stater in Oxford, but of different style. Both should probably be attributed to the reign of Croesus. Analysis of the metal of this and other lion- and bull-forepart coins revealed an unusually low amount of lead. It is very probable that the gold and silver for these came from separating the component metals in the natural electrum that came from the beds of the river Pactolus.

(c–d) Silver stater and half stater once attributed to Croesus. The smaller denomination is found in hoards of the early fifth century in such quantity that it cannot be questioned that such pieces were being manufactured under the

Persians. Differences in style suggest that the staters and very small fractions were struck a little earlier than most of the halves, but there is no evidence to take them back to the time of Croesus.

(**e–g**) Silver staters from Lycia (**e**) and Caria (**f**), and a third stater from Caria, all from a recent hoard said to be from near Olbia in south-west Turkey, which also included (**c**) and numerous small fractions both of the lion- and bull-forepart type from Sardis and of the Carian issues. It is clear that the Sardis and Carian issues in the hoard were contemporary. The latter would normally be dated to the last quarter of the sixth century, and the sign on the shoulder of the lion is a feature which could not be paralleled on coins before 525 B.C. The style of (**e**) with the prominent triangular eye and herring-bone mane, links the issue to the early electrum third stater of Sardis (**303b**) and provides evidence of a smooth transition from the use of electrum as the main coinage medium to that of silver.

((**a**) Fitzwilliam Museum, Cambridge; McClean 8635. (**b,d**) British Museum. (**c,e–g**) Private collection, USA, from the 'Olbia' hoard.)

(**b**) M. J. Price, 'Croesus or Pseudo-Croesus? Hoard or hoax?', in A. Houghton *et al.* (eds.), *Studies . . . Mildenberg* (Wetteren, 1984) 211–21.

307. The Persian gold Daric and silver siglos introduced at Sardis under Darius I, were to become well known to the Greeks of the fifth century, who gave the Great King's name to the gold piece. The coins derived their fabric from the earlier lion- and bull-forepart coinage of Sardis, and the siglos was the same weight as the half stater.

(**a**) The half figure of the Great King was chosen for the siglos. No gold has yet been found to parallel this issue of the last decade of the sixth century, but the rarity of examples in hoards, and consequently in collections today, suggests that the issue was fairly short, and that the design was soon changed to the more familiar bowman type.

(**b**) The earliest 'archer' gold Daric, probably not struck before 500 B.C. In the deposits placed in the foundations of the Apadana building at Persepolis in the early fifth century it was the lion- and bull-forepart gold, not the bowmen Darics, which were secreted. It would be surprising if the new coinage of Darius had not been used for such a foundation deposit, and this may suggest that these Darics began only in the later part of Darius' rule. Greek coins found in the same context, from Aegina, Abdera and Cyprus, confirm a date of 490 or a little later for these deposits.

((**a–b**) British Museum.)

D. Stronach, 'The Apadana: A signature of the time of Darius I', in *De l'Indus aux Balkans, Recueil Jean Deshayes*, 433–5.

308. A hoard found on the island of Santorini (Thera) in 1821 is one of the earliest documents for the spread of coinage to the west of Asia Minor. Several of the issues are closely akin to the electrum and early silver issues of Asia Minor, with oval flans and two reverse punches. They were discovered with a large quantity of Aeginetan 'turtle' staters which probably place the concealment of the hoard at the very end of the sixth century.

308

a

b

c

a

b

(**a**) Crab, later the badge of Cos, to which this issue is therefore attributed. A small silver fraction of the Cos coinage was discovered in a tomb in Jerusalem with pottery that is conventionally dated 586–540 B.C. As with the Artemisium pot hoard (**303e**) there may prove to be some discrepancy between the accepted pottery dates and the apparent dates of the coins. (**b**) Cock. Silver stater of uncertain origin, but clearly of a later date than the electrum coins of the Artemisium pot hoard (**303e**). (**c**) Head of Dionysus. Silver stater attributed to the island of Naxos because of the connexion with the Dionysus legend.

((**a–c**) British Museum.)
    W. Wroth, 'The Santorin Find of 1821', *Numismatic Chronicle*, 3rd series, Vol. 4 (1884) 269–80.

309. Early Athenian coinage.
    (**a**) Small electrum diobol with head of a bull discovered in Euboea, and attributed to Athens, where the same design is to be found on the tetradrachm (**c**). The use of electrum is unusual in mainland Greece, and occurs otherwise only in Macedonia and Thrace. Another example has been found in Attica, and varieties

with an owl or a wheel may also be linked by type to the earliest Athenian silver.
    (**b**) Silver didrachm showing the head of the Gorgon. This issue is found overstruck by the earliest coinage at Corinth, and this suggests that Athenian coinage began a little before the Corinthian. The fashion of using a variety of designs, resulting in the modern name *Wappenmünzen* (heraldic coins) for the series, links the earliest coinage of silver at Athens with the electrum coinage in Asia Minor.
    (**c**) The first Athenian tetradrachms occur at the end of the *Wappenmünzen* series, and have fully developed reverse designs, the first such in coinage.
    (**d**) The earliest issues of the famous 'owl' tetradrachms must be placed in the last quarter of the sixth century. They share the general fabric and technique of the slightly earlier *Wappenmünzen* tetradrachms, but soon after their introduction there is a vast increase in the quantity of tetradrachms, suggesting that a dramatic increase in the sources of silver had occurred. This coincides with the known increase in the exploitation of the mines at Laurium at the end of the sixth and in the early fifth century.

309

a

b

c

d

e

f

(**e–f**) Two tetradrachms of the massive early fifth-century issues, both found in the Asyut hoard of 1969. The final deposit of this large hoard must have been made *c*. 475 or a little later, and it gives a good picture of coin circulating at the end of the first quarter of the century. This, together with much other evidence, proves that the dumpy tetradrachms, often with coarse style, must be later than the fine tetradrachms on thinner flans, such as (**d**) which introduced the series.

((**a–d**) British Museum. (**e–f**) Asyut hoard 346, 347.)

(**a**) C. T. Seltman, *Athens: Its history and coinage* (Cambridge, 1924) 80–2; (**b**) J. H. Kroll, 'From Wappenmünzen to Gorgoneia to owls', *American Numismatic Society Museum Notes* 26 (1981) 1–32.

310. The confederacy of the cities of Boeotia is symbolized by their use of common coin designs and weight standard. The Boeotian shield is the device on all the obverses, and the stater (didrachm) is the main currency unit. The minting of drachma, obols, and even smaller fractions provided a flexible system about 500 B.C.

(**a**) Silver stater, Haliartus. (**b**) Drachma, Tanagra. (**c**) Obol, Thebes.

((**a–c**) British Museum.)

a b

311. Aegina was one of the first Greek states to adopt the minting of coinage on a large scale. The large quantity of surviving materials allows a clear view of the development of the reverse punch from a rod, square in section, with a rough pattern of lines cut onto the end (similar in some respects to the punches on the later electrum of Asia Minor), to a carefully constructed design on a slightly raised square, which impressed a shallow reverse square onto the coin.

(**a**) Silver stater from the first issues, about 540 B.C. (**b**) Stater from the Asyut hoard, from the latest Archaic issues with 'skew' pattern in shallow incuse square, of the 480s.

((**a**) British Museum. (**b**) Asyut hoard 541.)
Kroll and Waggoner 335–9.

312. The development of the fabric of Corinthian coins is from flat, thin flans to more dumpy ingots, which parallels the pattern at Athens in the late *Wappenmünzen* and Archaic 'owls'. An overstrike by one of the earliest dies of the 'foals' of Corinth on a didrachm of the *Wappenmünzen* series, a coin in the Cabinet des Médailles, Paris, confirms that Athenian coinage started a little earlier than that at Corinth. The introduction of the head of Athena as a reverse design can be dated by a hoard from Taranto, buried about 495 B.C., in which the first dies of the new reverse type were present. A date at the very end of the sixth century may therefore be given to this

310

a

b

c

312

a

b

c

Aeneas carrying Anchises, and Creusa with Ascanius, fleeing from Troy. Tetradrachm, Aeneia, Macedonia, about 490–480 B.C. (d) 8-drachma piece, Abdera, Thrace. One of the earliest occasions on which the responsibility for the issue is marked on the coin, like a date, in the form of the official's name, Them . . . The griffin is the badge of the city itself, derived from the mother city from which Abdera was founded, Teos in Ionia, about 485 B.C.

((a–d) Asyut hoard 27, 105, 194, 139.)

314. Hoards may provide evidence for the contemporaneity of issues from different areas through a comparison of the wear displayed on individual examples. In this way, evidence for the chronology of one series may be interlinked with evidence for another in an intricate web which creates a picture of the whole.

(a) Tridrachm. Delphi. The heads on the obverse have been conjecturally linked with rhyta captured in the spoils after the battle of Plataea, but the dotted truncation of the heads may be widely paralleled on coins elsewhere. About 485–475 B.C. (b) Tetradrachm. Eretria, or possibly her colony Dicaea in Macedonia. The flat fabric of the Archaic Eretrian coinage parallels the early issues of Athens and Corinth, and a date before the destruction of the city by the Persians is demanded. The Eretrian coinage

important change in the coinage, which follows soon after the introduction of the 'owls' at Athens.

(a) Stater, Corinth, about 515 B.C. (b) Stater, Corinth, about 500 B.C. The earliest dies of this series have a linear border framing the head of Athena. (c) Stater, Corinth, about 480 B.C.

((a,b) British Museum. (c) Asyut hoard 573.)
   Kroll and Waggoner 333–5.

313. The Asyut hoard from Egypt is typical of Archaic hoards from the Near East in containing a great mixture of coinage from the Aegean and other parts of the Greek world. The silver was clearly more valuable in the East than in those areas closer to silver mines, and the coins were cut to test their purity or chopped to make fractional amounts. In western Asia Minor (306b) silver was probably extracted from natural electrum to be found in the beds of the River Pactolus. Cupellation from silver-bearing lead ores was practised at Laurium (309) and the Cyclades (308), but one of the largest silver-producing areas at this time was Macedonia.

(a) Warrior, 'Ares', and bull cart. 12-drachma piece of the Derrones tribe, Macedonia; early fifth century. (b) Stater, Thasos, depicting a satyr taking to himself the nymph of the island, a symbolic representation of the fertility with which the island was imbued; early fifth century. (c)

313

a

313

b

probably derives from the practice at Corinth (**312b–c**) introduced about 500 B.C.

((**a–c**) Asyut hoard 242, 255, 573.)

315. The influence of the designs of one city's coinage upon another may be taken to indicate that the original was popular in circulation and that the design represented good money.

(**a**) An octopus from Eretria (**314b**) used on a coin of Cyprus, with the Cypriot sign *ka* replacing the Greek E. About 485 B.C. (**b**) The lion and bull foreparts of Sardis (**306a,c,d**) on a stater of the Lycian dynast Teththiveibi (480–460 B.C.), the design reversed having been cut in the die as the engraver saw it in front of him.

((**a**) Asyut hoard 817. (**b**) British Museum.)

316. Stater and siglos recently attributed to Histiaeus of Termera, Caria, clearly inscribed with his name on the reverse. The Achaemenid origin of the king and lion design echoes the pro-Persian sympathies of the Histiaeus who refused to take part in the Ionian Revolt (Hdt. v.37) and later played a major role in Xerxes' expedition (Hdt. vii.98). A date of 490–480 B.C. is fairly

c

314

a

b

c

comes to an abrupt halt with issues of this type. About 500 B.C. (**c**) Tetradrachm, Cyrene, about 480 B.C. displaying the silphium plant and the head of Zeus Ammon. The head placed in the reverse square, unusual for Greek coinages,

d

certain for this issue, and provides a useful view of the development of coinage at this particular time.

((a) Stater. Royal coin collection, Leyden. (b) Siglos. British Museum.)

M. J. Price, 'Histiaeus, son of Tymnes, tyrant of Termera, Caria', *Norwegian Numismatic Journal*, Sept. 1979, 4–12.

317. A key point in the chronology of Archaic coinage is the influence of the exiles from Samos who settled at Zancle in 494/3 (Hdt. VI.22ff.).

(a) Drachma of the earliest coinage of Zancle on the local Chalcidian weight standard, and depicting the sickle-shaped harbour, a pun on the name of the city. The fabric is notably thin and flat, and the pattern of the reverse suggests that this was derived from early Corinthian coinage, but with the shell added as a reverse design.

(b) Tetradrachm of the Samian exiles at Zancle. The weight was changed to the Attic standard. The dumpy fabric contrasts sharply with the earlier coinage of Zancle, and the designs reflect their Samian origin. The lion scalp derived from the island's earlier coinage, and the prow of the galley is a reference to their journey westwards. The letter Δ is the fourth in

an alphabetical sequence that is found on this issue. The tetradrachms display A–E. It is a fair assumption that this sequence should be years of issue, based upon an era beginning with the Samians' arrival at their new-found home. An obol in Oxford with Z may be evidence of a sixth year, or possibly a letter denoting the name of the city. The recent suggestion (Vickers, 1985, 39) that this might be an issue commemorating the victory of Syracuse over the Etruscans at the battle of Cyme in 474 B.C. is most implausible. The fabric of the coins is certainly not that of Syracuse, but fits very well that of Samos and of the later coinages of Anaxilas.

(c) Tetradrachm of Samos overstruck about 495 B.C. on another coin. Signs of the undertype, possibly the silphium plant of Cyrene, may be discerned to the left of the reverse square. The reverse design may be compared to the first issues of Corinth with the head of Athena.

((a) British Museum, Lloyd 1074. (b) Asyut hoard 22. (c) British Museum, Barron, *op. cit.*, **305**, p. 176.7.)

318. Anaxilas of Rhegium drove the Samians from Zancle, and renamed the city Messana. This episode is clearly reflected in the coinage.

(**a**) Tridrachm on the Chalcidian standard, Rhegium, about 490 B.C. (**b**) Tridrachm in the name of Messana, but with the designs and weight standard of Rhegium imposed by Anaxilas, 489–480 B.C. (**c–d**) The mule biga, a design common to Rhegium (**c**) and Messana (**d**), is said to have commemorated Anaxilas' victory in the Olympic Games (Aristotle fr. 578R). The hare is a reference to Pan, presumably reflecting the Peloponnesian origin of the Messenians whom Anaxilas settled at Zancle. Tetradrachms on the Attic standard, about 480 B.C.

((**a–d**) British Museum.)

E. S. Robinson, 'Rhegion, Zancle–Messana, and the Samians', *JHS* 68 (1948) 13–20. C. Arnold-Biucchi, 'Appunti sulla zecca di Messana dal 480 al 450 a.C.', *Numismatica e Antichità Classiche: Quaderni Ticinesi* 12 (1983) 49–64.

319. The earliest coinage of southern Italy adopted a technique borrowed from repoussé work to produce the designs on the flan of silver. The reverse punch bore the same design in relief as had been engraved into the anvil die for the obverse. Such a technique clearly preceded the appearance of reverse designs at Athens and Corinth, and may have influenced the development towards reverse designs. The flans for such pieces had to be thin, and the method was abandoned by the mid-fifth century in favour of the more normal method of engraving the reverse design into the punch die. The defeat of Sybaris by Croton in 510 appears to have brought to an end the short first phase of Sybaris' coinage. The introduction of these incuse coinages should probably not be placed much before 525 B.C. The coin of Sybaris illustrated here is of *c.* 515 B.C. Other examples are illustrated above, **267b–d**.

320. The earliest coinages of Sicily share the thin flans of the incuse coinages, but Naxus (see **267a**) and Syracuse open their mints with a fully developed reverse design.

(**a**) Celery leaf, a pun on the name of the issuing city, Selinus. Stater, about 510 B.C. (**b**) The cock, herald of day (*hemera*), Himera. Drachma, about 510 B.C. (**c**) The chariot that was to become so popular in fifth-century Sicilian coinage, and the head of Arethusa set into an incuse of a form derived from Macedonia. Syracuse. Tetradrachm, about 510 B.C. The famous Demareteion decadrachm, which used to be associated with the offering made to Queen Demarete for her part in the negotiations with the Carthaginians in 480, must now be dated about 465, and so is removed from the events of 480. As a result, the late Archaic coinage of Sicily in general must also be brought down a little in date.

((**a–c**) British Museum.)

(**b**) C. M. Kraay, *The Archaic Coinage of Himera* (Naples, 1984).